EIGHT DAYS IN
DARKNESS

THE TRUE STORY OF THE ABDUCTION, RAPE, AND RESCUE OF ANITA WOOLDRIDGE

ANGELA ROEGNER, LCSW
AND ANITA WOOLDRIDGE

Synergy Books

Eight Days in Darkness: The True Story of the Abduction, Rape, and
Rescue of Anita Wooldridge
Published by Synergy Books
PO Box 30071
Austin, TX 78755

For more information about our books, please write us, e-mail us
at info@synergybooks.net, or visit our web site at www.synergybooks.net.

Publisher's Cataloging-in-Publication
(Provided by Quality Books, Inc.)

Roegner, Angela.
    Eight days in darkness : the true story of the
abduction, rape, and rescue of Anita Wooldridge / by
Angela Roegner and Anita Wooldridge.
    p. cm.
    LCCN 2009937949
    ISBN-13: 978-0-9840760-3-1
    ISBN-10: 0-9840760-3-4

    1. Wooldridge, Anita. 2. Kidnapping victims--Indiana
--Kokomo--Biography. 3. Rape victims--Indiana--Kokomo--
Biography. 4. Missing persons--Investigation--United
States--Case studies. 5. Steele, Victor Thomas.
6. United States. Federal Bureau of Investigation.
7. Peace officers--Indiana--Kokomo. 8. Kokomo (Ind.)--
Biography. I. Wooldridge, Anita. II. Title.

    HV6601.I6R64 2010   364.15'4'092
                               QBI09-600192

The events recounted in this book are true, although some names have
been changed to safeguard certain individuals. While some artistic license
has been taken in devising the thoughts and motivations of some characters, the personalities, events, actions, and conversations in this book
have been constructed using interviews, police report records, and the
victim's firsthand account.

10 9 8 7 6 5 4 3 2

This book is dedicated to God, the heroes
who saved Anita's life, and the loving memory of
my grandma, Gertie Roe, my guardian angel.

And in loving memory of Deputy Don England,
a true hero. December 16, 1961–August 13, 2009.
May he rest in peace.

FOREWORD

I am often asked what investigation stands out most to me during my thirty-eight years in law enforcement. My answer is always the Anita Wooldridge case. The accomplishments of the various officers and FBI agents who were involved in this investigation are still regularly talked about in the halls of the Howard County Sheriff's Office and the Kokomo Police Department. I am proud to have been on the team, and I feel privileged to write the foreword of Anita's amazing story. The real story here is about her faith and strong will to survive. She confided to me after her rescue that she had prayed her way through the ordeal and knew the whole time that we would come for her.

Another test of will came for Anita during the federal court trial to convict her captor. Anita remained strong, courageous, and focused in her role during the days in court that followed. In my opinion, her captor's cross-examination was the ultimate test of Anita's strength. She stood her ground and won the day in grand style. Anita continues to volunteer assistance to law enforcement by telling her story to hundreds of police officers, prosecutors, and victims' advocates across the country. In 2003, Anita appeared before the International Conference on Violent Crimes in Ontario, Canada. There, she was able to educate investigators from around the world on a successful rescue case.

Locally, Anita serves on our Howard County Community Corrections Advisory Board as a victims' advocate. We value her input and hold her opinions in high regard. She is an asset to the board and to our community at large. I believe that Anita survived her ordeal for a purpose that she is fulfilling every time that she tells her story.

—**Major Steve Rogers**, director of investigations on the Anita Wooldridge case, Howard County Sheriff's Department

INTRODUCTION
BY ANITA WOOLDRIDGE

Out of evil must come good. Though I do wish that this had never happened to me, it did, and because of it, I have been given the opportunity to travel across the nation and meet many wonderful people. My mom always taught me that there is a reason for everything in life. Therefore, when I was kidnapped, I knew that there must be a more divine plan in the works. I knew that this was not just happening so that I would become a victim. After I was found, many people asked me how I was able to survive the daily torture I had endured. I always answered that my faith in God and constant prayer were the only things that got me through it, and thus, I began to understand that I was kidnapped so that I could be a witness to God's amazing work.

I thought about all the people who would read my story in the newspaper who would not normally hear about God's love or attend church. I began to hope that these people would read about the way God has worked in my life experiences, and then question what God could do for them. I was also contacted by the FBI to go to their headquarters in Quantico, Virginia, to speak to their profilers and behavior specialists in a training seminar they held. I told them what I did to stay calm and how I got my abductor to continue communicating with me so that he would ultimately want to keep me alive. Once again, I was able to share God's love with a large audience of people.

I feel like I make the most impact when I speak to various youth groups and at Butler and Ball State Universities here in Indiana. I realize that I help professionals at the conferences and training seminars, but I can see that I truly make a difference in the lives of adolescents and college students. They often tell me that hearing my story makes them more cautious and better aware of their surroundings. When I speak to them, the two things that I emphasize are God's love and the importance of being a more responsible person. I tell them that I never could have survived if I had not accepted God as my personal savior prior to this ordeal. When everything seems to be going wrong, I know for sure that God will never give me more than I can handle. He came close, but he helped me through it the whole time. I was never truly alone.

Being more responsible is also crucial. When this happened to me, I had just turned twenty-one, and given my young age, the police naturally thought that I might have gone off with friends without telling anyone. But my parents were adamant that I was always responsible—I would never run off without telling anyone, and I always checked in if I was not home on time. After corroborating what my parents said with every person that they spoke with, the police started to take my disappearance more seriously, and a few hours after I was reported missing, they suspected that foul play was involved. If I had not lived my life this way, my parents might not have reported it so quickly, and the police would have lost the precious time that is so vital within the first forty-eight hours of any investigation.

I try not to scare the young adults that I speak to. That is not my purpose in telling them my story. Instead, I encourage them to be accountable to someone in their lives. One person is better than none. I realize that not everyone has such a close relationship with their family, so I suggest a roommate, friend, or someone that they can trust. Sometimes they tell me that they feel like it takes away from their newfound independence at college. I assure them that this small sacrifice could save their lives.

I hope that as you read this book, you will realize how much God has worked in my life. I feel like this is the final chapter in my ordeal. I know that I will never give up on the lifelong process of healing or trying to help others, but this is my way of letting go. Thank you for reading this and taking this last step with me in my journey toward recovery.

God bless all of you!

AUTHOR'S NOTE

Anita and I decided early on in writing this book that we wanted to refer to her abductor, Victor Steele, as "the mole" in his interactions with Anita. We chose this name for the sexual predator in the book because of the striking similarities between him and this creature. Much like Anita's captor, moles have beady eyes, are unattractive, and prefer to only come out from their holes at night. We believe that all too often in books or movies of this nature, perpetrators receive fame or recognition that gives them a sense of importance or gratification. Our goal in this book is to portray him as the deranged sociopath that he is so that any recognition that he might gain from this publication will be negative.

Out of respect for their privacy, we have changed the names of everyone in the book, with the exception of Anita and her abductor. Though the events and major facts are real, some dialogue had to be elaborated upon and some inner thoughts of the characters invented to help the story flow. Most of the information for this book regarding the investigation and Mr.

Steele's history and mental status was obtained from interviews with various high school peers of Mr. Steele, military records, police report records, and in-depth interviews with the officers and FBI agents involved on this case. The most crucial pieces of information come from Anita's firsthand account of what she experienced during those eight days of terror through interviews and her personal journal. This book also contains actual crime scene photos from Anita's case.

All Bible quotes come from the King James Bible.

PROLOGUE
JUNE 26, 1998

Anita awoke to find herself in absolute darkness. Instinctively, she tried to sit up, but the top of her head cracked against something metal. She let out a whimper as a rush of pain and fear coursed through her body. *Am I dead?* she wondered. *This must be what it feels like to be buried alive.*

At once, the memory of the previous day came spinning back to her. Her prison, she remembered, was actually a metal storage cabinet. Anita's T-shirt and shorts were drenched in perspiration from the heat and lack of oxygen within her cramped quarters. There were only three small slits at the top of the box that allowed her to breathe. Every breath that she inhaled or exhaled was laborious, and she began to hyperventilate. *Just breathe*, she told herself. *In and out.*

As her breathing became more regular, she began to pray. "Please Lord, hear my prayers," she begged in a whisper. "I'm scared. I'm not ready to die yet. Please be with my family, and help the police to find me. I have to get out of here! Please help me to be strong and have the courage to trust in you no matter what happens. Amen."

The darkness still enveloped Anita, yet a sense of peace washed over her. She could hear her captor snoring soundly, and for a moment, she felt relieved. Although the box was confining, it also offered her respite from the monster who had imprisoned her in it. As she lay in the dark, a plan formed in Anita's mind. She would say or do whatever it took to stay alive long enough for the authorities to rescue her. She would take it one day at a time and never give up her hope of surviving this ordeal.

CHAPTER 1

SUMMER 1984

It was approximately 7:45 p.m. in Kokomo, Indiana, and the sunlight was losing life as dusk made its push to overthrow the day. As this ritual played out, Tom silently crept out of his hole. Opening his door, the slow and eerie creak provided a soundtrack for the light as it danced over the threshold and spilled out into the otherwise dark hallway. All the hallways in the upstairs of his mother's run-down, two-bedroom farmhouse were bathed in blackness, as Tom consciously kept the blinds closed over all the windows. Maybe the sunlight would illuminate what Tom actually was, and surely that was something he did not want to see—something he could not see. But here in this dimly lit house, Tom obviously felt a sense of comfort. In this closed-off world, he controlled everything. No one could tell him what to do. No one could tell what he was capable of doing.

Tom's childhood was an unhappy one. In this very house, he had grown up with two siblings, an older sister and a younger brother, and a pill-popping mother. His father, a truck driver, had been an infrequent presence in the house, only breezing through long enough to tell his family how worthless they were, knock his wife around a bit, and annex the last of her pain pills and cigarettes. His father had been dead for fifteen years now, but his mother still flinched every time someone walked through the door. He had died of cirrhosis of the liver from all the alcohol he had poisoned himself with over the years. Tom had laughed when he had heard the news. He thought his ol' pop had gotten what he deserved.

Tom hated this house—especially the attic, where he currently lived. Growing up, he had shared the attic with his siblings, and it had been way too small for the three of them. At least it was *his* attic now, and his alone. Without two siblings to share it with, the walls seemed to have expanded. But despite how spacious the attic now felt to Tom, he knew the four walls couldn't contain him. For him, living in his childhood home was a temporary measure—a stepping stone along the path to greatness.

At eighteen, Victor Thomas Steele graduated from high school and joined the navy. Though he went by "Tom," his superiors called him "shithead," and his peers called him "faggot." Tom Steele's enlistment in the navy had started off all wrong from the get-go, although he had done well enough in boot camp and had extended his enlistment by one year to advance to Third Class—a sacrifice he made so that he could have some authority over others.

As Tom always told the military examiners who questioned him during his frequent mental health reviews, the group that they had thrown him in with was packed with complete idiots. His supervisor, Chief Peterson, reminded him of his loudmouth, redneck dad. Both men were full of bravado, which, Tom assumed, hid the cowardly inferiority they felt when they were in his presence. Tom *knew* that he was smarter than his supervisor, but he was required to obey when Peterson ordered him around—something he did quite often.

"Drop and give me twenty, shithead!"

Reluctantly, Tom dropped and began doing push-ups while Chief Peterson continued talking.

"You tell me if I've got this right, shithead. You came out of the showers yesterday and started shaking your cock at everyone around? What in the hell was going through that tiny mind of yours, shithead?"

"Sir, if they call you a queer, then you should act like one, sir."

"But they didn't call *me* a queer—they called you a queer."

"Sir, then *I* will act like a queer, sir," Tom said defiantly.

For several weeks now, a few of the other guys had been spreading rumors around that he was gay, and that he and another guy from his hometown were lovers. The rumors had started after Tom had told the chief that his shipmates used drugs on a daily basis. When his shipmates caught wind of this, he quickly became the target of their aggression. As Tom told the examiner on multiple occasions, he felt threatened and ostracized every single day by both his peers and his supervisors.

Finished with his push-ups, Tom hopped to his feet and stared directly at the chief.

"Listen here, faggot," the chief said. "You will be written up for talking back to your superior, and I hope they demote you to E-3 status."

The chief soon got his wish. Written up, demoted, and then tossed back into the ravenous pack of his peers, Tom clenched his teeth when he thought back to how his prior request to transfer to a different ship had been denied. He had been a rock for quite some time, holding his emotions in and not letting his anger show. But his shipmates' jeering had really started to wear at his façade. He felt like a rock that was about to crumble.

Chief Peterson was in mid-sentence when the door burst open. There was no time for the men in his office to be startled because a visibly angry Tom was standing over them within three strides.

Looking right into the eyes of the chief with a searing stare, Tom screamed, "You have got to make those assholes stop!" To emphasize his point, he grabbed a nearby screwdriver and stabbed it clear through the table.

Every man in the room was frozen in silent astonishment—except, of course, for Tom, who felt alive and righteous, savoring the sweet taste of power and control. He had shut those bastards up. It was his first real, outward experience of dominance, and it felt good to him. Yet, shoving a screwdriver through a table, screaming at superior officers, interrupting a meeting—basically hurdling over the careful lines drawn between superiors and subordinates—aren't things that go over well in the navy. And so, forced into another mental evaluation, Tom put on his game face once again. It was him versus the examiner in a chess game of wits.

"And I guess I just, overall, um…feel like I don't fit in because I'm misunderstood," Tom answered the examiner, finishing up an explanation of his actions. Calm and with a forced inflection of remorse, he performed for the know-it-all sitting across from him. In his head, the explanation—the truth—was far different. *I feel I showed mercy by only attacking the table. I wanted to wet the walls with their blood and see red all around me.* But he never said any of this. He remained committed to his act, and it worked. The shrink cleared him mentally, and in his files, the diagnosis listed was "adjustment issues."

Apparently, these "issues" were ongoing. The very next week, he was reprimanded after arguing with someone on the crew and then blatantly ignoring his chief's orders to "shut the fuck up!" Tom was docked daily for his poor grooming skills and stained clothing. He also admitted to his superiors that he carried a piece of steel pipe around with him at all times for protection, which was also against the rules.

Tom was convinced that the navy was out to get him. He was sure they were just looking for a reason to get rid of him. *I just need to keep my mouth shut for now, play their game, and follow their stupid orders.* And during this period of pseudo-submission, he found some sick comfort in daydreaming about the inevitable opportunity he would have to mutilate each and every one of them. Sometimes entertaining these thoughts caused Tom to laugh out loud. The other guys in the unit who witnessed his unprompted, maniacal laughing fits quickly labeled him the crazy guy—a more accurate conclusion than the shrink had come to.

Tom Steele believed that it was more than his thoughts that separated him from those in his present company; there was also a division and a hierarchy separating them. In Tom's mind, they were all complete rejects. If there was any communication between them, it was because he chose to come down to their level. He acted as if it would be an impossible task for them to elevate themselves to his level. To him, they were simply spiders—creatures he could, with the swipe of a hand, wipe out. All of them were just tiny little spiders that crawled around building webs for others to fall into. To him they were all disposable.

Despite Tom Steele's delusional God complex, his appearance was nothing special. At twenty-eight, he was already balding and overweight. To his chagrin, he was also still a virgin. Rejected by all the girls he had asked out in high school, Tom mentally added them to his list of people who would someday regret passing up the opportunity to be with him. Once he published all the science fiction books he had been working on, he would use the proceeds and his newfound fame to open up his own bookstore. Any woman he wanted would be his—they'd see.

As he quietly crept around the house, Tom hoped that his mother would be passed out in her recliner. The last thing he wanted was to have to explain to her where he was going. His mother had no idea that he was planning on attending his ten-year high school reunion, and she'd have a million irritating questions for him if she found out. *Good Lord*, he thought as he paused in front of the mirror, *has it really been ten years since I graduated?* Tom hadn't set foot in Taylor High School since graduation day, but he couldn't wait to go back now. *I'll wipe every fake fucking smile off their faces*, he thought, smiling to himself. *They are in for a real treat tonight!*

In high school, Tom had been a loner. His looks had been average, his attire hadn't been anything out of the ordinary, and he had been a decent student. But he had become a magnet for his peers' cruelty simply because of his mediocrity. He had been nothing—never a standout in any way. In high school, he had acquaintances but no real friends to speak of. There were a few who claimed to have tried—either out of genuine interest or pity—to befriend him, but they all had failed. Wary of the motives of those around him, Tom had closed himself off and slowly turned inward, which led, eventually, to complete social ineptness.

The only activity that Tom had enjoyed in high school was being on the chess team. And though Tom had generally trusted no one, on rare occasions he had confided in another student on the team, Bruce. Bruce had felt sorry for Tom, who had always walked home after chess practice since his parents refused to pick him up. It was a two- to three-mile trek, and it would take him over an hour to get home. Bruce had often offered Tom and his younger brother a ride home, but Tom had always refused the kindness. Tom hadn't wanted Bruce's pity, and he didn't want Bruce to see their run-down house.

Tom's thinking, even back then, had been delusional and grandiose in nature. He had honestly believed that he was superior to other people—to the entire human race, in fact. He was certain that he was a more evolved form of being. After all, he never got cavities—proof enough, at least in his mind, that he was genetically superior.

In high school, this genetic superiority had never been more apparent to Tom than during chess matches. When he had competed in chess, he had never doubted that he would beat his opponent; his elevated level of intelligence would not allow it. And that's really all that life was to him: a chess match full of disposable pawns and calculated maneuvering. Success in life boiled down to the ability to bait the opponent and then swoop in with deliberate precision and no remorse to claim victory. Pity for the prey? Please.

Dressed in his Sunday best—khaki pants and a stained blue polo shirt he hadn't worn in years—he made his way to the living room, the room where his mother spent most of her time. Luckily for him, she had already taken her pills and was snoring with a lit cigarette dangling from her hand. "She's gonna burn the house down one of these days. She never listens," he said under his breath, careful not to wake her. Plucking the unfiltered Marlboro, the same brand she had smoked since he was born, from her hand, he hastily snuffed it out. With the shades drawn and the glowing cherry extinguished, the only light in the room was the flickering picture on the TV. He turned to walk away but stopped as his mother suddenly coughed and readjusted her position. It was a hacking, persistent cough that she had also had since he was born.

Continuing his stealthy exit, he gently closed the door behind him. Spinning around on his heels, he squinted into the bright red glow of the sunset. He had to take a minute to catch his breath—not because the beauty of it was breathtaking, but because this was the first time in months that Tom had emerged from the isolation of the house. Even in the fading light, he could see the stain on his shirt over the midriff area. What could he do? Go change? It wouldn't have mattered, as he had stained all his shirts. Sans napkins, he frequently feasted on his favorite foods: fried chicken or a big stack of ribs.

This habit not only explained the stains, but also why Tom continued to stay overweight despite daily exercise (within the confines of his bedroom, of course). He religiously followed the strict workout routine that he had garnered from his time in the military. In his mind, it was worth the time and effort it took to gain the strength and stamina he would need to evoke pain and fear in others when the time came.

CHAPTER 2

The excitement that flooded through Tom on the night of his reunion was very different than the excitement most people feel when they attend their high school reunions. Walking with a bounce in his step, he could hardly contain the energy that coursed through him. Three years in the making and tonight was the night. Ever since the San Ysidro McDonald's massacre, he had planned a way to harness that level of power and direct it at those who had made his time in high school torturous. He recalled, fondly, watching the coverage of the massacre on television.

San Ysidro, a San Diego community, had been permanently and notoriously put on the map that fateful day. On July 18, 1984, an unemployed security guard named James Oliver Huberty walked into a crowded McDonald's and, armed with three guns, began shooting for no apparent reason. He killed twenty-one people, including five children and six teenagers. Nineteen other victims were injured before Huberty was shot and killed by a police sniper. The seventy-seven-minute shooting spree and standoff had gone down as the largest single-day, single-gunman massacre in U.S. history. With news of the massacre spreading nationwide through television sets and newspapers, a very unsettling realization loomed. Awareness was now heightened that such a massacre could occur again at any time or any place—even in small Indiana communities. And so, the week of Tom's reunion, people around the nation were on alert.

The high school reunion could not have come at a better time for Tom. It was almost a sick favor that some unknown entity had granted him, gathering all his former classmates in the same building under the pretense of reconnecting and having a blast. They were all, unknowingly, right where he wanted them—a real-life chess match with plenty of pawns and all the pretty queens and kings perfectly positioned for him.

Muffled music and indistinguishable chatter emanated from the packed auditorium of the tiny high school. Tom entered the building with more strength than it required, pushing the double doors open with unnecessary force. His eyes scanned the room, catching some of his old classmates as they nudged the people next to them and tossed their heads in his direction. Tom strode in with an uncharacteristic confidence as he made his presence known in the packed room.

As Tom made his way through the crowd, he noticed a former classmate, Suzie, standing near the stage. In high school, Suzie had been one of the popular, rich kids that Tom had always hated. As he watched, she turned to the woman standing beside her, another old classmate. "Isn't that that freak Tom?" she asked. "Yeah, I thought he was in jail or something," the other woman replied. "He always gave me the creeps." They must have thought that Tom couldn't hear them over the music. But Tom simply grinned and walked on.

Though Tom was unshaken by the banter, he was actually a bit surprised when he ran right into Bruce, his old acquaintance from the chess team. Seeing Bruce sent a small shock through his system, because he had had some level of respect for Bruce and, if he was honest with himself, a bit of admiration as well.

But that was then, and this was now. Snapping back to the present, he realized that there was no room for pleasantries in his mission tonight. Unaware of Tom's desire to completely avoid him, Bruce spoke first. "Hey, buddy! How ya been? I wondered whatever happened to you."

"First of all, Bruce, I am not your buddy. If I was, you'd know how I've been and what I've been doing. We clear on that?" Without waiting for an answer, Tom continued, "And secondly, screw you!"

Mouth agape, Bruce stared at Tom, silently processing how horribly wrong that conversation had gone. After several seconds, Bruce simply shook his head, spun around, and walked to the back of the room as quickly as he could.

Tom made his way up to the stage and, with great force, yanked the cord to the music system out of the wall. There was a loud screech from the feedback of the speakers, and then there was silence. With the music stopped so abruptly, everyone's eyes were now on "Tom the freak" as he stepped up onto the stage.

A sweaty hand clutching the microphone and a completely captive audience in front of him, Tom launched into his speech.

"Everyone needs to shut up and listen...right...now." His voice sounded surprisingly steady and almost an octave deeper, nearing a growl. But telling them to shut up was unnecessary, as his actions had already taken care of that.

In an instant, Tom's sense of calm disappeared, and his rage took over. Pointing and shaking a finger at each one of them, he began to shout irrationally, "I remember you, and you, and you, and every last one of you motherfuckers! You all made my life hell! You all thought that you were so much better than me, but we all see who's in control now, don't we? I am!"

And now, completely forgetting that the microphone was right in front of his mouth and that he didn't need to shout, he continued even louder, making the speakers shake with a demonic distortion.

"Mark my words, you bastards…If you ever have another one of these stupid reunions, I will slaughter every one of you! I'll enjoy watching all of you breathe your last breaths! Consider this your one and only warning!"

As if this threat wasn't clear enough, it was time to drive the point home.

"I promise you that it'll put the San Ysidro massacre to shame!"

With that final thought embedded in their minds, his former classmates looked on as Tom threw the microphone down. It landed with a *thunk*, echoing throughout the auditorium. As he jumped down off the stage, everyone in his path scattered like roaches. Tom's exit was purposefully slow; he made eye contact with everyone he passed. No one stopped him or dared to speak to him. Finally, he came to the double doors he had entered and again shoved them forcefully. They swung all the way open, bouncing off the walls as he stepped through, and then slamming shut behind him. As Tom stepped out into the cool night air, he let out a whoop of joy and accomplishment.

The Taylor High School class of 1974 never met for another reunion after that night. Tom was never questioned by the authorities regarding this incident, and this success seemed to embolden him. Now that he had a taste for terrifying others, it would just be a matter of time.

DAY ONE
THURSDAY, JUNE 25, 1998

(FOURTEEN YEARS LATER)

CHAPTER 3

It was shaping up to be a scorching hot day in Kokomo, Indiana. By ten o'clock in the morning, it was already seventy-four degrees, and the air felt as humid and sticky as a sauna. Considering the record-breaking highs of late, the heat advisory warnings broadcasted over the radio and printed in the morning paper weren't a surprise. Local weather personalities started off the morning news predicting the heat index to reach 104 degrees. Scorching, indeed.

Kokomo is located in Howard County, about an hour north of Indianapolis, the state capital. The city is nicknamed "City of Firsts," largely because of the inventiveness of one of its most famous residents, Elwood Haynes. In 1894, Haynes invented one of the first successful gasoline-powered automobiles, and in 1906, he invented stellite, an alloy widely used today in spacecrafts, jet engines, dental tools, and nuclear power plants. Six years later, to appease his wife's desire to have tarnish-free silverware, Haynes invented stainless steel.

In 1887, Kokomo was put on the map when the largest natural gas gusher in U.S. history struck in what is now southeast Kokomo. The city was immediately transformed into a center of industry. Not surprisingly, a small suburb sprang into existence on this southeastern side of town. Since its founding, this town—Center, Indiana—had been considered a safe place to live. Neighbors in Center treated each other like family, often because they were family. The few major crimes and dangers that existed were near the heart of the city of Kokomo, not out on its fringes where Center was located. It was the kind of town where people left their doors unlocked and their car keys in the ignition.

On this hot morning, the mole drove his old, beaten up '81 Datsun to the nearby post office in Oakford, Indiana, only a mile from his house. Inside was an attractive female who he knew worked the morning shift alone. These were the kinds of details that the mole had recorded with an eerie efficiency.

Brazenly, he walked into the building at nine o'clock sharp. Visually startled, the woman faced the mole.

"Sorry if I scared you, but my car needs to be jumped. My battery is dead. I couldn't find anyone else, and I hate to even bother you, but could you help me out?"

The woman looked around to see if Jeff, the custodian, was around, but she didn't see him. An awkward silence was growing in the air.

Trying to keep her from panicking, the mole continued to lure her out.

"I promise it will only take a second. I have jumper cables in my car, and I've done it a million times." He offered a not-too-convincing smile.

"Sorry, but my boss won't let me leave the building when I'm here alone," she said, trying to work the shakiness out of her voice. "Walk over to the church. There might be someone there who can help you."

The mole started to sweat. He had not expected the woman to be such a stickler for the rules. Determined, he tried again.

"Look, it's so hot out here today. Can't you just bend the rules a little? You'll be back in no time. I'll make it worth your while...I'll give you twenty bucks," he said, sticking his hand in his pocket and pretending to fish around for some cash.

Now her fear was mixing with irritation. "I told you I can't, buddy," she said firmly. "I'm not getting in trouble with my boss for you." She surprised herself with how convincingly she delivered this last line.

More angry than impressed, the mole contemplated throwing himself across the counter and choking the woman, but he kept himself in check. After all, all these federal buildings had surveillance cameras inside. He sighed and then walked briskly to the door to exit the post office.

"Have a nice day, bitch!" he said, smiling smugly. The mole quickly dismissed Plan A and set his sights on Plan B.

Plan A was supposed to work like this: Get the pretty little clerk to come out to his car. Immobilize her with a stun gun. Put her in his car with him and whisk her off to let the games begin.

Without rhyme or reason, he started whistling as he pushed his car out of the clerk's view and then hopped in, started it up, and drove off. Little did the woman at the post office know that by following the company policy, she had saved her own life.

Tick tock, tick tock. Today is the day. Time is wastin.' That cunt whore don't want to come and play? She wasn't worth my time anyway.

Driving back to his mother's house, he tried to let go of his anger and focus. To stay on track, he needed to be determined and confident. His mother was on the tail end of one of her trips to the gambling boats in northern Indiana. Time definitely was ticking. *On to Plan B*, he thought.

CHAPTER 4

The ten years following his high school reunion had not been good to the mole. Soon afterward, he had been arrested for raping and assaulting a woman in Bloomington, Indiana. The ten years he had spent in prison for these charges had given him ample time to read multiple books from the library on police investigations and to devise plans to outwit the legal system. He had learned his lesson since then. This time, he would be more careful.

He parked his old beater in the front yard of his house and put a For Sale sign that he had dug out of his mother's closet that morning on the hood of the car. He would have to remember to call his mother in a few days and tell her that if anyone called about it, he would take no less than five hundred dollars for it. He would make her give a starting price higher than that and then settle for less if he had to. He would need some extra cash to get his bookstore and new relationship off to a good start.

The mole went inside the old house and got out his trusty gray backpack, which he had carried around since college. It was a handy mode of transporting all the essentials to abduct a woman, if the opportunity presented itself, no matter where he went. It was unassuming, and whenever he was asked about it, he just told people that he loved to read and that it was filled with books.

This morning, he filled it with a stun gun, nylon electrical ties, and the handgun that his mother had kept in her night-stand for the past twenty years. The mole also added a sharp Swiss Army knife, electrical tape, a wig, a dress, and a bra. He threw in a pair of gloves as well so he wouldn't leave fingerprints at the scene. He had only used ropes and a knife in his first rape toolkit in 1984. This one was much more sophisticated. He was determined not to get caught again. This time, he wouldn't let the girl escape like the last one had. He would kill this one if she ever tried to get away from him.

The mole retrieved his old, rusted Schwinn bicycle from the garage. He knew that the bike ride to his next prospect's home was just a little over a mile, but it could take him longer since it was so miserably hot and he was overweight. He had been watching her and taking note of her daily routine for the past year, so he was fairly certain that she did not go into work until five thirty in the evening. She lived with her parents, but they left by nine in the morning for work. It was around ten o'clock now, and he hoped that he could make it there before Anita left the house that morning.

The mole climbed onto his bike and set off toward Center Road. After several minutes, he was panting hard with every pump of his legs. It was a bit windy, but in these temperatures, it only stirred the hot air around. It wasn't a good day to be do-ing much outside, but the mole was already on his second trip of the morning.

As he pedaled closer to her house, he heard the familiar and comforting squeaking of the bicycle spokes with every turn of the wheels. He concentrated on the soothing rhythm of the sound, and soon he was passing rows and rows of cornfields and the occasional soybean field. It was typical midwestern Indiana scenery. A cloud of humid fog lingered directly over the cornstalks. There was a stark contrast between the lush green of the grass and the golden hue of the corn husks that were towering high by now. The cornstalks were, as Hoosiers say, "knee-high by the Fourth of July."

It had been a rough season for the local farmers. On June 11, just two weeks prior, a tornado had ripped through the eastern side of Howard County. The tornado's destructive, zigzag path had left large gaps in the rows of crops, but as the bright sun began to clear away the hovering fog, highlighting all the vivid colors of the land, it was still a breathtaking sight to see. The mole, however, paid no attention to the scenery surrounding him, and he was not remotely concerned about the plight of the farmers. He had his eyes on the prize that lay a mile down the road.

Although the strong breeze coming off the fields produced a wave of delightful fragrances, a bouquet of pollen, sunflowers, and sweet corn, all the mole could smell was his own rank breath as he took long breaths in and out. His grooming skills had gotten even poorer over the years, and he was now accustomed to only showering once a week and brushing his teeth when he felt like it. His shirt, a white tank top, was drenched with sweat, and he had a putrid body odor. He never even put on deodorant; what would be the point?

The mole took his hand off the handlebars and wiped the dripping sweat from his brow onto his soaked shirt. He smiled at his own foul odor. He liked the freedom of showering when he damn well felt like showering—even if it meant reeking to high heaven. As the mole rode on, he came upon a carcass lying in the road. It appeared to be a dead kitten, and three black crows were already devouring the remains. The smell of the decaying, rotting flesh combined with the heat smoldering off the asphalt road would be enough to turn most people's stomachs, but the mole watched this activity intently and delighted in the odors. The crows waited until he was just inches from them to leave their breakfast. As they flew away, they seemed to give the mole a look of disgust and loathing.

This damn heat is gonna kill me, he thought angrily. *Maybe I should have planned this for the fall.* The mole stopped pedaling about a half mile from the girl's house, pulling his bike off onto the side of the road. He made sure that he was right in front of cornfields with no houses in sight. At this time of day, Center Road was fairly deserted, though there had been a group of teenagers that had zoomed by him several minutes before, shouting for him to "get off the fucking road." The look of scorn they had given him had just fueled his already present fury at the human race. The mole looked around, and seeing no cars present, he swiftly zipped open his backpack, removed the Swiss Army knife, and slashed the front tire of his favorite bike, letting the air escape. If his brother happened to pass him on the road or if the girl's family was home, the flat tire would act as his excuse for being there.

The mole quickly threw the knife back in the bag and slung his backpack into position. He started walking, slowly at first and then a little more briskly, his thoughts and heartbeat quickening with each passing step. *Tick tock, tick tock*, he thought. *The time has come, little Miss Anita. You will either learn to love me or I'll kill you…*

CHAPTER 5

That morning, Anita Wooldridge had planned to head over to Taylor High School—the school she had graduated from in 1995—to help on the tornado clean-up crew. Helping others came naturally to Anita. A very empathic person, she had always looked for the good in others, and she was the type of person that other people wanted to be around. Modest and humble in nature, she never took herself too seriously. She had an easy laugh and a quick wit, with a good sense of humor about herself and others.

With her pale skin, mid-length red hair, and full lips, Anita was often told that she resembled Molly Ringwald. She had a thin, fit figure—in high school, she had competed in volleyball, softball, and basketball—but she had developed rather large breasts at a young age, much to her chagrin. Over the years, she had gotten attention from many boys, but for the past eight months, she had been dating Scott Miller, her second serious boyfriend.

Anita's family was a tight-knit one, and Anita, the youngest of three children, had remained close with her parents and her older brother and sister even as she grew older. Now that Anita was twenty-one, her mom, Carrie Ann, wondered where the time had gone. It seemed like just yesterday that Anita was running around with her flaming red pigtails flapping in the air, asking incessantly, "Mommy, what we gonna do today?" Now, Anita had graduated from college. She was planning to move out soon to get her own place or to live with her friends, and though her parents would miss having her in the house, they trusted their daughter and knew that it was time for her to leave the nest.

Anita's mom poked her head in her daughter's room before she left for work that morning at eight forty-five. She stared lovingly at her youngest daughter, who looked very peaceful in her slumber with her long, pale legs sprawled out on her bed. Though she hated to disturb her, she entered the room and shook Anita gently.

"Honey, are you still going over to the school this morning?"

Anita had been out late the night before, catching up with friends at the local Applebee's, but she managed to wake up enough to stretch her arms over her head and give a big yawn. It took her several seconds to figure out who was in her room and what her mom was asking her. Anita hastily wiped at her eyes to clear the crust that had formed on her eyelids overnight. "No, it got cancelled because of the heat advisory," she mumbled groggily. "I'm gonna get some more sleep. Can you set the alarm for me for ten thirty? Scott's coming over at noon, and we're gonna go have lunch at Grandma and Grandpa's today."

"Sure. What time do you go into work today?"

"I have to be there by three thirty. I'm gonna be so tired, so please, Mom, let me sleep!"

Carrie Ann set the alarm for her daughter.

"Okay, okay. I'm going. I love you, sweetie. Have a good day."

"Love you, too."

Anita fell back into a deep sleep for another two precious hours. This would be the last deep sleep she would have for some time.

CHAPTER 6

Anita was tossing and turning in her sleep, drenched in sweat. She was scantily clad with only a white T-shirt and underwear on, but without central air, her room was becoming stiflingly hot. She was dreaming that she was surrounded by flames and couldn't escape from her grandmother's upstairs bedroom. In her dream, the house had caught on fire during the night, and though she kept trying to yell for help, she couldn't catch her breath from all the smoke she inhaled. She gasped for air and jerked straight up in bed, relieved by the sudden awareness that it had only been a bad dream. "Whew! Just a dream," she said out loud. "Man, I'm so hot!"

Anita squinted to see her surroundings, as she was not wearing her contact lenses and her glasses were nowhere to be found. Everything was blurry, but she could see the blazing sun streaming in through her window and illuminating her small bedroom. Aware that it had to be close to ten thirty, Anita sighed deeply and leaned down to put her face close to the alarm clock on her bedside table. This allowed Anita to see the big red numbers: 10:13 a.m. Though she had only had one Long Island Iced Tea last night, she had stayed out until two in the morning because she was having such a good time catching up with some of her old friends from high school. She rarely stayed out that late during a work week, and she was feeling it this morning.

Anita had just swung her long legs over the side of the bed to get up when she heard the doorbell ringing. She was slightly irritated to hear it, thinking that it must be her boyfriend showing up several hours early. *I told him I wouldn't be ready until noon*, Anita thought to herself. *What is he doing here so early?*

She hastily threw on a pair of old jogging shorts and trudged down the hallway to the front door. In mid-step, Anita suddenly felt a sharp pain in her right toe. "Ow!" she yelled. She looked down and realized that she had stepped on a tack. The tack, she recalled, had fallen off her calendar weeks before, and though she had looked for it, she had been unable to find it. *Oh, this is turning out to be a great morning*, she thought. *What else is going to go wrong?*

As Anita stood in the hallway, the doorbell rang a second time; at the exact same moment, the telephone rang. With the tack still lodged in her toe, Anita should have remembered her grandmother's old saying, "You step on a tack and the devil is comin' back." If she had, she might have thought twice before answering the door. But Anita wasn't thinking about her grandmother's saying. Instead, she was thinking, *What is this, Grand Central Station? Everyone needs to leave me alone!*

Anita reached the door first, yanking it open without checking to see who was behind it. To her surprise, it was Tom, a guy she had known from her days at the sports club she had worked at a year or so prior. Anita had not seen or talked to him at all for the two years since he'd stopped coming to the gym. It was as if he had vanished for that period of time. Now, here he was, waiting on her doorstep.

Anita's best friend, Sarah, was getting married in less than two weeks, and they had discussed sending Tom an invitation. He had always seemed in desperate need of some friends. His name had popped into their heads while they had been reminiscing about old times at the club they both had worked at. Anita thought that maybe Sarah had invited him after all, which could explain why he was stopping by unexpectedly; maybe he wanted to see if she was going too. This is why Anita felt comfortable and safe when she willingly let the mole into her family's home.

CHAPTER 7

The first time she had checked in Tom Steele at the fitness center, he had seemed odd but harmless. He had walked in and, without making eye contact, had asked her if any hot girls worked out at the gym. "I don't know. I don't check out girls," Anita had replied sarcastically. "You'll have to let me know." He had ignored her and walked on past her after scanning his ID membership card. *Well, he's got no social skills*, she had thought. But as Tom's visits to the gym became more and more regular, Anita started to feel sorry for how backward and lonely he seemed. He would talk to her on occasions about celebrating holidays alone and how he had gotten used to it. Tom had never had the best grooming skills, and to avoid his powerful stench, Anita would often have to hold her breath for as long as she possibly could while he was standing in front of her.

Weird and a little obnoxious, Tom annoyed most of Anita's coworkers. Every time he came into the club, the other female staff members would flip a coin to see which one of them had to check in "creepy Tom." But unlike her coworkers, Anita thought that everyone just needed to give him a break, so she always tried to be nice to him. Often, Tom would bring her science fiction stories he had written and ask for her opinion on them, but he never seemed to want to hear any of her constructive criticism.

Honestly, Anita just couldn't follow his way of thinking in the stories—it was all way too "out there" for her. The one time she had told him as much, Tom had seemed offended at first, but he had recovered quickly, saying haughtily, "That's okay. I haven't found anyone yet that can think the way that I can." After that encounter, he had left the gym without working out and did not come back for weeks.

Tom's membership at the club was terminated a few weeks after his return to the club. Anita's boss told her that it was because of complaints from some female employees that Tom "creeped them out." Anita, who was back on good terms with Tom, since he had returned to the gym and started talking to her again, felt sorry for him. He had recently told her that he liked the way she was always there to talk to and how she was so giving to other people. He had mentioned to her that, although he would never attend her church like she had asked him to do, he respected Christian girls for how submissive they seemed to their men. Anita had quickly started talking about her boyfriend so that he would not try to ask her out. She did not want to have to reject him and get on his bad side again.

Anita never saw Tom again after his gym membership was terminated. Early on, she would occasionally wonder what had ever happened to him, but she never felt like she should try to contact him as he might not want to be bothered. As time went on, she stopped thinking of him altogether until, years later, she and her friend Sarah reminisced about old times at the gym and his name was brought up.

CHAPTER 8

With the telephone still ringing in the background, Anita greeted the mole. "Hey, Tom," she said. "What are you doing here?
I haven't seen you in forever." He was the same balding, overweight, smelly guy that she remembered.

"I was riding my bike and got a flat tire. It's so hot out!
Could I have a drink of water and use your phone?"

"Sure. Come on in. I just have to take this call first."

Anita answered the phone. It was her uncle, the town fire
marshal, calling with some questions for her dad about the fireworks display they were putting on for the annual Fourth of
July festival in town. She told her uncle that she would leave her
dad the message and hung up the receiver. Anita started to lean
down, finally getting the chance to pull out the tack still lodged
in her throbbing toe.

But as Anita bent over, she felt an electric shock go through
her backside, followed by a violent shove. "Stop!" she screamed.
She tried to fight back, kicking her attacker with all her might.
"You're hurting me! Why are you doing this?"

The mole, now lying on top of her with all his weight, said very calmly, "I'll kill you if you scream again." When Anita continued to struggle, he reached around and shocked her in the stomach with his stun gun. "Listen very carefully," he said slowly. "I mean it. You're dead if you fight me anymore."

The shock to Anita's stomach had completely sapped her strength, and she lay limp, unable to fight anymore. She lost control of her bladder and urinated all over the floor. Though he hadn't planned for this, the mole responded with swift efficiency, removing Anita's sodden underwear and shorts and wiping up the mess from the floor with a towel he found in the bathroom. He threw the soiled towel inside the laundry room hamper, where it mixed with the other wet towels, and then, as if he had been there hundreds of times, he walked into her room and pulled out a pair of running shorts from an old white dresser that had been in her room since she was a child. Anita used to draw on that dresser with magic marker as a kid—a habit that had driven her mother crazy—and the pink marks were still visible. Anita, in utter shock, was still too weak from the blow to her stomach to attempt an escape.

Holding the shorts, the mole returned to Anita and slid them on her without underwear. For the first time, she noticed the black gloves on his hands. He quickly removed the electrical ties and tape from his backpack, and as a reminder not to mess with him, he snapped Anita's head back with such force that she was sure he was trying to break her neck. In a state of total shock, Anita couldn't make a sound, so the mole broke the silence.

"I can kill you, and I will if you don't cooperate. I'm in some financial trouble, and I need some money."

The news came as an instant relief to Anita.

"You can take all the money I have. My bank card's in my purse, and my pin number is 1709. I have around a thousand dollars in there. And you can have my mom's jar of coins and bills. It's in her closet. There's probably a few hundred dollars in there. Take whatever you need—just please let me go."

The mole stood directly over Anita and pretended to write in a small notebook. When he was finished, he opened his bag and pulled out a wig, women's clothing, and a handgun. He changed into his disguise as she watched him, even taking care to stuff the bra with Kleenex tissues he had brought with him from his mother's bathroom. Picking up the loaded gun and putting it against Anita's head, he contemplated his next move. His thoroughness perplexed Anita. *Why is he going to all this trouble if he's only going to rob me?* she wondered. The mole put the gun down on the table. He gagged her mouth with a sock and electrical tape and bound her hands and feet with the electrical ties. As he did so, Anita thought that she was going to get sick from the excruciating pain and choke on her own vomit.

"I'm going to carry you to the garage. I assume your car is in there. Are your keys in your purse?"

Anita nodded her head, and the mole reached into her purse to grab the car keys. Anita was surprised and confused when he did not touch her bank card or her mom's money. Keys in hand, he threw Anita over his shoulder and carried his captive prize to the kitchen. The mole was out of breath and growing impatient.

"Where's the damn door that leads out to the garage?"

The mole hadn't realized that the garage was detached from the house; from outside, it appeared to be attached. In the kitchen, he found only a window that opened up to give him a view of the inside of the garage that he so desperately wanted to reach. The mole seemed to panic as he realized his mistake, becoming so agitated that Anita feared he would drop her.

"I don't have a choice now. I have to kill you. Your neighbor across the street is out, and he'll see us if we try to get to the garage," the mole said as he ripped the tape and gag from Anita's mouth.

"Please don't kill me," Anita pleaded. "There has to be another way."

As he tried to formulate a new plan, the mole sat Anita down on the floor and pulled the tack out of her toe. Although he didn't notice it, one tiny drop of her blood went splat onto the linoleum floor. It was the only DNA evidence that the police would find at the crime scene. The tack, which had so irked Anita earlier, was in fact a blessing in disguise, a single clue for the police to find her.

After several seconds of contemplation, the mole made up his mind. He ripped the screen out of the kitchen window, threw it on the kitchen floor, and attempted to shove Anita through the tiny window. Unfortunately for him, his new plan failed as well; the window was too narrow for her to fit through.

"You could take me out the back door and around to the garage."

"No, that won't work," he snapped.

The mole rushed into Anita's parents' bedroom and grabbed the comforter off their queen-sized bed. He tried to wrap Anita up in the comforter and carry her out, but his prey was too heavy. The mole was becoming visibly frustrated.

"Dammit! Why does this have to be so hard? I'm about done with you."

The mole put Anita down and untied her feet so she could walk on her own. He forced her into her own room, where he grabbed her favorite red robe, the one her mother had embroidered penguins on, from her closet. He wrapped the robe around her, trying to hide her bound hands, and retied her feet with the zip ties. The robe, which reached the floor, covered her feet as well.

The mole led Anita out the front door slowly, as she had to shuffle her bound feet forward and stumbled several times. Her captor placed his arm securely around her. His tight grip ensured that she wouldn't have the opportunity to fall or run away, and also, if anyone saw them, it would appear that they were good friends. The mole looked hideous in his disguise as a woman, but from a distance, he could probably pass for her aunt or grandmother. He led her to the garage and opened the door with a strong pull, letting it shut behind them. Out of view once again, he removed the red robe, leaving Anita in just a T-shirt, shorts, and her favorite bracelet on her arm.

The mole picked Anita up and placed her in the trunk of her 1990 dark blue Buick sedan. "Listen carefully," he said before he closed the trunk. "I'm going to drive you way out to the middle of nowhere and leave the car, so I'll have time to get away before you're found. I'm taking your purse with me, and I'll get the money out before I leave town in my own car."

The mole paused for a moment and gave Anita a rueful look. Making his best attempt at an apology, he added, "Sorry it had to be this way. You were always nice to me." He slammed the trunk door with a *thunk*, and she could hear his wheezing breaths through the door. The mole was elated that his plan was working. *I am so brilliant*, he thought to himself. *They'll never catch me this time. I'll always be one step ahead of those stupid pigs.* Ironically, at the very same moment, Anita heard him snorting with delight. *He sounds just like a pig,* she thought.

Left alone in the trunk, the darkness enveloped Anita. She was trapped, and for the first time in her life, she found herself in a situation with no perceivable way out. Her body began to shake uncontrollably. This was actually happening to her, she realized. For several seconds, she was completely immobilized by intense fear. She couldn't think or speak, and she was beginning to lose her breath from the lack of oxygen in the tiny, stiflingly hot trunk. She gasped, and the rush of warm air to her lungs was enough to snap her out of her panic. *I will be out of here soon,* she thought. *Someone will find me. I just need to breathe.*

Feeling calmer, Anita began to quietly recite her favorite Bible passage, Psalm 23, which she had memorized as a young girl in Sunday school. It had always brought her comfort.

"The LORD is my shepherd; I shall not want. He maketh me to lie down in green pastures: he leadeth me beside the still waters. He restoreth my soul: he leadeth me in the paths of righteousness for his name's sake. Yea, though I walk through the valley of the shadow of death, I will fear no evil: for thou art with me; thy rod and thy staff they comfort me. Thou preparest a table before me in the presence of mine enemies: thou anointest my head with oil; my cup runneth over. Surely goodness and mercy shall follow me all the days of my life: and I will dwell in the house of the LORD forever. Amen."

Anita could now breathe again. *Please, dear Lord, let me live through this. I'm not ready to die,* Anita begged silently.

CHAPTER 9

Captain Jack Roberts had joined the law enforcement agency right out of high school. Growing up, there was never any question what field he would go into. He had been a part of the force for twenty-eight years now, and not once during those years had he ever regretted his decision. In fact, his father had always urged him to go and make more money at one of the two automobile plants in Kokomo, but Jack wanted to be out in the field fighting crime. He often almost felt bad taking money for the job as it was mostly fun and exciting to him. Hardworking and intense, Jack Roberts never gave up on a case.

His determination came from the fact that he strongly believed in justice and felt like victims and their families needed the closure of a solved case in order to move on. Jack was a man who went by the facts and evidence and tried not to get emotionally involved in any case he worked on. He felt like it clouded an officer's vision and interfered with the investigative process. Jack was a very loyal man with old-school beliefs; he believed that a handshake meant something. If he gave his word to someone, then he would come through for them. He had good relationships with his fellow sheriff's department officers, as well as with the Kokomo Police Department officers, a rare thing given the competition and rivalries between the two departments and jurisdictions.

People respected Jack, which helped him solve cases; he had contacts who were willing to help him from both departments and support from his boss, Tim Madison, the chief sheriff's deputy. Over the years, Jack had been in charge of several murder, robbery, and drug cases. He had been in dangerous situations, but he prided himself on following procedures for safety to keep himself and his men alive.

He and his wife, Dorothy, had been married for twenty-five years and had raised two daughters and a son together. Jack had always been a strict but loving father, and his expectations for his children had been greatly exceeded. He was extremely proud that they had all gone on to college and were now starting to make families of their own. Jack was a very private man and fiercely protective of his family.

Thus, it was important to Jack to mentally separate his professional life from his private life so that he did not bring home all the chaos and violence he witnessed on a daily basis at work. Jack and Dorothy lived in Kokomo on the outskirts of Howard County in a serene setting. Their modest but beautiful one-story home sat about a mile back from the road, surrounded by woods, providing them with a sense of privacy and allowing them to view all the wildlife in its natural setting. It was always such a nice reprieve to come home to a peaceful house away from the hustle and bustle of the city. The twenty-minute drive to work allowed him the time to mentally prepare for the day, and the drive home allowed him the time to unwind and let the frustrations and excitement of the day go.

To balance these two sides of his life—work and family—Jack maintained a very structured household and a rigid routine. Every day, he and his wife woke up at seven in the morning to the beeping of the alarm clock they had used for the past twenty years. He would rise first, and after stretching his aching limbs, he would take a long, hot shower. When Dorothy heard her husband step into the shower, she would go downstairs to start brewing their caffeinated coffee. After retrieving the *Kokomo Tribune* from the driveway, she would scramble eggs and make buttered toast. The couple would read the newspaper over breakfast. Dorothy always started off with the upcoming community events section, while Jack was always anxious to read about the top news stories first. Then they would trade off.

On this particular Thursday, Jack came downstairs in his starched, long-sleeved sheriff's uniform, looking dignified and attractive, despite the fact that he was nearly fifty years old. He had remained physically fit, due in large part to the daily walks he took with his wife and their three dogs and his regular workouts in his home gym. He was only five feet eleven, but his natural charisma and authoritative air made him seem taller.

Dorothy was standing at the stove when Jack approached her and kissed her tenderly on the top of her head. "Good morning. That smells good," he said, leaning over the skillet. "So what's on your agenda for today?"

His wife turned to look at him over her shoulder. "You look good today," she said with a smile. "I've got to get groceries and then go over to Beverly's house to help her with her mom. She can't lift her by herself to get her cleaned up, and the insurance won't pay for an in-home nurse yet. I really feel for her. If she doesn't get any help, she'll have to put her mom in the nursing home. She'd really hate to do that to her mom, though."

Jack looked up at his wife. As always, he was amazed by her beauty and compassion for others. His love for his wife—who stood by him despite her fear that the perils of his line of work would catch up with him one day—had continued to grow over the years. He knew that she prayed everyday for his safety, and he prayed every day that she would not worry so much.

"Well, I hope it all works out for them. I'm sure that her insurance will kick in soon. Try not to worry about it too much, hon," Jack told Dorothy to console her. Dorothy returned to her cooking, and Jack turned his gaze toward the back sliding glass doors. In the bushes near the house, he had spotted a cardinal, its color such a vivid crimson that it had immediately caught his eye. He watched as a blue jay landed on the same bush. As soon as the new bird landed, the cardinal flew away. *How funny*, Jack thought. *Even birds have turf wars!*

After breakfast, Jack checked his watch—he had to be at the station by eight thirty—and rose from his seat. "Gotta go," he said to Dorothy. "Love you. Have a good day." She walked over and gave him a kiss and a hug. "Love you too," she replied. "Be careful." As he drove to work, Jack's mindset was peaceful. He knew that he would deal with whatever came his way that day.

CHAPTER 10

Anita was trying to lie as still as she could so she would stop flopping from one side of the car trunk to the other. Each time the car came to a stop, made a sharp turn, or hit a bump, she went flying. She lay crammed toward the back of the trunk and tried to focus on which way her captor turned and where he was taking her. Anita was familiar enough with the roads to sense that they had just gone down Center Road and come to a stop sign. They kept going straight, driving over the railroad tracks that she had sped over a thousand times before. She knew this route like the back of her hand.

Soon, they reached what Anita knew had to be Highway 31; she could hear the loud, speeding traffic zooming by. She heard people's voices from nearby cars. She envied each and every one of them, knowing that they were probably headed out to lunch or on their way back to work. *Why did the relief team have to be cancelled?* Anita thought earnestly. *I should have gotten up and gone over to Scott's house when my mom woke me up this morning. If only I could wake up from this nightmare like I did the last one.* But she couldn't. Anita was trapped, at least for now.

Anita felt her captor turn her car left onto the highway. She flew to the right side of the trunk, landing with a loud thud. Her elbows and hips were getting banged up and badly bruised, and she frantically grasped for anything to hang onto but found nothing. The mole made another left, this time onto what Anita knew must be the familiar State Road 26. *He's probably heading out into the country near Oakford,* Anita thought, trusting his promise to leave her stranded. When he came to an abrupt stop and turned into what she thought was a gravel driveway, she was surprised. She heard the crunching of the tires grinding into the gravel rocks. The rocks were being pelted at all sides of the car, and the sound was deafening from inside the trunk.

Anita heard a garage door going up, and her car drove forward slowly. Until that moment, she had kept up hope that the mole had been telling her the truth—that this whole ordeal was going to be over soon. She had been grateful that he was planning to leave her for dead and believed that someone would have eventually found her stranded car and rescued her if she prayed hard enough.

The mole turned the engine off, and in the trunk, it became deathly quiet. *Why is he sitting in the car?* Anita wondered. *What's he planning to do with me?* Though terrified, she was unable to scream or move. *He's left me in here to suffocate, and he hid the car. No one will be able to find me now. Oh, God, please save me from this crazy maniac. Don't let him hurt me!* She whimpered and began to repeat, over and over, in a soft, desperate whisper, "I don't want to die!"

The frightened girl heard the mole open the car door and shut it with a *bang*. She heard his footsteps as he approached

44

the trunk, jostling her keys. Anita's thoughts went briefly to the photo on her keychain. It was her favorite picture of her and her boyfriend, Scott, taken on a canoeing trip in Tennessee this past October. They both were smiling broadly in the photo—it had been a great day, and they were very much in love with each other. That day, Anita had felt the happiest and most content that she had ever felt.

The mole interrupted Anita's thoughts as he put the small key in the hole and turned it; the trunk popped right open. The light from the garage poured into the trunk, and Anita was forced to squint to see a blurry vision of the mole standing over her. She could barely see him without her contacts in, but she could tell he had changed out of his disguise.

The mole picked Anita up out of the trunk and flung her over his shoulder like a bag of trash. He carried her over to the other side of the garage and placed her, sitting up, on the filthy, oil-stained floor with her back up against the wall. Pulling over a fold-up lawn chair, he sat down facing her. He looked at her for a few moments, and then he rose, grabbed a dirty, old cup from the shelves, and went to the garage sink to fill the glass full of lukewarm water for her to drink.

The mole placed the drink in Anita's trembling hands. Still standing, the mole cradled his face in his hands for a moment, as if to collect his thoughts. With new resolve, he picked up the terrified girl and carried her over to the lawn chair. He sat down in the chair first, and pulled her down with him so that she was sitting on his lap. Staring into Anita's brown eyes, he cleared his throat before speaking. "Well, I know you've already heard about my prior conviction," he said with no emotion in his voice.

"I have no idea what you're talking about," Anita stammered. "If you just let me go, I won't tell anyone about any of this."

"Don't play dumb," he replied. "I know that your boss at the sports club told all of you that I have a criminal record. It was for rape. I have an unusually high need for sex, and I chose you because you were always so willing to give of yourself for others."

After a slight pause, the mole continued, "Now, you have an important decision to make. If you choose not to have sex with me and give me what I want, I'll have to kill you and find a woman that will. It's your choice."

For a moment, Anita considered her options. She quickly decided that she would do whatever it took to stay alive—long enough for the police to rescue her and for her to be reunited with her family and Scott. She would do whatever she had to do to stay alive. Anita knew that if she could just endure this, if she could become her captor's friend like she had in the past, he might keep her alive long enough for her to be rescued. So Anita accepted what she had to do to stay alive and asked him only one question that she felt like she deserved to know.

"Do you have AIDS?"

"No. I've only been with one woman, and that was thirteen years ago."

As if the mole could be trusted. He threw a ratty, blue blanket onto the filthy garage floor. Anita began to beg. "No," she pleaded. "Please, not here."

But the mole ignored her pleas. Gruffly, he said the four words that she would hear repeatedly over the next eight days: "Take your clothes off."

Anita made one more attempt to talk him out of it. "Please," she cried, "just forget about all this, and let me go. You're really a good person, and I won't tell anyone about this."

"Then I'll have to kill you," he replied.

"Can you at least loosen the straps on my hands first?" Anita asked. Both of her hands had gone completely numb and were now a deep shade of purple. The mole reluctantly agreed. But the relief of having her straps loosened quickly subsided.

"Kiss me," the mole said, pulling her head forward to his and meeting her lips with an eager, open mouth. He forced his tongue inside her mouth, causing Anita to gasp. When he felt her tensing up, he pulled her head back with a jerk to let her know that she had better start cooperating. Anita knew then that she had to succumb to him. She parted her lips reluctantly, and his tongue reentered her mouth.

After several minutes, the mole began to squeeze Anita's breasts. "You have beautiful tits," he told her. "Just the way I like them." Anita felt like a new car that he was trying out. He pulled her T-shirt over her head and pulled off her black running shorts, leaving her completely naked and exposed to him. His eyes roamed over her body, and a strange, glazed look—a look of deep desire and evil intentions—crossed his face. "I made a good choice with this one," he muttered to himself. "She's so sweet and soft."

Anita closed her eyes and tried not to think about what was happening. The mole took off his jean shorts and underwear and pointed down to his naked penis, which was hanging limply. "Suck it," he ordered, and she complied, putting it in her mouth as he rammed her head down on it, causing her to gag and choke. Anita felt like she might vomit from the combination of this gruesome act, the sweltering heat inside the garage, the strong fumes from the nearby gas cans, and the pain that she already felt from his earlier blow to her neck.

But the mole didn't care. Moaning with pleasure, he continued to thrust his penis in and out of her mouth. His penis smelled of some sort of fungus mixed with the acrid smell of urine and body odor. The taste was salty and made Anita cringe. She was hopeful that the mole would climax soon and be done with her. Unfortunately, this was not the case.

The mole was struggling to keep his erection, so he laid his victim down on the blanket and retightened her hands. He entered her roughly with his fingers. After several seconds, he attempted to push his penis inside her, but it was too limp. Highly frustrated, he abruptly yanked his hostage to her feet and bent her over two antique trunks that were stacked on top of each other against the garage wall. After stroking his penis himself to get it hard, he tried to ram it in her anally. Anita, who had never experienced this act before, screamed out in pain and begged him to stop. "Shut up!" he scolded. "You'll learn to like it." But the mole—unable to keep an erection—could not fully penetrate her.

"Dammit!" he cursed. "It's just too hot in here! I'm taking you in the house where it's cooler. Then we can really have some fun, honey."

The mole picked Anita up, carried her over to a large cardboard box, and placed her inside. Loading the box onto a dolly, he transported her from the detached garage, across the large yard, to his mother's house so that no one passing by would see her. The dolly hit several bumps as he crossed the uneven yard, knocking Anita around inside the box. Once they reached the house, her captor used his foot to scoot the large box off the dolly and into the house; once inside, he forced Anita to crawl out, still naked. As she obeyed him, she felt degraded, exposed, and dirty.

Although Anita tried to become aware of her surroundings, she saw no way to escape from this unfamiliar house. She had no idea where she even was at this point. The mole picked her up off the floor and carried Anita up several steep steps, through a doorway, to the entrance of a second stairway, where she had to duck her head to go under a blanket that the mole had hung to give himself a sense of privacy from his mother. He had an understanding with his mother that she was never to go upstairs to his room.

The mole dragged Anita further up the stairs into a dark, musty attic, which Anita guessed was his bedroom. It was a filthy mess, with clothes strewn all over and rotten food left out on the nightstand. The stench was powerful. Everything Anita saw seemed bizarre and out of place in a forty-two-year-old man's room, including the posters of young pop stars that adorned the drab walls. He seemed obsessed with Britney Spears in particular.

Inside his bedroom, the mole again ordered Anita to suck his penis. She did as he said. He then laid her on her back on his old mattress and began to rape her. As he thrust himself inside her over and over, the bedsprings creaked loudly, and Anita was bounced up and down, despite her efforts to remain still. As the mole raped her, Anita took herself unconsciously to another place. Her eyes caught a blurry glimpse of a shiny, gold chess trophy that sat on his shelf, and she fixated on its color, which conjured up images of her own happy childhood and the many trophies that she had won in sports. Anita was flooded by all the emotions and good memories of her life up until now. She thought of her dad and how proud he had looked the night that she had graduated from high school. Tears flooded down her cheeks, but she did not make a sound. She was too afraid.

Her rapist's moaning finally stopped, and his body shook in ecstasy. Although her body could still feel the hot pain of the thrusts, Anita's conscious mind was in a state of shock. The mole had taken a precious, loving act and turned it into something evil and wicked. It felt as if she were floating and could see herself from above. It was the only way she could cope with this experience. Like so many other sexual victims coping with trauma, Anita pretended that she was out of her body—pretended that she was just an observer of this horrible scene. Her mind and body began to shut down, and she started to block out the thoughts, images, and smells, even as they were happening.

The only sexual experience she had to compare this to was with her ex-fiancé, Mitch. Their relationship had lasted two years, and they had waited a year before they had gotten to that "next step." They broke up mutually, and Anita had moved on and was happy with Scott now. She had been with him for almost nine months now. Mitch and Scott both had always been so loving and gentle with her, unlike this monster. They had always been extremely considerate of Anita's comfort and wanted to please her. Fireworks of passion and pleasure had gone off instantly when she had first kissed Scott. She prayed that she would be able to kiss and caress him again someday. Anita missed him and wanted him to help her get this guy off her.

Anita lay motionless, completely stunned by what had just occurred. She could not look at her rapist. Moving mechanically, the mole got up and wiped himself off with a towel. He—like many sociopaths—expressed no emotion and showed no concern toward his victim and her feelings. He came over and untied her hands, as they were visibly swollen and purple again. "You'll do just fine," he said. "You might even grow to love me. You'll see."

Changing his mind, the mole bound her hands again. "Sorry," he said, "but I have to go and ditch your car, honey."

The mole dressed Anita in her clothes and then dragged her across his cramped room to a metal storage cabinet that was lying down on its side. It was no larger than five feet long and three feet wide. Opening its doors, he yanked out a dozen of his hanging shirts from the rod inside it. He pushed Anita down inside the cabinet, shut the metal double doors, and secured it by placing a wooden dowel through the door holes. There were several slits at the top of the cabinet that let in a small amount of air. Anita had no idea what the actual time was, but she guessed that it was probably around three o'clock by now. She was supposed to be at work at UPS at three thirty, and she was praying that they would be looking for her now. She'd already missed lunch with Scott and her grandparents. They had to be worried.

Through the doors, the mole issued Anita a warning. "Don't try to get out or I'll kill you, honey." She heard his footsteps recede, and stop. "I might not leave right away to see if you'll try to escape," he threatened again.

Anita heard the front door slam, but after a period of silence, she again heard his footsteps inside the room. Her captor did this numerous times, hoping to scare Anita into submission. His tactic worked, because even when the silence lasted for the next twenty minutes, Anita was too frightened to move. Of course, she couldn't have moved even if she wanted to—she couldn't fully stretch out in the cabinet and had to scrunch her five-feet-five-inch frame into a ball. The metal box was a prison for her, but it was also her safe haven from the monster that had put her in it. It protected her from her captor's touch and gave her a reprieve from being civil to someone who had just assaulted her. Still, it didn't take long for the air to grow sparse, and she had to stifle the impulse to scream. In her mind, she prayed to God. *Why me, God? Why is this happening to me? Where are you, God? Help me!*

CHAPTER 11

"This is 911. What is the nature of your emergency?" Mary asked, answering the call that came in around twelve thirty on Thursday afternoon. It had been a slow morning, so the operator was surprised by what she heard next. "My daughter is missing," a frantic woman told her. "I just got home. Her boyfriend was supposed to meet her for lunch around noon. When he got here at eleven forty-five to pick her up, she wasn't here. She's supposed to be at work at three thirty today, and we just called them, and she didn't go in early. Something has happened to her. This isn't like her at all. Please send the police out now." The woman on the phone, who had barely paused to breathe, now took a sharp breath before continuing. "We have to find her. Please! Oh, please help us!"

Mary had heard this type of plea all too often, and she attempted to calm down the hysterical mother. Mary quickly learned that the woman's name was Carrie Ann and that her missing daughter, Anita, was twenty-one and allegedly very responsible for her age.

"When was the last time that anyone spoke to Anita?"

"I talked with her around nine this morning before I left for work. She was in her room sleeping. That's all that I know. Please hurry. We have to find her. Something terrible has happened."

"Okay, ma'am," the operator responded. "I need you to try to calm down. Is there any way that she could have just gone to the mall or something? Does she have a cell phone you've tried to contact her on?"

"No," Carrie Ann said emphatically. "She doesn't have a cell phone, and she would never just blow off her boyfriend and her grandparents. Like I told you, she is very responsible. She would have called first if she were going to change her plans."

The operator sighed and continued, "Okay, ma'am, are there any signs of forced entry to your home?"

"Well, Anita's car is gone from the garage, and her contact lenses and glasses are both in her room. She can't see well enough to drive without one of them. And I found the comforter off our master bedroom bed on the floor, and her favorite red robe that I got her for Christmas last year is gone. And we found the kitchen window screen removed and on the floor. There is also a drop of what looks like blood on the kitchen floor."

Hearing this, the operator began to take the call much more seriously. "Ma'am, I think that we have enough information now to warrant an officer coming out to do an investigation. I'm sending an officer out to your residence immediately. Just don't touch or move anything. Stay outside until the officer arrives."

Carrie Ann burst into tears. "Please tell them to hurry! Please find my baby! Oh, dear God, please let her be alive!"

"God bless your family, honey," the operator said before hanging up to dispatch an officer.

CHAPTER 12

The mole was in his element. His heart raced with the excitement and thrill of staying one step ahead of those pigs. His plan had worked thus far, and his fantasy was now a reality. He was sweating profusely from the activities of the day and the adrenaline rush they were providing him. He walked briskly across his mother's lawn (which was really just a few patches of grass among large patches of dirt). Upon entering the garage, he pushed the button on the wall, and the garage door opened with a familiar creak. The mole then got back into Anita's car. He knew that he had to dispose of her car immediately, and he knew just where to hide it.

The mole backed her car out of the long driveway and turned right onto State Road 26. After passing several houses, he turned into a large subdivision called Indian Heights. There were hundreds of small houses situated so closely together that they seemed like they were piled on top of each other. In this neighborhood, an unidentified car would not appear conspicuous—and could possibly sit there for weeks before anyone would even notice it or report it to the authorities. He found a convenient cul-de-sac at the end of the street and pulled Anita's car over to park it.

The mole turned the key to shut off the car engine. He took a quick glance around to see if anyone was in the street or watching from a window. Nope. He was golden. He opened the door, stepped out onto the street, and strode away from the car, quickening his pace with each step. The only sound he heard was a dog yapping in a nearby yard. *Shut up, you nasty mutt!* the mole thought. He had never liked dogs; they reminded him too much of his father. His dad had made their own German shepherds as mean as he was by kicking them regularly with his steel-toed boots. The mole had been forced to care for the dogs when his father was gone, and his father would have killed him if anything had ever happened to them. The dogs were a constant reminder of his father's presence, so even when his dad was on the road, it was like he wasn't really gone.

No, the only animal the mole had any fondness and respect for were cats. His cat growing up, Chester, had always seemed able to sense his loneliness and would often comfort him by snuggling up to him and purring in delight when the mole would pet him. He planned to get a cat for him and Anita once they got settled in. It would be good for both of them. He would mention to Anita later on that a cat would help her to forget about her family and friends. This would be their new life together, and he was confident that she would grow to love him soon.

It was only a short walk back to his mother's house. Pleased that no one seemed to notice him, the mole became more confident with every step. A wave of relief washed over him when he saw the house in sight. *Whew! Next step is to get out of Dodge.* He couldn't wait to see Anita again, smell her, touch her, and know that she was his for as long as he wanted her.

Anita lay, trapped and cramped, inside the metal storage cabinet. She tried to pass the time, and stop herself from panicking, by humming some of her favorite gospel songs, like "What a Friend We Have in Jesus," "Amazing Grace," and her favorite hymn from Sunday school, "He Lives." The words to these songs soothed Anita. She feverishly prayed that God would keep her safe and help the police to find her.

Anita knew that the police had to be looking for her by now. She should have already been at work. Surely they would know that she would never stand up her boyfriend and skip work without telling anyone. Silently, she prayed, *dear God, please hear my cries for help. I know I can do and endure all things through Christ Jesus. Nothing is impossible for you, God. I pray that it is your will that I will be rescued soon. I will take up my cross daily for you, dear Lord. Just please get me through this so that I can carry out your works. I have so many things that I can still do here on earth for you, dear Lord. Please don't let him kill me.* Then she began to whisper, "I will trust in you, Dear Lord. You are my strength—my rock." Anita repeated these words over and over until she felt at one with the words and sounds echoing inside the depths of the box. Peace and comfort began to wash over her, despite her horrific surroundings. She would make it through this; she knew it. God would teach her something in this awful experience. She just wasn't sure yet what it could possibly be.

CHAPTER 13

At approximately one in the afternoon on Thursday, Sheriff's Deputy Barry Watts arrived at the Wooldridge residence on Center Road after receiving a dispatch from the 911 department. The dispatcher had told him that it was a possible abduction of a twenty-one-year-old female. Deputy Watts was new on the force and had never witnessed an actual abduction case, but the rookie was optimistic about his ability to handle the situation. It might all turn out to be nothing anyway—you never knew in this field of work. When Deputy Watts arrived, the girl's parents, Carrie Ann and Gerald, were outside waiting for him.

"She was in bed when I left home for work around nine this morning," Carrie Ann told him. "She and her boyfriend Scott were supposed to go to her grandparents' house for lunch around noon."

Gerald interrupted his wife, "I just talked to my brother, and he says that he called and talked with Anita around ten thirty this morning, and she sounded fine. Scott told us that

58

he showed up around quarter to twelve and couldn't find her in the house. He says that he went out to his car to wait for her to return. He was there until around twelve thirty when my wife came home for lunch."

"Scott asked me where Anita was when I got home, and I told him that I had no idea," Carrie Ann added. "We went inside the house and began noticing things out of place. The comforter from our master bedroom was thrown onto the floor. We noticed that Anita's favorite bracelet and her red robe are missing from her room. Her contacts and glasses are still in her room, and she can barely see without them. The screen above the kitchen sink was torn out and is lying on the floor. Anita's car is missing from the garage too. We also noticed a spot of blood on the kitchen floor. I sent Scott home because he was so distraught. He was going to call around to all their friends and see if anyone has seen her. He just called and said that no one has." After taking a deep breath, Carrie Ann continued, her voice becoming more frantic, "We know that something's happened to her! She would never leave without telling someone or stand her grandparents and her boyfriend up. She's always been very responsible."

"Does your daughter have any enemies that you know of?" Deputy Watts asked calmly.

Both Carrie Ann and Gerald shook their heads no.

"Could I get a list of people whom Anita is close to?" Deputy Watts continued.

The worried parents gave him the names and contact information for Anita's closest friends, coworkers, and pastor. "I'll be right back," he told them. "I just need to call these people and make sure that Anita hasn't contacted them recently."

Watts walked over to his squad car to make the calls in privacy. He talked to everyone on the list, and they all told him the same thing: No, they had not heard from Anita today. Yes, she is a very responsible person. A call to Anita's boss at UPS absolutely confirmed this—she had only missed three days of work in the two years she had been employed there and had always called in if she wasn't going to be there.

Armed with this information, Deputy Watts quickly determined that this was the real deal. The drop of blood on the floor and the ripped-out window screen both suggested foul play, and he knew that time was of the essence now. Watts hurriedly made two more phone calls: the first to Don Howell, the senior deputy investigator for the sheriff's department, and the second to Captain Jack Roberts, the detective coordinator for the sheriff's department and the lead investigator in county cases like this one. While waiting for them to arrive, the deputy ordered Anita's parents to leave the area until it had been thoroughly investigated for crime scene evidence.

Deputy Watts entered the Wooldridge home and quickly discovered signs of a struggle in the living room. There were sofa cushions strewn across the floor, and a picture frame with a family photo lay on the floor with the glass shattered. He also found a spot of blood on the kitchen floor and a scuff mark near the bottom of the refrigerator. Watts saw the pushed-out screen and confirmed that Anita's car was not in the garage, where it supposedly had been parked all morning. After making careful notes and taking pictures, Deputy Watts and his fellow sheriff's deputy, Don Howell, spread out to question the neighbors. Neither man doubted that something out of the ordinary had happened that morning at the Wooldridge residence. But as they set out to look for witnesses, they both wondered if anyone had been there to see it.

CHAPTER 14

Silence filled the rooms of the old house when the mole crept back in. He was out of breath and anxious to get back upstairs to make sure that the girl was really his to do with what he wanted. He could barely believe that his plan had worked out and that this was really happening. Entering his room, he had to step over the mess on his floor—old army figures strewn about over a layer of dirty clothes and trash—to get to the box. The mole removed the quarter that he had placed on top of the box prior to leaving the house as a means of keeping his victim honest. If the quarter had moved at all, he would have known for sure that she had tried to escape. He quickly removed the wooden dowel and opened the doors, feeling just like a little boy opening up his present on Christmas morning. As he eagerly peered in at her, Anita looked up at him with wide eyes and started to whimper. "You can get out now," the mole told her. Since Anita's legs were still bound, her captor grabbed her arms and pulled her out. He sat her down on the couch nearby and turned on the TV for her. "I'm going to make us a nice barbecued dinner on the grill outside. I bet that sounds real good, doesn't it? I'm starving," he called out to Anita as he headed outside to start the grill.

While the food cooked, he packed his things in several cardboard boxes and carried several loads downstairs. Anita could hear his truck door opening and closing. It was obvious to her that her captor was making preparations to leave the house soon, but he did not appear to be in a rush, and even whistled as he worked.

"People are going to start looking for me," Anita said to her captor. "I should've been at work several hours ago." The mole whipped his head around in shock.

"I…I thought that you worked third shift and didn't have to be there until around six."

"No. I've been on second shift now for several weeks."

In a panic, the mole rushed out of the room, and all Anita could hear was the sound of things being thrown into boxes. She heard him go out the door and reenter several times. When he came back upstairs, he said gruffly, "We need to leave sooner than expected. We'll have to wait another hour, though, because we're taking a trip, and it has to be dark out when we make our first stop for gas."

"Where are we going?" Anita asked, alarmed that he was taking her somewhere else. "You'll find out when you need to," her captor answered.

The mole paced rapidly back and forth across his messy room, kicking the clothes and trash up in the air out of frustration and anger. His eyes were blazing as he pounded his fists into his sweaty palms. Anita could tell that her captor was trying to devise a new game plan but he was aware that he was running out of time. "How could this have happened?" Anita heard him mutter to himself. "It was all going so perfectly. It'll be okay, though. We still have time to get out of here. Those stupid pigs aren't that quick." These words seemed to snap him out of the panic, and he picked Anita up off the couch and carried her to the downstairs bathroom. "Go pee if you need to," he said. "It's going to be a long drive."

After sitting Anita down onto the toilet and removing the electrical ties from her feet with a kitchen knife, he waited and watched her as she relieved herself. When she was done, he picked her up and placed her in the shower. "I'll need to get you clean in here since your hands are still tied behind your back," he told her. "You have dirt and grease all over you from the garage. I can't let you get that all over my truck."

The mole grabbed his mother's Pert shampoo bottle and, after working a lather into his palms, he began soaping down her body and long hair like Anita assumed he would his car or bike. As he cleaned her, his hands ran over her body, lingering at her privates. "I like your tits," he told her. "You're so pretty." Anita cringed at the touch of his calloused hands on her skin. She kept her head down and stared at the water collecting at the drain by her feet. *In a way*, she thought, *this is worse than the rape. Just breathe*, she told herself. It'll be over soon. *Please God, give me strength.*

When the mole seemed to feel like she was clean enough, he took her out of the shower and dried her off with an old towel hanging on the back of the bathroom door. He reached for the T-shirt and shorts that Anita had been wearing, and then untied her arms and feet so that he could redress her for the second time that day. He then put a pair of his own white tube socks on her bare feet. "I thought you might want to wear these," he said, feigning concern for her comfort. "Your feet might start to get cold tonight."

Anita knew that dressing her in his socks was just another way to control her—not a true act of kindness—but she paused and said, "Thanks. They were getting cold already." She knew that she had to converse with him and make him believe that she was his friend, but her own voice sounded far away to her, as if someone else was speaking and she was just listening from a distance. If he thought they were friends, maybe she could talk him into letting her go eventually—at least that was the thought she tried to console herself with.

After she was fully dressed, the mole put his arm around Anita and squeezed her tightly. "If you scream or try to run from me," he said calmly but forcefully, "I will put a bullet in your back. Don't ever think of screwing with me!" Anita could feel his hot breath on her neck and smell his rank odor as he talked. Instinctively, she turned her head away from him, but nodded that she understood and would be a good girl. Anita had no way of knowing that the mole was bluffing. Though he was armed with several knives and a stun gun, he had replaced his mother's handgun in her nightstand drawer a few minutes prior; he didn't want his pesky mom to get suspicious.

The mole walked Anita outside to his truck and, after opening the front passenger side door, gestured for her to get in. She obeyed, stepping up and onto the front seat, which made a *whoosh* sound as she plopped down on the vinyl covering and sank into it. The truck looked like it had not been driven in years. It smelled musty, and trash was strewn all over the floorboards. *Why in the world did he care if I got the seats dirty?* Anita wondered. *It was probably just another excuse for the pervert to feel me up.* It took a while for the motor to start, and Anita was hopeful that the mole's plan would be ruined. No such luck, though. Once it started, the truck purred like a kitten.

The mole pulled out of the driveway cautiously and turned right onto State Road 26. He soon got to Highway 31, turned left onto it, and then quickly took a right onto an old country road. Once it got dark, and no other cars were in sight, he took one hand off the steering wheel and swiftly cut off Anita's arm straps with his pocket knife. To ensure that she could not escape from him, he pulled over on the side of the road and rebound her feet with the electrical ties. He would leave these ties on her for the remainder of the seven-hour trip.

As the tires hit the random potholes scattered along the old country roads, Anita closed her eyes tightly and made herself focus on the steady hum of the engine and the *thump, thump, thump* of the tires, trying to block out the thoughts swirling around in her head. *Should I try to jump out of the truck?* she wondered. *Should I make him crash and take my chances as far as surviving? Is anyone looking for me? Am I going to die?* The thoughts were too much for her to handle, and she forced herself to try to get some much-needed rest.

The mole did not seem to mind the silence. In fact, he seemed rather comforted by it. *I hope he doesn't fall asleep and run off the road,* Anita thought. *Or maybe that wouldn't be such a bad thing.* These were Anita's last thoughts before she dozed off for the next several hours. As Anita slumbered, she was taken farther and farther from her home and the family that loved her. The mole knew that with every mile that passed, he increased his chances of getting away with his brilliant plan. Pure adrenaline kept him awake and alert. He felt more alive than he had ever felt before.

CHAPTER 15

Violent winds jerked the old, red pickup truck around as it continued west at a steady speed of around sixty-five miles per hour. The mole had kept to country roads and had not seen another vehicle in at least an hour. It was now after ten o'clock and pitch black out. He was starting to get very tired and found himself nodding off several times, despite the loud sounds of the wind whipping against the truck's windows. He had been so rushed that he hadn't had time to watch the weather before they left. He hoped it was not another tornado heading toward them.

The mole needed company to stay awake, so he jabbed his sleeping passenger in the side. Anita did not stir. "Hey, wake up!" he said. "I need you to keep me awake. Come on now, wake up!" Anita fought hard to stay in dreamland, where she was subconsciously safe. She had been dreaming of a squirrel that was running through some sort of maze. The squirrel would make turns at full speed and—when it appeared that at the next turn he would find the exit and be free—he would inevitably hit a wall and have to start all over again. Even in her

67

dreams, Anita was desperately trying to find a way out of this situation, but she kept hitting a wall.

Anita begrudgingly awoke. It had taken her a long time to fall asleep in the truck, as her already sore neck was uncomfortable from resting on the door at a strange angle. Also, her bound feet throbbed with pain.

"What? Where are we now?" she asked groggily.

"Don't worry your pretty little head about it. I just need some company to stay awake. Do you have to go to the bathroom yet?"

The truck's headlights illuminated row after row of cornfields. Everything else was a cloud of black surrounding them.

"Yeah," Anita answered. "I have to go at the next gas station."

"Oh, no. You can go right out here in these cornfields. That way you can't yell for help or run away."

The mole pulled the truck over onto the side of the road and came around to her door to carry her out. He sat the girl down at the front of the corn rows and stood over her as she relieved herself. After she was finished, he peed into the wind, his urine spraying out over the fields. To Anita's chagrin, several drops landed on her leg. "Yeah, I can do whatever I want out here," the mole said. "There are no rules here. I'm in charge now, motherfuckers! Yeah!" Anita was disgusted by her captor's behavior. He was a forty-two-year-old man acting like a teenage boy. Had she not feared for her life, she might have decked him and told him to grow up. When he finished playing around, he picked Anita up and put her back in the truck.

As they set off again, Anita sat back in the seat with a heavy heart. She knew that she was now expected to carry on a conversation with this vile man—a man whom she had once felt sorry for. Now, it was clear to her that he was off his rocker. She knew that if she didn't pretend to like him, he would kill her and find another victim. The mole broke the silence first.

"So, are you still friends with Sarah from the sports club?"

"Yeah. I'm supposed to be maid of honor in her wedding next week."

"I got an invite too. I wonder why she invited me. I haven't talked to her in a few years."

"We decided that she should invite you because you'd always told us you didn't really have any friends or family to do things with. We wanted to include you so that maybe you could meet some friends there."

Anita thought back to how, just three weeks ago, she and Sarah had deliberated on whether to invite Tom. They had felt sorry for him and had wanted to reach out to him so that maybe he would one day accept Jesus into his heart. They had no idea at the time that they were inviting a convicted rapist back into their lives.

"You know," the mole said, interrupting Anita's thoughts, "if you hadn't been home, I was going to Sarah's house next. I always liked her. You were just closer since she moved to Kentucky with her fiancé and all." Hearing this sent chills down Anita's back. She couldn't believe that Sarah had been next on his list and that he even knew where she now lived. Sarah was like a sister to Anita. They had been inseparable since elementary school—both girls had loved to climb trees and could run faster than all the boys. Anita would gladly endure this torture to prevent this despicable man from hurting her best friend.

"Yeah," the mole said, "I got her a present. I brought it with me. Maybe you could help me wrap it, and then I can send it to her."

"What'd you get her?"

"Can you believe it?" he asked with a chuckle. "I got her a damn skillet. That way if she gets mad at that son of a bitch she's marrying, she can crack him over the head with it."

"Have you ever even met Jared?" Anita asked defensively. "He's a really nice guy. They're in love."

"I don't have to meet him. All guys are the same. Just wait till they've been married for a few years. Then his true colors will surface."

Anita tried to keep the conversation going by talking to him about when he worked as a dispatcher at the local community college in Kokomo. For nearly twenty minutes, they compared stories about their workplaces, UPS and International Resources. Then, they talked about their college days. "I have an accounting degree from IU Bloomington," he told her. "I used to work for H&R Block. That was a great way to check out women, let me tell you." Anita had a degree in computer programming, and she told him about her skills on the computer. The mole was glad to hear this, he told her, because he would need her help in setting up his computer at their new place.

Curious, Anita decided to ask her captor a personal question. "Have you ever had a serious girlfriend?"

He grunted. "Yeah, I had one girlfriend in Bloomington," he replied. "She wouldn't kiss me. I know that all girls just play hard to get so I *made* her kiss me. She tried to say that she hadn't wanted it, that bitch. I know that whore wanted me. I was the best thing she ever had. You should've seen the trash she brought home to her trailer. She was just another slut in the end."

The mole began to bang his palms against the steering wheel. Sensing his agitation, Anita decided to move on to the next subject.

"So, how long have you been living with your mom?"

"Since I had to move back in temporarily in 1995. That was three long years ago. It was time to move on."

Soon they came upon a small town that had a few fast food restaurants still open for business. He quickly turned into the parking lot of a Kentucky Fried Chicken and pulled the truck up to the drive-through window. He scooted his hostage close to him on the seat, gripping her tightly around her neck. "I'm real hungry," he warned her, "so I don't want any funny business from you. I'll kill you if I have to."

The mole got his food, and they were back on the road within minutes. At his request, Anita passed her captor the greasy chicken wings one by one. As she handled the chicken, she felt her stomach turn from nausea. "You want any?" he asked. "You need to eat, girl."

"No thanks," she replied. "I'm not hungry." He proceeded to scarf down every last bite of the twelve-piece chicken bucket, gnawing each wing down to the bone. Anita felt like she was watching a wild animal on the Discovery Channel devour its prey. The mole let out a loud belch. "Whew!" he said. "Now that was good. I'm going to sleep like a baby tonight, if we could ever get there."

After a little while, he turned the truck onto an interstate highway. Anita began to see tons of lights and knew they were approaching Chicago. She had made this trip several times to visit her older brother, who lived in the city suburbs with his wife. The mole was going too fast for her to jump out, but she considered it for a moment.

They did not go through the city but rather around it on the outskirts. She had never been on this side of Chicago before. He turned off the interstate and headed down an old side road. Eventually, they came to a remote area surrounded by fields with a train track nearby. Terrified that he was going to carry out his threats to kill her, Anita began to shake, but she was relieved when the mole said, "I've got to drain my radiator again. You have to go yet'?" Anita decided that she better, since she could be in the car all night. She nodded her head yes, so he walked around the truck, picked her up, and placed her down in the grass next to the train track.

Anita was still relieving herself when she heard a faraway train horn going off. The mole leapt up. "Oh shit," he exclaimed. "Get down. Here comes a damn train. What are the chances of that?" He lay on her chest to cover her and put his head down in the grass to mask his identity. He did not want to take any chances until they got further away.

Anita felt like another chance of being found was gone, and her heart sank further. She looked up and caught a blurry glimpse of a child with wide eyes and an innocent look on her face peering out of the passenger window. Anita wished that she could be that little girl, in awe of all the passing lights and buildings. Instead, she was stuck here with this pig smashing her ribs with his full weight. She looked up and pleaded to the people on the passing train, silently mouthing the words, *Help me!* But once the train finally passed, her captor put her back in the truck, and they were on their way again.

As he drove on, the mole confided in Anita. "We're heading to a town in Wisconsin," he told her. "I have a room in our house that I'm going to keep you in until I can trust you." Petrified, she wondered if he had one of those hidden, soundproof rooms. Even if the police found him, they would never find her.

After twenty minutes of silence, it began to storm. The truck was besieged by heavy rain for the next hour. The mole turned the ancient radio on in the truck and quickly discovered that there were tornado warnings and hazardous conditions in the area. But this would not deter him—even though he could barely see the road at times, he kept the old truck going, pulling over only a few times to let the rain die down. As the storm raged outside, Anita hoped and prayed that a funnel would overtake the truck and give her an opportunity to escape. Half an hour later, though, the storms passed, and she remained trapped.

When the rain subsided, the mole pulled off onto the side of the road to retie Anita's hands. *This can't be a good sign,* Anita thought as he rebound her hands. *What else is he going to have me do? How much more can I take?* Anita wondered.

"I've got to get some gas down the road here," he told her. "That's why I have to tie your hands again, so you won't try to roll down the window and yell for help or something. I know how you females are. I've had to learn the hard way my whole life. I won't get burned again."

"Why don't you just pay at the pump with a credit card?" Anita asked him coyly. "That would be a lot easier." She prayed that he would be dumb enough to take her advice and leave some sort of trail for the police—if they were even looking for him. But the mole played dumb.

"Nah," he mumbled. "I can't do that. I can't remember my damn pin number." He pulled into the gas station. She could only see one lone male attendant inside. "I'll be right back," the mole warned her as he got out of the truck, "so you be good now." He put his finger to his neck and made a gesture, silently threatening to slit her throat if she dared to mess with him. Anita had no doubt this madman would follow through if she disobeyed him.

As the mole went inside to pay, Anita prayed that a squad car would miraculously pull up to arrest him and pull her to safety. It happened all the time in movies. Why couldn't she have the same good fortune? No such luck. Her captor came back with a Mountain Dew and forced her to take a sip of it. He got back on the road, pulling over shortly to untie her swollen, purple hands. They throbbed as the blood rushed back through her veins, and she rubbed them to soothe the pain. Back on the road they went.

Anita tried to sleep, but was awakened twice by the mole's demands. "Hey. I'm bored again. Suck it," he said the first time as he pointed down to his exposed penis. When she hesitated, he grabbed her red hair by the fistful and yanked her head down. Anita complied, but like before, the mole was unable to ejaculate. She complained several times that her neck and throat were hurting, but each time she asked for a reprieve, he ignored her and pushed her head back down. Eventually, the mole became visibly frustrated by his inability to climax. "What kind of slut are you?" he asked derisively. "You can't even make a man come?" After what seemed like an eternity, he finally gave up trying.

Anita curled up into the fetal position in her corner of the seat. She remained there—as far away from him as she could possibly get—hoping that he would leave her alone, but an hour later, he flicked her on the bottom. "Get back over here and finish me up, woman," he said. "You just going to leave me hanging?" He pulled out his penis again and made her suck it until he came all over her. He insisted that Anita leave her head resting on his penis. While he stroked her head gently, he tried to reassure her. "Things will get better, hon," he told her. "I promise. You'll forget all about your family, and we can be happy together. You'll see." He handed her one of his fast food napkins and said, "You need to wipe yourself off, though. You're a mess!"

As they drove on in silence, the hate Anita felt toward her abductor grew with every mile. She did not know how to deal with all the anguish and fury that she felt inside her. She had never hated anyone, but she did now, after what he had made her do. She let this anger make her more determined to outwit him. Whenever Anita had resolved to do something in the past, she didn't give up. She would use that same approach now. She knew that God would help her through this, that he would help her to escape. She clung to this conviction during the remainder of the journey.

CHAPTER 16

Captain Jack Roberts arrived at the station promptly at eight thirty and brought his coffee in with him. He went directly to his office, calling out greetings to all the staff as he passed by. The previous night had been uneventful, and nothing needed his immediate attention. He spent a few hours catching up on the mounting pile of paperwork in his office. Around noon, Jack walked over to the conference room with several of his deputies to brief one another on the progress of their various cases. It was a slow day, and he was beginning to wonder if he would be able to leave work early. His yard at home needed mowing, and he wanted to get a head start on it before the weekend.

It was close to one in the afternoon when they finished up, and Jack was heading out the door to pick up some lunch when his secretary called out to him, "Hey, Jack. Barry's on the phone. He says he really needs to talk to you. It's urgent." Jack sighed. *So much for an easy day at the office*, he thought. But Jack knew that Barry was a rookie deputy, and rookies tended to operate with a mixture of extreme caution and eagerness to crack a big case—a recipe for false alarms. *So it could still be nothing*, he reminded himself as he returned to his office to take the call in private.

Jack picked up the receiver. "Hey Barry," he said. "It's Jack. What's up?"

"Hey Jack," Barry replied, his voice full of urgency. "Sorry to bother you, but you should probably get over here right away. I got a call from a 911 dispatcher about a possible kidnapping off Center Road this afternoon. I've already spoken to the girl's parents and several neighbors and checked out the inside of the house. There are signs of a forced entry, a spot of blood, and the girl's car is missing."

"Okay, I'm on my way," Jack said. "Don't let anyone else in the house until I get there." Jack hung up the phone and rushed out to his squad car. This sort of thing never happened in Center, Indiana. Especially in broad daylight off a well-travelled highway.

Jack's lingering doubts about Deputy Watts's judgment were erased when he received a call while in route from Don Howell, a veteran sheriff's deputy investigator. "Jack, it's Don," the deputy said. "I'm at the Wooldridge residence, and I'm familiar with the family. Anita is a very trustworthy girl. She's twenty-one, but she's not the type of girl to just run off. Something has happened to her. I'm here now. We'll see you as soon as you get here. I think we've got the real deal." Jack hung up the phone. He knew that he could be up all night if this was truly a case of foul play.

Jack arrived at the Wooldridge home and pulled his cruiser up the long driveway to the residence. After greeting Don at the front door, they went inside to review the evidence. Deputy

Watts had already called Anita's friends and coworkers, and she checked out to be a reliable girl. Jack headed over to talk with the neighbor, Fred Taylor, who had informed Don this afternoon that he had witnessed a stocky man with a backpack walk up to the Wooldridge residence around the time she disappeared. Jack walked across the street, went up to Mr. Taylor's door, and knocked on it. Fred opened the door and immediately asked, "Did you find Anita yet?"

"No. Not yet," Jack replied. "I need you to tell me exactly what you saw this morning, sir."

"Well, I told the other officer that I was outside getting my mail, and I saw a stocky male walk up to the Wooldridge's front door. He was carrying a gray backpack. I just thought he was a salesman or something. I went back inside and then left to get gas for my mower."

"Did you see Anita or her car at all this morning?"

"No. She usually parks in the garage, and I never saw her leave today. Sorry, but that's all I can tell you. She's always been a real good girl. She'd never just leave and not tell her parents. I've known her since she was little. I hope you guys find her. Let me know if there's anything my wife or I can do to help. Her parents have to be worried sick."

Jack returned to the Wooldridge home and asked Deputy Watts when Anita was supposed to be at work. "Her boss said three thirty," he said. "He also said that she didn't show up early. We called the local hospitals too, and she hasn't been admitted to either one of them." It was almost two in the afternoon. Jack decided to drive to Anita's workplace to see if she had arrived and to talk to her coworkers while he waited. As he pulled out of the driveway, a picture of one of his own daughters, Emily, popped into his head. She was only two years older than Anita, and the mere thought of this ever happening to her gave him chills down his spine. It was then that Jack decided that he would have to distance himself from the victim's family so that he would not get too emotionally involved. He had to stick to the facts to find her, not emotions.

Jack arrived at the UPS building and began debriefing Anita's coworkers. None of them had seen or talked to Anita since the previous day. One coworker, Stephanie, said, "Anita told me once that one of our male coworkers, Craig, would constantly ask her out and say perverse comments to her. He even smacked her on the butt one time, and she almost punched him. Anita tried to just blow him off when he did things like this, but she jokingly told me one day that if she ever came up missing, I'd know it was Craig." Stephanie added, "Anita never took him seriously. I'm not saying that Craig did anything to her. I just thought that I should mention it. I really do think he's harmless, just a little strange."

"Thanks for the tip," Jack said. "We unfortunately have to take every statement like that seriously right now. Is Craig here right now?"

"No," Stephanie replied. "He has the day off. He'll be in tomorrow."

When Anita failed to show up for her shift at three thirty that afternoon, Jack was positive that she had been abducted. He knew that time was of the essence and that he had to get back to the office to talk with his boss about alerting the FBI and putting out an all-points bulletin for Anita and her car. He sped back to the station, and at five o'clock, his boss and his deputies met him in the conference room. All of them were in disbelief that something like this was actually happening in their small hometown of Kokomo.

As the lead investigative coordinator for the sheriff's department, Captain Roberts was in charge of the meeting. He issued an all-points bulletin for the five-feet-five, auburn-haired female and her blue 1990 Buick Century vehicle. He also dispatched a private pilot to search for her car in the surrounding counties. As a group, the officers began to compile all the information they had on a dry-erase board so that everyone in the room could see it. It helped Jack to see it all visually.

Jack stood up and cleared his throat. "Okay, guys," he began. "I know that it's been a long day for most of us, but we're all in for a long haul here. This is a kidnapping of a twenty-one-year-old female. We do know that the screen from the kitchen window was removed and found lying on the kitchen floor. There is a drop of blood at the crime scene. We have sent the blood sample away to the forensic lab, but it could take days to identify whose blood it is. There was a bedspread taken off of her parents' bed. Anita's red robe and favorite bracelet are missing. Her car is missing. Her glasses and contacts were left behind, and she can barely see without them.

"She has a reputation for being a wholesome, responsible girl," he continued. "She has a boyfriend named Scott Miller. They've been together for around nine months now. The victim has an ex-fiancé named Mitch. They were together for several years. Don talked with both young men today, and Mitch claims that they ended on good terms and that he had not spoken to Anita in almost a year. He was unaware of any enemies that Anita might have. Scott was visibly shaken and had significant stress in his voice tone. He claims that he showed up at her house to pick her up around eleven forty-five. He entered her house and called for her. He alleges that he went back out to his car and waited there until her mother arrived home a little after noon for lunch. According to both Scott and the victim's family, Scott and Anita get along well, and Anita did not seem upset this morning.

"The uncle is the last one to have talked to Anita on the phone at around ten-thirty this morning. Again, he claims that she did not sound distressed at all, just winded from running to the phone from her room, she had told him. So, we know the window of time she was taken in is from ten thirty, when she got off the phone with her uncle, to eleven forty-five, when her boyfriend claims that he arrived. It is now five thirty, so our victim has been missing for six or seven hours. We also know that a neighbor saw a stocky man that he could not identify walking up to the Wooldridge residence a little after ten this morning. He was carrying a gray backpack. Anyone else have anything that I missed?"

Don Howell piped up. "Jack," he said, "I also found a piece of black tape in the Wooldridge driveway and an old, abandoned bicycle with a damaged tire lying along Flowing Wells road. You know that's nearby Anita's residence."

Jack jotted all of this down on the dry-erase board in his own organized scribble. When he was finished, he turned back to his men. "Good work!" he said. "Now we have to establish prime suspects and wait for the calls to start flooding in. Of course, we'll have to weed through all the crank calls, but we have to take them all seriously at first. I'd say that Scott is our number one suspect at this point. I think it's odd that he disappeared right after her mother arrived and seemed so shaky. He's only twenty so he could've just been in shock, but we need to keep pressing him for answers to see if his story changes at all.

"We also need to look seriously at Anita's coworker Craig," he added. "He apparently made lewd comments to her at work almost every day and even touched her inappropriately recently. She was supposedly creeped out by this guy, and he had the day off today. We need to question him as soon as possible. We also need to find a male friend of Anita's whom they call 'Snake.' Anita was out with Scott, Snake, and a group of other friends last night at Applebee's. Several of Anita's friends told me we should question Snake as a suspect since he's kind of an odd character who she's close to.

"Everyone Anita was with last night alleges that Anita drank a Long Island Iced Tea at the restaurant, and then Scott drove her home, tucked her into bed, and went back to his parents' house as far as they knew. All of Anita's friends describe Snake as a nice but weird guy. He apparently has multiple tattoos and piercings and may be into drugs. I tried to reach him with no success. I left him a message to return our phone call immediately. I even stopped by his house in Indian Heights today before I went to Anita's workplace, but no one answered the door. None of their mutual friends have any idea where he might be."

Jack paused. "I hate to put Fred Taylor on the suspect list," he said, "but he needs to be there since he's claiming that he saw someone else approach the home. We just need to check him out a little further and see if anything comes up just to be sure." Wrapping up the meeting, he added, "Okay then. I need all of you back in here at five a.m. to finish where we left off. See you all in the morning."

Jack's boss, Tim, stayed behind to talk to him briefly. "You do know that the Kokomo Police Department and the media are going to be hounding me for information tomorrow?" Tim asked.

"I know, Tim," Jack replied, "but we can't give the media any information yet. It could jeopardize our case, and I still can't decide who I need from the police department. I want to comprise the best investigative team possible. And look, with your permission, I'm going to alert the FBI tomorrow to get their assistance in the case. Anita could already be in another state by now. Just give me some time, and I will let you know as soon as I know. Okay?"

"I trust your judgment, Jack," Tim said. "That's the only reason I'm willing to take all the heat for you. Just remember that the police department's going to be upset that you alerted the FBI so soon, and several of their veteran officers probably aren't going to be happy when they're not asked to join the team on such a big case. I'm just letting you know, buddy."

Jack nodded his head. "I know," he replied. "I'll probably be here all night thinking about it…trying to figure out the right way to proceed with this case. The way I see it, this case is like a basketball game. The suspect got Anita away from us. Now we just have to play the basics for the long haul to find her. The suspect will eventually slow down or slip up in some way, and we'll be right there to take Anita back from him. I'm confident of that."

Tim, as always, was impressed by Jack's determination. "Try to get some sleep yourself, Jack," Tim said. "You're not getting any younger, buddy. We can't do all the things we once could."

"Speak for yourself, old man," Jack replied defensively. "I'm far from being washed up. You wait and see."

Alone in the building, Jack called his wife. "Sorry, hon," he said regretfully, "but I won't be home tonight. I can't go over the details yet, but it's a kidnapping case of a twenty-one-year-old girl."

"Oh my goodness," Dorothy replied. "That's awful. That poor girl's parents."

"Yeah, well I'm just going to take a quick nap in my office and get a fresh start early in the morning. I'll wash up in the sink or something."

"If you need anything from home, just let me know. I love you. Be careful and take care of yourself. Promise?" Dorothy said.

He hesitated, not wanting to lie to his wife, and then said, "Okay. Okay. I promise. I love you. Goodnight."

Jack didn't fall asleep until nearly two in the morning. He had three hours until the staff would return to the office. He drifted off into dreams of chasing a train that kept getting farther and farther away from him.

CHAPTER 17

Anita awoke from an uneasy slumber when the car engine stopped. As she roused herself from sleep, she heard her captor talking to her. "We're getting close," he said.

Anita sat up in the truck. "What?" she asked. "Where are we?" Her half-open eyes darted to the dash; she leaned closer to see the bright red numbers on the clock. It was two in the morning. She had dozed off for several hours and had no idea where they were. She looked out the window and saw that they were at a gas station, but it was closed.

"We're in La Crosse now," the mole said. As he spoke, he tied a black handkerchief around her head, covering her eyes. "This is where we'll live now. I can't let you see our new home, but I think you'll like it. It's out in the country, where no one will ever bother us. Don't even think of trying to run off. There isn't a single house or person around for miles. That's why I chose it. It's perfect." The news weighed on Anita. The doubts and fear crept back in as she thought, *How will they ever find me way out here?*

What Anita did not know was that the mole was once again bluffing. He had actually rented an old church parsonage right in the middle of downtown La Crosse. His plan was to open up a bookstore in the house, so it had to be in town. He would wait until his victim was not so apt to leave him to tell her the truth. She would want to stay soon; he was sure of it. For now, he would just have to leave the television on loud enough that she wouldn't hear the cars or people around them. The mole put his hand on her knee as they drove the last few miles to the house. It was still windy out, and he had to be careful to keep the truck from being tugged to the right by the strong wind gusts.

The mole pulled up to the house and parked his truck out on the street right in front of it. There was no one in sight at this late hour. He opened Anita's door and carried her to the front door, which was the only accessible entrance to the house. The back door had already been boarded up when he had rented the home a few weeks ago. It was one of the best qualities of the house to him.

The mole had no real reason for choosing La Crosse, Wisconsin, as their new home. A few weeks prior, he had been driving around, searching for a new place to live, when he had nearly run out of gas. He had stopped at the same gas station that he and Anita had just stopped at to fill up his tank. Afterward, he had driven around La Crosse, and liked the way that everyone there seemed to mind their own business. La Crosse had a population of about sixty-five thousand at that time, making it the twelfth largest city in Wisconsin, situated on the east side of the Mississippi River.

A flat prairie town surrounded by towering bluffs, it was wedged between the two major cities of Chicago and Milwaukee—

perfect for the mole if he needed to flee from the authorities. In his sightseeing of the area, he had found three regional colleges and universities. The mole had assumed it would be good to have educated people around who enjoyed reading and would want to purchase his books. He also liked the idea of living so close to the river. As a young boy, he had always wanted to go fishing with his father and brother, and now he figured that he would take Anita fishing as part of their new life together.

The mole carried Anita into the rented house, sat her down on the floor, and locked the door behind them. He finally cut the straps off Anita's swollen legs. They were almost completely numb by now. He took the blindfold off and turned on the television with the volume on high. Anita, who hadn't used the restroom in hours, asked desperately, "Could I please use the bathroom again? I really have to go."

"Yeah," he replied. "The bathroom is in our basement. I'll take you down there." He led her to the bathroom, and she noticed with dread that there was no shower curtain to provide privacy.

He watched her as she sat down to relieve herself. Anita was humiliated. The experience reminded her just how trapped she really was. When she finished, he led her by the arm back up the dark stairs into a room with wood-paneled walls and old wallpaper covered with brown trees. The décor was from the seventies, and the room was filled with boxes and trash. The whole house needed to be updated and repaired.

In the corner of the room, there stood a metal cabinet, similar to the one he had confined her in at his mother's house in Indiana. He pointed to it and said, "This is where you'll be sleeping from now on. I'm going to keep it locked up when you're in there so you'll never try to leave me. If you ever try to get out and I catch you, I'll be forced to hurt you. Now, I don't want to have to do that, so you just be good. All right?" Anita nodded her head in agreement.

The mole tried to lay the metal cabinet onto its side, but he started to drop it, so Anita helped him ease it down. He looked up with appreciation and said, "Thanks, hon."

It almost made Anita gag, but she forced a smile and said, "You're welcome."

Mismatched blankets and clothing covered the bottom of the tan box, and he forced her to lie down on them. The box was no more than five feet by two feet, and there was a metal bar to hang clothes on. She could not stretch out her five-feet-five-inch frame with the bar in it, so she curled into a ball with her head resting on the hard metal bar.

The mole bent down and kissed her forehead. "Goodnight," he said, smiling down at her. "Enjoy your first night in our new house. I'll be sleeping on the floor right next to you, so don't be scared. This is the start of our new life together." He shut the metal doors and placed a wooden dowel and a butter knife through the door handles to lock them shut. Then he placed a quarter on top of the box. After giving a great yawn, the mole placed a pillow and blanket on the floor beside the box and lay down. He was snoring loudly within minutes.

From within the dark, cramped box, Anita could tell the mole was sleeping soundly. How unfair that he should be so peaceful when she was suffering beyond belief. The tiny slits at the top of the box provided Anita with just enough air to breathe laboriously. As she struggled to remain calm, she turned again to prayer. In a whisper, she pleaded to Jesus, "Please help me through this. Thank you for keeping me alive. I know that I would be dead if you hadn't given me the strength to survive. I remember reading in the Bible that you said if you have faith as small as a mustard seed, nothing is impossible to you. I have faith, dear Lord, and I believe that you will get me through this and guide the police in finding me. Please let them find me, dear Lord. Please give me peace like a river. Amen." This prayer gave her the peace and strength she needed to fall asleep and make it through her first night of hell on earth.

DAY TWO
FRIDAY, JUNE 26, 1998

CHAPTER 18

Captain Jack Roberts awoke to the sound of his alarm on his watch beeping rather loudly. He had fallen asleep at his desk with his head on his arm, his left ear pressed against the watch on his wrist. His face was lying in a puddle of his own drool, and he had only a vague recollection of where he was or how he had ended up there. It was four thirty in the morning, and he only had thirty minutes until his guys would be back. Standing up, he found that his neck was stiff from sleeping on it at such an odd angle. His bones creaked as he walked over to the coffeemaker in the hallway. *Man, Tim was right,* he thought. *I'm not a young pup anymore! This old body can't take overnighters.* Jack had spent many overnighters at the office in his years on the force, but he had not worked on a case of this magnitude in a long time. He knew that he might not get a good night's sleep for a while.

Jack turned on the coffeemaker, and as he waited for the coffee to brew, he went to the bathroom to wash up. Luckily, the station bathroom was equipped with lockers and a large sink. Always prepared, Jack pulled out a pair of jeans and a polo shirt from his locker. He knew that he would get more information from people if he was wearing civilian clothes, rather than his police uniform, when he questioned them. He would bring his badge to look official, but not too intimidating. He looked in the long mirror and cringed. He could see stubble starting to form over his typically clean-shaven face, and the corners of his eyes were crusty from sleep. He wiped the crust out of his eyes and splashed some cold water over his face. The water revived him; he was ready to get started again.

Jack took his coffee cup back into the conference room. He called his wife to say that he would come home for a few minutes around lunchtime. Dorothy was still asleep when he called and had responded groggily. As he hung up the phone, Jack heard voices filling the corridors. A minute later, Don and Deputy Watts appeared in the doorway. They each carried several boxes of doughnuts, the good Krispy Kreme kind. Tim and the captain of the Kokomo Police Department, Curtis Hoover, followed behind them. Deputy Major Phil Lyons and Deputy Ron Eastwood came in shortly after with two special investigators, Detective Monroe and Sergeant Kellar.

"Okay. Now that we're all here we can get started," Jack said, sitting back in his chair. "I think that we've all been briefed as far as where this case is, so now we need to find out if any leads came in over the phone last night." Jack assigned Deputy Watts to this job. "I also need a few of you to go find Anita's friend Snake," he continued. "I'm going to try to locate the co-worker, Craig, to interview him. Don, I want you to interview Anita's family, close friends, and especially the boyfriend again, okay? The rest of you can weed through some of the phone calls and try to get us some sort of lead. We should probably all meet back up here around noon. Sound good?"

They all nodded. As they rose to begin their various tasks, taking final bites of doughnut and sips of coffee, Curtis reminded, "If anyone gets a lead, call Jack or me immediately. We really need to get going on this case. The media's going to be all over us real soon!"

"Oh, about that," Jack added. "Tim and I have agreed that no one is to talk to the press yet. I don't want any leaks. It could jeopardize the investigation, maybe even Anita's life." They all agreed to keep things quiet, but Tim looked worried that he would have to take all the heat for this code of silence.

Most of the guys had already left the office by six thirty that morning. Jack was headed out the door to talk to Craig when Deputy Watts came in with a notebook in his hand.

"Hey, Jack," he said. "The dispatcher said they had hundreds of calls last night. She said that most of them were crackpot calls like, 'Well, my neighbor always seemed strange. You should check him out,' but one caller had seen a man riding his bike on Highway 31 yesterday morning. The caller said that he seemed odd."

Though this news interested Jack—the public did not know about the abandoned bicycle—he thought he might know the identity of this strange fellow spotted on the bike. He had gotten to know many of the homeless population around Howard County over the years, and there was a man named Bobby who rode his bike on Highway 31 daily, and had for the past twenty years.

Jack told Deputy Watts to find Bobby and ask him where he had been yesterday morning. "And go to all the gas stations off Highway 31 and ask the clerks whether they saw anyone else riding a bike around yesterday morning," he added. Watts rushed off to carry out his orders. As a rookie, he was very eager to please Jack and to impress the guys in the department who gave him a hard time about being wet behind the ears. Jack liked Watts's enthusiasm and drive—it reminded him of his own attitude when he was just starting out on the force. *We all need that kind of attitude to solve this case*, he thought. *This one will take stamina for sure.*

Anita had been missing for close to twenty hours, so Jack did what he knew was necessary before the twenty-four hour window passed. He called in the higher-ups—the FBI. Anita could be in a different state by now and communicating with the FBI would give the case national coverage. The whole nation would be on the lookout for Anita and her missing vehicle. The FBI could also provide expert knowledge in profiling and a database of information that it would take their department weeks to get. Though Jack might receive some flack for his decision, he knew that it was the right one. The FBI could have all the glory if they wanted it; Jack just wanted to get this girl back home.

Jack spoke to Ray Montgomery, an FBI agent from Quantico, over the phone and briefed him on the situation. After Jack had finished speaking, Ray said, "We'll have one of our profilers contact you within the next twenty-four hours. That will give you guys more time to nail down suspects and leads. We'll also send out a national bulletin on the victim and her vehicle." *He seemed to be taking the situation seriously*, Jack thought. "Good luck," Ray added. "You'll hear from us soon." Jack thanked him and hung up the phone. He took a deep breath. It was a relief to have the FBI working with them on this one. Time was ticking by, and he would take any help that he could get.

Jack walked out the door into the bright sunlight. It was already seven thirty, and he wanted to catch Craig before he headed out for the day. Jack put on his sunglasses and got into his squad car. Before pulling out of the parking lot, he made sure his pistol was still in its holster. *You never know on a case like this if you might need protection,* he thought. Craig's apartment was in the Kingston Green complex on the east side of town. According to Craig's coworkers, he had lived there alone for several years, but his older brother had been staying with him for the past few months.

Jack found the apartment easily and banged on the front door to the townhouse apartment. No one answered, so he waited several minutes and then banged harder. Finally, he heard footsteps from inside the apartment. "Who is it?" a male's voice said. "I'm trying to sleep before work!"

"It's the sheriff's department," Jack replied. "Open up!"

For several seconds, there was complete silence on the other end of the door, and Jack could sense that the man was looking at him through the peephole. "Why don't you have on a uniform if you're the police?" the man asked.

"Open the door so I can show you my badge," Jack said. After a moment, the man unlocked the deadbolt and opened the front door cautiously.

Jack was appreciative that he had not had to exert any physical effort to talk to Craig, as he was still rather worn down from the previous night's lack of sleep. The man who opened the door was tall, blond, and slightly overweight. He appeared to be in his midthirties. Rubbing his eyes as if he had just woken up, he was wearing boxer shorts and a T-shirt, and his hair was sticking out in all directions. Jack's presence at his door seemed to perplex him.

"What's this about?" he asked. "Did someone break into one of the apartments again?"

"No. I just have a few questions for a man named Craig, and then I'll be on my way. Are you Craig?"

"Yeah. Why?"

"Good. I have the right place then. Where were you all day yesterday, Craig? Why did you ask off from work?"

Craig was clearly growing defensive, but he tried to keep his cool. "Look," he said, "I don't know what this is all about. I hadn't taken a day off in months, so I asked off so I could go with my brother after work Wednesday night to see his girl-friend, Susan, in Indianapolis. We got there at about one and spent the night at her house. The next morning, we got up and went out to breakfast at Waffle House with a few of her girl-friends. We hung out at the Castleton Mall in Indy for a few hours after that and then went to see a movie."

Jack interrupted him. "Can I ask what movie you saw?"

"Titanic," he replied. "A total chick flick. Never go see that one on a first date. Talk about being uncomfortable. Anyway, then we went back to Susan's house to play cards. We stayed there until about one in the morning. We just got home around two, and it's now what, about eight?"

Jack checked his watch and said, "Correct. Now, do you by chance have any proof that you did all these things?" Craig thought about it for a minute, and then walked over to a pair of jeans that was lying on the dining room table in the next room. Jack followed closely behind him. He wasn't taking any chances. Craig pulled a black wallet from the back pocket and threw a wad of receipts and tickets out onto the table.

"Is this good enough for you?" he asked. Craig sorted through the receipts and handed Jack his receipt to the Waffle House and the movie tickets. He even gave him a gasoline receipt from the Indianapolis area. Stamped on each receipt was the date and time of purchase. It looked like Craig's story added up—he really had been out of town.

It was Craig's turn to ask questions. "So, now do you mind telling me what all the questions are about?"

"Sure," Jack replied. "I appreciate your time and cooperation. You must not have heard that one of your coworkers, Anita Wooldridge, was reported missing yesterday morning. It looks like she's been abducted, and your name came up as someone who repeatedly asked her out and propositioned her."

Craig laughed uneasily. "No, you have the wrong idea here," he said, rubbing his temples. "I just always have some fun with Anita. She's like a little sister to me. We always joke around with each other and stuff. That's all. Wow! I can't believe that she's missing."

"Do you know of any enemies that Anita might have had?" Jack asked.

"No. Anita is a real easygoing, sweet girl. I don't know how someone could dislike her. She would never intentionally make anyone mad."

"Do you know her boyfriend, Scott, at all?"

"Yeah, I met him a few times when he picked her up from work. He seems like a young, quiet, shy guy. She told me he's really sweet and that they had taken a few trips together. That's all that I know about him."

"Well, you can get back to sleep now. If you hear anything about Anita that could be useful, please give me a call," Jack said as he handed Craig his business card. Craig took the card and walked him to the front door.

"I will. I hope you find her. I'm really gonna miss seeing her at work." Craig shut the door, and Jack walked back to his squad car highly frustrated. *Man*, he thought. *One less suspect and no further leads. She couldn't have just vanished in broad daylight—someone has to know something. I hope my guys are having more luck than I am.* Jack got in his car and started the ignition. He was driving back toward the station when his cell phone rang.

Jack answered it on the second ring. "This is Jack. Can I help you?"

"Hi, Dad." It was his daughter Emily.

"I just talked to Mom," she said. "She told me that you've been up all night working on a big case. I wanted to let you know that the missing girl is in my prayers, and so are you. She's only a few years younger than me. How scary."

"I know. It's good to hear your voice, though, hon. We miss you and Todd. Are you still planning on coming over on the Fourth for a cookout?"

"Of course. We wouldn't miss your barbecued ribs."

"Good. Well, thanks for all your prayers. It means a lot to me. This is going to be a tough case."

"Well, if anyone can find her, it's you, Dad. I know you won't give up. Just try to get some rest soon. You're not as young as you think!"

Jack laughed. "People keep trying to tell me that. My body is too. I'm going to try to get home at a decent hour tonight. Don't worry about me, okay?"

"Okay. See you soon. I love you!"

Jack told his daughter that he loved her and hung up the phone. He wished that Carrie Ann and Gerald Wooldridge could receive a similar reassuring phone call from their daughter, but for now, they could only sit by the phone, waiting to hear Anita's voice again.

CHAPTER 19

Anita awoke, gasping for air, and hit her head on the metal doors when she tried to sit up. She could still hear the mole snoring loudly just outside the box. She did not want to move or scream for fear of waking up her sleeping captor. She did not know how much longer she could lie still, though, as she had to go to the bathroom again.

From inside the metal box, Anita could hear the mole begin to stir. Soon he removed the stick and butter knife from the double doors to unlatch them, and they squeaked open. Anita braced herself to face her captor again. The mole looked down at her and wiped the sweat from his brow with his stained white T-shirt. "I'm starving," he said groggily. "How about you? Want any breakfast? I'm having cereal and toast."

"No thanks. I'm not hungry," Anita replied. "But I do have to go to the bathroom really bad."

The mole led his prize down the stairs and watched as she relieved herself. Anita just wanted his eyes off her—even for five minutes. When they got back upstairs, he ate in the nearby kitchen while she sat quietly on the worn couch in the living room. The small room had a desk and an old TV with a VCR next to it. He had several old movies on top of the VCR. She also saw a few old board games and books strewn about the room. Like his bedroom in his mother's house, this room was a pigsty; it was clear to Anita that this was the way he preferred to live.

When the mole finished eating, he returned to the living room, sat down on the couch next to Anita, and pointed at his crotch. With dread, she realized that this must mean he wanted her to perform oral sex on him again. He took off his pants, and she begrudgingly knelt down and did as she was told. Moaning, the mole pushed her head down on him and pulled her hair. "You like it, you nasty girl," he said. "I knew you would."

Despite all his dirty talk, he could not ejaculate. "Take your clothes off," he demanded. He pointed down to the floor, indicating that Anita should lie down once she was undressed. When she complied, he roughly fondled her breasts for a few minutes before putting his fingers inside her to get her wet and raped her again. After he ejaculated inside her, Anita thanked God that she had gotten her Depo Provera shot just a month ago and that it was good for another few months. The thought of conceiving a child with this monster was unthinkable.

Satisfied, the mole dragged Anita down to the basement and commanded her to take a shower. As he sat and watched, she scrubbed herself clean, trying to block his eyes from her body as best she could. There was no razor in sight, and she hated the feeling of the stubble growing on her legs and armpits. She hated all this and was beginning to feel like she would rather die than to live like this much longer. Her captor dried her off with a towel when she was done, grabbing her breast in the process.

"Now don't you feel better?" he asked. "You're all nice and clean. You smell great." He took a long whiff of her hair, nuzzling his face in it, before leading her back over to the stairs. "I have to put you back in your box so that I can shower now," he told her. "I feel like I just had a great workout."

As they were heading back up the creaky basement steps, they heard a loud knock at the front door. "Oh, shit!" he exclaimed, clearly startled. "Who could that be? I'll shoot you and whoever is at that damn door if you scream for help. Remember that." He rushed her into the bedroom and shut the door before he cautiously walked to the front door.

The mole opened the door slightly and peered out of the crack. He immediately recognized the short, stocky man. "Hey, Pete," he said to the man. "How's it going?"

Pete, his landlord, replied, "Hey, Tom, glad to see you got moved in. How was your trip here?"

"I hit a few snags, but I made it. I hate moving."

"Tell me about it. My next move hopefully won't be till they put me in the nursing home."

The mole, trying to appear at ease, chuckled. He hoped that he had scared Anita enough that she'd keep quiet.

Pete, having exchanged sufficient pleasantries, got to the real reason he had come over. "So, did you bring your first month's rent with you?" he asked. "I need to get it today if I could."

The mole grabbed his wallet and pulled out a crisp stack of bills—five hundred dollars. He handed it over to Pete and said, "Thanks for letting me move in on such short notice, man."

"No problem. I think we're going to get along just fine as long as you pay your rent on time and don't make a lot of noise."

"Don't worry about that. It's just me living here for now, and I don't know a soul around here yet, so you won't even know I'm here. But is it okay if I build some bookshelves for all my books? I may want to sell them all someday. Maybe make a business out of it or something."

"Look, I don't care what you do, within the law, as long as you pay your rent on time." The landlord's statement didn't seem to faze the mole.

"Hey, while you're here, could you hook up my computer for me and help me with the phone jacks?" he asked "I haven't been able to figure it all out yet."

"Sure," the landlord replied. "I've got a few minutes before I've got to go on to work."

As Pete got started, the mole went into the bedroom on the pretext of cleaning out some boxes. He closed the door behind him. Anita was sitting on a pile of sofa cushions and blankets that he had thrown on the floor beside the cabinet she slept in. She looked as white as a ghost.

"Get in the box now!" he ordered in a whisper. "The landlord is here, and if he finds you, I'll kill you both and hide your bodies in the woods."

Anita obeyed, climbing into the dreaded box once again. The mole closed the doors and latched them with the stick. Feeling safer now, he went back out to the living room. Pete had already hooked the computer and phone up and was brushing his hands on his pants when the mole returned. "Well, it's all ready to go," he said. "You'll just have to call the phone company to get a line installed. They always take forever, so I'd call soon. Also, my last tenants ran their business out of here, so they left their copier and fax machine. They'll be by to pick those up tomorrow. Okay?"

The mole was rather irritated by this, but said calmly, "That's fine. But I don't like visitors, so they need to make it quick."

"Sure. I understand," Pete said. "We won't bother you at all after that. Again, I'm glad you made it here safely. I'll get out of your hair now. If you need anything, just holler. Here's one of my cards with my cell phone number on it." Pete handed him the card as he walked toward the door. "See you later," he said, stepping outside into the bright sunshine.

The mole waved good-bye and shut the door, breathing a sigh of relief. He had escaped being caught one more time.

The mole let Anita out of the box and said to her, "Whew. What a morning. I'm ready for some lunch now. How about you?" Anita, who had not eaten since Wednesday night at Applebee's, was starving.

"Sure. What do you have?"

"I'll make you a peanut butter and jelly sandwich and some water. I'll be right back. You can sit on the couch and read one of my books."

Anita sat back and tried to relax her aching muscles. It felt so good to stretch out and be out of her captor's sight. He came back after a few minutes with two sandwiches and a glass of water. She forced herself to say thank you. The peanut butter felt strange on her tongue and stuck to the roof of her dry mouth. She had to drink the whole glass of water to get the sandwich down. Anita only ate the food out of necessity; although she was hungry, she had no real desire to eat.

Anita took a chance by complaining to the mole about her other necessity: breathing. "It's really hard for me to breathe when I'm in the box. Is there any way for me to get more air?"

"Well, I guess I could put my fan where it'd blow directly toward the vents in the box," he replied in an agitated tone. "Maybe that'll help. If not, you're out of luck. That's the best I can do for you." *How thoughtful of him*, Anita thought.

"Do you want to watch a movie now or play a game?" he asked her. *He is crazy*, she thought. *He wants to play games and act like everything is just perfect? How am I going to do this?* When she hesitated, he said, "Hey, if you don't want to do those things, we can have sex again. It's up to you."

Considering her options, Anita quickly said, "Let's watch a movie."

The mole put in *Showgirls*, and Anita tried to stay focused on the movie, even though it had no plot and the acting was awful. She tried to sit as far away from him as possible on the beat-up, bright orange couch. Just as she was starting to relax and tune him out, he abruptly scooted over right next to Anita on the couch.

"I'm bored," he informed Anita. "I'm ready for you to suck me again."

Tears of disbelief and anger welled up in her eyes. "Please, no," she said. "My throat is killing me. Let's just play a game now." But he yanked her flaming red hair and said, "You will do as I say. I told you what I wanted. Now do it."

Anita knelt down and went through the motions once again, but her mind and body went elsewhere. She imagined that she was a child, swinging with her friends on a hot summer day. Drifting in and out of consciousness, she was snapped back into reality by a slap across the face. Anita could hear the mole talking, but his words sounded far away. "Hey. Wake up," he said. "You passed out and fell on the floor, but at least you took care of me first."

As she came to, Anita hoped that he was done with her, but he dragged her semi-conscious body over to his room and laid her on the blankets on the bright green carpeted floor. He took off her clothes and began fondling her breasts and forcing his fingers inside her. He began to rape her with such force that she screamed out, "No! Stop it. I can't take it anymore!" The mole covered her mouth and ignored her pleas for mercy. When he was satisfied, he got off her and left the room. Anita lay alone in the dark, cold and shaking with fear and anger. *How could anyone be so callous and cruel? she thought. He's a monster!*

It was several minutes before the mole returned from the bathroom. "All right," he said. "Let's go play that game you were just dying to play. I'm bored again."

Her captor's selfishness stunned her. It was all about entertaining him at all times, and he had absolutely no consideration of her feelings. As he roughly pulled her limp body off the floor, Anita thought he was going to yank her arm out of its socket. "Ouch," she complained. "Okay, okay, I'm coming. Just let me get my clothes back on." Her clothes were damp with perspiration and beginning to reek of body odor. Though she felt disgusting, she either had to wear these stinky clothes or walk around nude with him watching her every move. No, she would wear these rank clothes for as long as it took for the police to rescue her. Maybe, she hoped, her putrid smell would keep him away from her eventually.

They sat down on the floor in the living room, and the mole set up the game of Monopoly on a cardboard box that he had turned upside down to make a table. He insisted on being the banker and in charge of the cards. Anita noticed that he cheated whenever she started to build up any houses or hotels on her properties. He was very competitive, and seemed unwilling to lose to her. It was a long game, but she let him win in the end because she was afraid he would take it out on her if he lost.

When the game was over, the mole got up and cheerfully said, "That was fun. We'll have a rematch soon. You need to redeem yourself. But for now you're going back in the box for a while. I've got to go into town to buy some Sunny Delight and something for dinner. I worked up another appetite. Is there anything I can get for you while I'm out?"

"I like to chew gum. I like Juicy Fruit."

"You got it. Now be a good girl and get back in your box, sweetie. I'll be home in a few hours."

Anita climbed willingly into the box. Now that she had the fan blowing on it to provide her with just enough fresh air, she was actually relieved to be in there. Relishing the next few hours away from him, she passed the time by reciting Bible verses from her memory. One verse was from the book of Joshua 1:9: "Be strong and of a good courage; be not afraid, neither be thou dismayed: for the LORD thy God is with thee whithersoever thou goest." As she held onto this thought, she began to sob uncontrollably. Scrunched up into a fetal position, Anita rocked herself over and over until she fell asleep, sucking her thumb. Although she wasn't aware of it, this type of behavior is common for victims of sexual abuse or other trauma. She was regressing into a childlike state as she could not cope and desperately wanted to be comforted like a baby.

When the mole returned, he woke her up and let her out again. His breath smelled like an unpleasant mixture of greasy food and Sunny Delight. "Come on," he said. "Let's finish our movie and then get to bed. Tomorrow is going to be a long day. I have to get my computer going, and people are coming over to get their equipment out." Anita, suppressing a desire to run for the door and scream bloody murder, followed him into the living room.

Anita sat through the rest of the movie, but her thoughts were elsewhere. In her head, she played out scenarios of ways she could possibly escape from this monster when the right opportunity came along. Maybe tomorrow she would be able to get away when the people came over. She would never give up trying; she would find a way to outwit him. She had to.

These thoughts continued even after he placed Anita back in her metal box for the night. She had survived her first day in this new house. *Please find me soon. I can't make it much longer,* she frantically thought. *Help me, God. Help me to get some rest.* Within minutes, she was asleep, despite being cramped up in an uncomfortable ball and forced to listen to the blaring TV left on in the next room. The mole snored while lying on cushions right beside the box. He had placed the quarter on top of the box again, and he slept securely, knowing that his lovely prisoner would be honest throughout her second night of captivity.

CHAPTER 20

Captain Jack Roberts went home to see his wife, check his mail, and play around with his dogs before he returned to the station at noon. He needed just a few minutes of normalcy to get him through the day. Dorothy hugged him and forced him to take a ham sandwich for the road. He walked into the conference room a little early, and Deputy Watts was waiting to brief him on the homeless man on the bike.

"It's a no go on the bike suspect," Watts said. "It was just Bobby, riding his bike along 31 and picking up cans along the side of the road like he does every day. He says it was him yesterday, and he has an alibi. I talked with the rescue mission's staff, and they confirmed that Bobby rode his bike over for lunch a little bit before eleven. They say he stayed there the rest of the afternoon, counting his cans, playing cards, and then taking a nap. He's innocent."

"I thought so," Jack replied. "Just wanted to be sure. Well, we can cross two suspects off our list now. Craig's alibi checked out too. He was out of town Wednesday night and didn't return until late last night." Jack walked over to his dry-erase board and crossed their names off the dwindling list.

Jack's closest allies on the force, Captain Curtis Hoover and Deputy Major Phil Lyons, walked into the conference room. They had worked side by side with Jack on several big cases over the years. Despite their different personalities and lifestyles, they trusted each other and worked well together. Curtis was a good cop; he had good rapport with people and was competitive by nature. He hated to lose and therefore gave each case 100 percent of his time and energy. Unlike Jack, he was a bachelor; he liked to wear flashy clothes and drive sports cars, and he was always ready to hang out with the guys or pick up women. He reminded Jack of Don Johnson on *Miami Vice*. That was his personal life, though, and it didn't bother Jack as long as it didn't interfere with a case. It never had yet.

Jack had a deep respect for Phil as well. He was a family man, like Jack, and they had often gotten their families together over the years. He was older than Jack and had more knowledge and experience. Jack often went to Phil for advice or to run things by him when he had no further leads.

Curtis and Phil sat down. "Well, that son of a bitch Snake you sent us after is sure hard to find," Curtis said. "We went over to his house in the Heights and knocked on his door for hours. His neighbor came out and told us that Snake often disappears for days without telling anyone. The guy said that Snake was probably on another drug binge and that he'd likely come back home to crash by tonight or tomorrow morning. He said that he'd call us if he sees him pull in the drive."

"Did you ask the neighbor when the last time he saw Snake was?" Jack asked.

"Yeah," Phil replied. "He said Snake went out with a group of friends on Wednesday night and hasn't returned yet."

Jack went over to the dry-erase board and circled Snake's name. "We have to find this guy to talk with him!" he said. "It's odd that he was out with Anita the night before and then never returns home when she comes up missing too. As far as I'm concerned, he and the boyfriend are our prime suspects here."

Don Howell, the sheriff's department senior deputy investigator, walked into the conference room, shaking his head. He sat down and announced, "No luck with any other neighbors. Nobody other than Mr. Taylor saw anything. How is that even possible?"

"Did you talk with Fred further about his own alibi?" Jack asked.

"Yeah," Don said. "He says that he went to get gas for his lawn mower right after he saw the man approach Anita's home. He has a gas receipt from the nearby Shell station right off 31. Then he went over to the Furrows hardware store and bought a new chain for his mower. He showed me that receipt as well with the date and time on it. He didn't leave the store until about noon. That clears him as a suspect."

Jack wasted no time in erasing Fred's name from the board. He had hated to question him in the first place, but it was procedure. "Okay," he said. "That leaves us with Scott, the boyfriend. Did you get him to come in to talk to you, Don?"

"Yep. That boy was scared shitless! I've never seen anyone shake as badly as he did. He had his parents with him, and they said he's just distraught over the whole thing."

"That kid has to know something. Maybe that's why he's so scared. Did his story change at all this time?"

"No. He still swears he came over to pick Anita up and waited in his car until her mom showed up. He says he has no other information to give us. He cried and said he loves Anita and would never hurt her."

"Did you threaten to hook him up to a lie detector test?"

"I told him and his parents that would be the next step. His parents are now saying that they are going to get him an attorney first."

"Let them," Jack said, his voice beginning to rise. "He's our prime suspect. We'll get that test done tomorrow if he doesn't tell us anything by then. I'll bring that kid in here every damn day until he gives me something to go on. He has to know something!"

"Calm down, Jack," Don said. "Don't forget. He's young, and he might just be in shock. I'll take care of it. I'll get him back over here in the morning."

Detective Rick Monroe and Sergeant Doug Kellar walked into the conference room. "No new leads, even though thousands of people called in today," Rick reported. "People don't quite understand that we don't want their condolences. We set up these phone lines for information only. Word spread through the community fast! People are just devastated, and they're scared their child could be next. Someone's going to have to make a statement to the press soon. It's quite a frenzy out there!"

"Humphrey's Printing stayed open after hours last night with Anita's family," Kellar added. "They printed thousands of 'missing posters' with Anita's picture on them. The posters are already posted all over town and even in several surrounding counties. The community's really going above and beyond on this one. You would think that, with the posters and the reward money put up by local businesses for any information, someone would come forward soon with something for us to go on."

"We'll hear something soon," Jack replied. "We just have to keep our eyes and ears open, but no one speaks to the press yet. I'll set up a conference with the media tomorrow. Let's all go and take some calls and see if we can't find another lead."

They all headed to the dispatch room and stayed there until almost eight thirty at night. They weeded through hundreds of calls with no further success. Jack sighed as he stood up to go home for the night. *Her poor parents will have to get through another sleepless night not knowing anything,* he thought. *That son of a bitch better not hurt her! I'm going to find him, no matter what!*

Jack prayed the entire twenty minutes home that God would give him the strength and knowledge to find Anita, even though he had no idea how he was going to pull this one off. He believed that God knew and would open the doors for him when it was time. This helped to ease his mind and allowed him to get some much needed rest for the night.

DAY THREE
SATURDAY, JUNE 27, 1998

CHAPTER 21

The mole was listening to the radio in his old red truck this bright and sunny morning. The deejay was saying that today was going to be another scorcher in La Crosse, but rain and thunderstorms were predicted for later tonight. He wiped the sweat from his brow with the back of his arm. It was only eight o'clock in the morning, and the truck, which had no air conditioning, was already sweltering hot. The rental house was also without air conditioning, and the only relief was from the two fans that he had brought with him to cool the house off. He kept the windows shut and barred with steel rods to prevent his girl from escaping or peering out the windows. Unfortunately, the bars that kept Anita from getting out also kept a breeze from getting in.

The mole had woken up around six thirty and had creaked open the box to ask his girl if she needed to go to the bathroom. "No. In a few more hours, I will," she had said. He had then left the house—leaving the TV blaring so that Anita couldn't hear the outside noises—without telling her.

The mole drove to Menards, a hardware store, to buy nails and rent a power saw to get started on building his bookshelves. He then drove over to a gas station payphone to call his landlord. Pete answered on the second ring.

"Hey, Pete. It's Tom. What time should I expect the guys to come by and get their stuff today, so I can make sure I'm home?"

"I'll tell them to come around one, if that's okay."

"Sure," he replied. "That sounds fine. Thanks, Pete. Bye." Well, at least the mole now knew when he would have to put the girl back in the box to hide her. He strolled into the gas station to pick up a pack of the gum she had requested.

The mole would later share with Anita how he drove back home in good spirits, singing along to the new Will Smith song on the radio, "Gettin' Jiggy wit It." He mentioned to Anita that he liked the song so much because Will Smith was in one of his favorite movies, *Men in Black*. In the movie, Will Smith and Tommy Lee Jones scour Earth to find aliens masquerading as humans. The mole told her that he felt that if they found him, they would find him to be an alien inside as well.

The end of the song snapped the mole out of his fantasy world. He made a mental note to call his mother the next time he was out to give her his new address and remind her to sell his car. He would need that money soon to get his bookstore going and for food and such. The mole had never been very good at budgeting money and only had enough with him to last a few months. Also, his mother would probably be dumb enough to call the police and report him missing if she didn't hear from him soon. She had always been nosy and wanted to know where he was at all times. It drove him crazy.

The mole entered the stifling hot house and tossed the bag of nails down with a thud. He charged into the bedroom and was pleased to see that the quarter was still in place. He went over to the box and opened the doors. Anita was lying inside, drenched with sweat. He could see right through her white T-shirt, which excited him. He reached out a hand to pull her out and then handed Anita the pack of Juicy Fruit he had just bought for her. "I got this for you. Is it the right kind?"

"Yeah. It's my favorite," Anita said, taking it from him. "Thanks." Her mom would have been shocked that she was able to hold back her sarcasm and rage when she talked to him. Anita had never been one to hold back on expressing how she felt; you always knew where you stood with her. But right now, she had to bite her tongue to stay alive. She was sure about that.

Her captor went through the morning ritual of asking her if she had to use the bathroom and if she was hungry. Anita said she needed to use the bathroom, so he took her down to the basement and watched her urinate again. It was still humiliating, but as time went on, she found herself caring less and less; she just tried to block his presence out as best as she could, since there was nothing she could do to stop him from looking at her. She did refuse to take a shower that day, even though she was desperately in need of one. Anita was starting to reek to high heaven, but she didn't care as long as she didn't have to shower in front of this pervert.

The mole forced her back upstairs and made her give him oral sex once again. Afterward, he pointed over to the bedroom and made her take her clothes off. Anita started crying as he took his clothes off and moved toward her. She went to the safe place in her mind again, and the room started to black out. She would randomly snap out of it every few minutes. Anita was so terrified of the pain of his thrusts inside her and seeing this animal on top of her moaning. It was too much for her mind and body to handle, so her brain would once again, miraculously, shut down, and the blackness would shelter her from the images, smells, and pain. Locked away in the deep crevices of her mind, those images would stay there until she felt safe enough to let them out for good years later.

When the mole was done with her, he stood up. "I'm going to eat something now," he said. "You can hang out for a while in the living room, but then you have to get back in your box. Some guys are coming over to get their equipment out of here." Anita felt relieved at the thought of being away from him, but at the same time, her body was sore from being so cramped up. Her neck, throat, back, and legs were in excruciating pain. Even her wrists and ankles were throbbing from having been tied up so long on Thursday.

The mole allowed her to sit on the couch and read a book while he ate. She could see up close if she put the book right up to her nose. She chose a thriller about a man who killed his wife and buried her remains. It was a very old, outdated book, and she wondered, *How in the world does he think that he is going to sell these crappy, old books to people? He is out of his mind.*

"Drink some of this water, and get yourself a piece of gum," he ordered her thirty pages in to the novel. "Then you're getting back in the box. I know you're starting to like me, but I'm not taking any chances yet." The water that he handed her was lukewarm and had a slight brownish tint to it. But Anita was so thirsty that she gulped it all down; she was beginning to feel dehydrated and dizzy from the heat and the trauma, and the water helped a little.

Anita submissively took the gum and got back into the box. Suddenly, the mole put a knife to Anita's throat, warning her, "I don't want to have to cut your pretty neck now, but I will if you fuck with me. You make one peep while those guys are here and I will gut you like a pig." He shut the doors forcefully and latched them. There was no way she was going to risk being cut to pieces, so she remained quiet. She quickly dozed off but woke up with a start when she heard the mole talking loudly with two other men. She heard the mole ask, "So are you moving your office somewhere else, or are you selling all this stuff?"

"We're just moving to a different location. None of it's for sale," one of the men replied.

"I was asking because I'm starting my own business here, and once it's up and running, I might need more equipment," the mole said. "Call me if you ever want to sell any of it."

"Will do," they both said in unison. The men carried it all out to their car and left. They were in and out within seconds.

Anita felt like she had been kicked in the stomach—another opportunity to escape had passed. She began sobbing, and was still sobbing when the mole opened up the doors to the cabinet.

Ignoring her tears, he said, "Let's play another game. Maybe cribbage this time."

"I can't play a game right now!" Anita wailed. "Please just give me a break for a while. I can't stop crying. I miss my family so much! Please, just let me call and talk to them. I need them, please!"

Looking at her sobbing face, the mole paid no attention to her pleas. "Well, I don't see any reason for us both to be so unhappy, do you?" he callously said. "I want to have sex again.

That'll definitely cheer me up. Soon, you won't even think of your family. We'll have our own." He pulled his victim over to the couch and raped her for the second time that day.

It was now almost three in the afternoon, but Anita had no idea anymore what day or time it was. She felt completely disoriented and dehydrated. *I will never let this creep see me cry again,* she vowed silently. *He is a coldhearted snake, and he'll just hurt me more if I don't pretend to be happy with him in his fantasy world.* From that point on, Anita became emotionless. She had to.

They began to play cribbage. It was a long, boring game, but at least it distracted her from having to think. As they played, it started to rain, and she heard the raindrops pelting the window panes. Anita had always loved to take leisurely naps during rainstorms—something about storms had always made her feel so relaxed and tired.

When the game ended (she let him win again), Anita yawned, stood up, and then stretched her stiff arms and legs. She had been sitting on the floor the entire game, and her legs were numb. "Good game, hon," the mole said. "Just give up thinking you're ever going to beat me, though. I never lose."

"Well, then why'd you have to spend years in prison if you never lose?" Anita asked. The words had escaped her lips before she could think about the dire consequences of such a bold statement.

Anita could tell that her comment caught the mole off guard; she could see from his face that he felt both hurt and angry. He stood up and charged toward her. "Look, bitch," he yelled. "That's something you know nothing about! That whore set me up. I believed we actually had a connection or something, and then she wouldn't even take my calls or see me anymore. Do you know how that feels? She was lucky to even have me, and it could have worked out if she hadn't been such a slut! Don't you ever talk to me like that again! You are disposable, and don't you ever forget it!"

The mole yanked Anita's head back and threw her into the wall. He jumped on top of her with all his weight and punched her hard in the stomach. She groaned and then vomited all over the ugly carpet. The only thing that came out was water, since she had not eaten since yesterday. Her captor stood up and kicked Anita in the side, and she rolled over to cover her head. "Stop," she begged. "I won't do it again. I'm sorry. Please stop hurting me!"

Anita's words seemed to snap the violent mole out of his fury. "Okay," he told her. "I hope you learned your lesson. I don't like hurting you, but you deserved it. You know?"

"I know," she replied. "I'm sorry."

"Okay. I forgive you. Now, I need to get out of here and cool off some, so go get in your box. I'm going to get some dinner."

"Okay. That's fine. Can you help me up? I can't move. It feels like my ribs might be broken."

The mole knelt over to lift his prey up off the ground and then assured her, "You'll be okay. You're just bruised up. You'll feel better soon." He put her into the box, and Anita was again enveloped by the darkness. She was beaten down, both mentally and physically, but she was growing desensitized to the pain and suffering. Unable to muster up the energy to pray, she suddenly blacked out.

CHAPTER 22

On Saturday morning, two days after Anita's disappearance, Captain Jack Roberts and Captain Curtis Hoover gave a joint press conference to make the media and the frantic community aware that they did in fact have several suspects, though not enough evidence yet to make any arrests. They also reported that they had not found Anita or her car yet, and they pleaded with the nation at large to be on the lookout. It was a scorchingly hot summer day, and the conference was held inside the police station in downtown Kokomo with the air conditioning cranked up high. The men—both wearing their uniforms—looked official, but they were unshaven and running on fumes. They had both gotten home at nine the night before and had to meet back up at five in the morning to take more calls and plan for the press conference.

By eleven in the morning, the press conference was over, and they were driving back to the sheriff's department together when Jack's cell phone rang.

"This is Jack," he said. Deputy Don Howell was on the other end.

"Morning, Jack!" he said cheerfully. "It's Don. I think that we just might have a lead."

"Really? Did you talk to Scott again? Did his story change?"

"Well, I spoke with him, but nothing new there. I set up the lie detector test for him for tomorrow morning, and he's willing to do it. No, I was interviewing one of Anita's old employers at a fitness center that used to be open here in town. Anita worked there from 1995 until they closed the gym in May of '97.

"The co-owner of the gym, Linda Noll, told me that it just came to her that there was a man named Victor Thomas Steele—he goes by 'Tom'—who was a member of the gym for a couple of years while Anita worked there," he continued. "She says she had problems with Tom in the fall of '96 when he asked Anita, her best friend Sarah, and another coworker named Danielle out on dates repeatedly. When Danielle turned him down, he apparently took offense and started stalking her. On Friday nights, when several girls were left to close the gym at nine, Tom would go get in the hot tub several minutes before closing. Linda also indicated that they had reason to believe that when Danielle was alone in the gym Tom would disappear to watch her.

"Based on his harassment of the female employees and the fact that they learned that Tom had a criminal history as a convicted rapist during a background check, they terminated his membership immediately. But they didn't tell the employees of his prior conviction."

"Okay," Jack said. "Are you on your way to the station? I want to hear the rest of this in person."

"Yeah. I'm pulling in right behind you guys. I'll see you in there in a few. Bye."

They hung up their phones and rushed inside to talk further. Jack updated Curtis on the newest information as they walked inside. The three men met up in the conference room and started in where they had left off on the phone.

"Linda said that Anita and Sarah were the only two girls that treated Tom nicely and that Tom trusted Anita enough to give her a book he had written to get her feedback on it," Don said. "Linda described Tom as a real loner who never seemed to socialize or have any friends or family around. She said that he would leave his aerobics instructors Christmas cards and small gifts, but he never asked them out. She described him as approximately five feet eight with blondish-brown hair. He's kind of bald and around forty years old. She also said she has no idea whether Anita kept in contact with Tom after they terminated his membership. They never heard from or saw Tom after around November of '96."

"We need to talk with Anita's best friend Sarah pronto!" Jack said. "We've got to find out whether they kept in contact with this Tom guy or not. Don, can you work on getting her in here?"

"Sure," Don replied. "I talked with her yesterday. She lives in Kentucky now but is actually getting married next weekend, so luckily she's back in town for the wedding events. I'll go call her now."

Don left the room, and Jack and Curtis gave each other a high five. This just might be the best lead they had encountered thus far. It was at least something to follow up on. "I'm supposed to go meet with Chuck Wilson at our buddy Snake's house. Chuck's a member of the regional drug task force," Curtis told Jack. "We got a search warrant for his house, so if he doesn't answer the door, we're gonna break it down. You want to come?" Jack knew that it was crucial to find this suspect, so he agreed.

When the officers arrived at the residence in Indian Heights, they immediately noticed a black Jeep parked in the driveway. It had not been present the day before and was listed as Snake's vehicle. The neighbor came outside as soon as they pulled up. "I was just gonna call you guys," he said. "Snake pulled up and went inside a few hours ago. He's probably crashed by now."

"Thanks," Jack said. "But please go inside. We don't know what to expect with him."

The neighbor cooperated, stepping back into his house, but continued peering out of his window to get a view of all the action. They banged on Snake's front door. "It's the police. We know you're in there, so come on out, Snake. We need to talk to you. It's urgent!" Hearing no answer, Curtis sent Chuck to guard the backyard, the only other exit from the tiny house. The three men knew they could not let this guy get away.

Jack and Curtis continued knocking and calling out to him for several minutes, but no one came to the door. "Screw this!" Curtis said finally. "I'm getting in there!" He and Jack busted down the lightweight front door by kicking it in with joint force. They entered the house with their weapons drawn, shouting, "Police. We have a search warrant. Put your hands up, Snake. Come out." Still no answer or noise of any kind.

Chuck joined the others in the house and they all three made their way down the tiny hallway to a closed door to what had to be a back bedroom. Behind the door, they heard faint sounds of rock music playing. They kicked the door open. A pale, skinny male was lying in the fetal position on the bed. He was wearing only earphones and boxer shorts, and his body was covered in tattoos and piercings. He appeared to be out cold.

Chuck went over to the bedside table and picked up a bag of what appeared to be about an ounce of weed and a few pills that he identified as Xanax. The room reeked of marijuana smoke, and a bong was lying right next to the bed on the floor. Some of the water had leaked out onto the dingy carpet. It created a foul odor within the cramped bedroom.

"Well, I think the neighbor was right," Curtis said. "Our friend here is obviously strung out on drugs and came home to take his downers and crash." They tried to wake him up, but all they could get from him were grunts and a few feeble swats in their direction. The suspect was still breathing but clearly unable to answer any questions in his current state. "You stay here and check his place out, top to bottom," Curtis told Chuck. "Call us if you find anything regarding Anita or if he wakes up. We need to talk with him as soon as he wakes up, okay?"

"You got it, boss man," Chuck replied sarcastically. He was not exactly thrilled by the thought of hanging out all day with this winner on his weekend. For all that Chuck knew, this guy might sleep for days.

Around two in the afternoon, Jack and Curtis walked into the conference room where Don and Sarah, who had just arrived at the station for questioning, were waiting.

"Are you familiar with a Tom Steele?" Don asked.

"Yeah. He used to work out at the gym Anita and I worked at. He was always a loner. We felt sorry for him. We were just talking about him a few weeks ago. Neither of us had seen him in a couple years, and we decided to invite him to my wedding so he could maybe meet some Christian friends and not be so alienated. I don't even know if he got the invitation. He never responded."

"So Anita had no contact with Tom for the past couple years?" Jack asked.

"No. I'm sure of that. She just told me two weeks ago. She would've told me if he had called her to RSVP."

"What does Tom look like?" Curtis asked her.

"He's around five feet eight, with a stocky build, and kind of a big gut. All the girls at the gym thought that he had creepy, beady eyes. They were all scared of him, but Anita and I always just saw him as a harmless, lonely guy."

"Were you or Anita ever aware that he had a prior conviction for rape?" Don asked.

Sarah's mouth dropped open, and she stammered, "N-N-No. I never knew he was a convicted rapist, or else I'd never have invited him to my wedding."

"How would Tom get to the gym?" Curtis asked. "Did he drive?"

Sarah's next answer floored them. She laughed and said, "No. We always made fun of his old Schwinn bike that he rode everywhere. He'd always lock it up right next to the building when he got there to work out. You never saw him without his bike or his gray backpack."

The three officers sat back, their mouths hanging open in shock. "Thanks so much for coming down, Sarah," Jack said.

"You've been a great help. Good luck on your wedding next week. We'll try to have Anita home by then."

Sarah began to cry. "Please find her!" she pleaded. "She is the best friend I could ever ask for. Nothing would be the same without her here!"

"It sure sounds like it has to be this Tom guy," Jack said after Sarah had left the building, "but she hadn't seen him in almost two years. We need to find out more about him. Don, get a background check on him and see where his prior conviction was, so we can request a hard copy of the details in his rape case." Jack was frustrated that their resources were so limited. They still lacked a computerized database of all sexual offenders, and it was time-consuming to locate where the crime was committed and to have the hard copy sent over to them by mail. Jack did not have that kind of time to waste.

"Okay. I'll get on it, but with it being a Saturday, it'll probably be tomorrow morning until I hear anything back on him," Don answered.

"Okay," Jack said. "Just get back with me as soon as you know anything further on him."

As the men were getting up to leave, Curtis's phone rang. It was Chuck Wilson, giving him an update on Snake. Chuck was still waiting for the suspect to wake up and would probably have to stay the night.

It was now nearly six in the evening, and they were forced to play the waiting game. "We might as well take this idle time to get some sleep," Curtis suggested. "It's going to be an early morning tomorrow. We get to start off with another visit to see our Sleeping Beauty suspect. Chuck told me that he didn't find anything unusual at the house other than drugs and porn. He didn't find any weapons or anything with Anita's name or number on it. He's probably clean. We just need to make sure that he doesn't have any information for us. If he hasn't burned off the last of his brain cells on his latest drug binge, that is."

"You're right," Jack replied. "I'm headed home to get some rest. Call me if you hear from Chuck, even if it's two in the morning."

The men left the station in better spirits than when they had walked in. They had a new lead, and that gave them both hope that they might be able to find Anita before it was too late. *If this Mr. Steele is our guy,* Jack thought, *I'm gonna nail him! I'm coming after you, Tom!*

CHAPTER 23

The mole stepped out into the pouring rain and jumped when he heard a loud boom right next to him. A bolt of lightning had hit a nearby tree, and he quickly hopped into his truck for safety. "Dammit!" he yelled. "That nearly gave me a heart attack." He was so angry at the girl for smarting off to him. *Who does she think she is?* he thought. At the same time, though, he surprisingly felt a twinge of guilt for beating the girl so badly. He had not meant to kick her so hard. He justified it in his mind by telling himself, *I'll make it up to her. I'll bring her back some KFC and take care of her. She'll be okay, just a little sore.*

The mole, soaked from the rain, started the ignition and sped toward the north side of town by the river. He just needed a few minutes to clear his head and calm down. He got out of the truck and walked toward the rising water. It was still pouring outside, but it felt good on his face. He was burning hot, and it cooled him off. *Damn her,* he thought. *Why did she have to bring up the past and get me so mad? I had put all those years behind me. I might have to kill her and find someone else now. But I guess I can give her one more chance. She's pretty nice to have around.*

The mole picked up some stones from the ground and flung them into the river. When he got back into his truck, he felt refreshed. He was sopping wet, and the seat became drenched when he plopped down into it.

He drove to the KFC in town and ordered enough food for an army at the drive-through window. He listened to the radio as he drove home. Hearing no news reports mentioning the missing girl whom he currently held captive at his home, he breathed a sigh of relief.

It was nearly seven o'clock when he returned, and with the rainstorm blocking any remaining sunlight, the house was dark. The TV was still blaring, but he heard no other noise inside the tiny house.

The mole threw the sack of food down on a box of books and went into his bedroom to let the girl out. When he opened the box, he found Anita curled up on her left side, sleeping soundly. "Wake up!" the mole said loudly as he turned on the lights to illuminate the room. "Wake up. The food is here. You said you were hungry, Sleeping Beauty." Anita slowly lifted her head up and had to shelter her eyes from the bright lights that illuminated the room. She was still in a great deal of pain, and she considered refusing to eat the food, but her hunger pangs won out in the end.

The mole gave his wounded victim a hand out of the box, and she walked with a limp into the living room. "I decided to give you one more chance," he told Anita cheerfully, "so don't blow it. I got you some chicken and macaroni and cheese. And you need to drink some more water to keep yourself hydrated. I don't need you passing out on me anymore."

"Okay, you're right," Anita replied submissively. "I really do need some water. I'll try to eat some food, but my stomach hurts so bad."

"You'll be fine," he said rather coldly. "Just eat whatever you can. That'll leave more for me anyway."

Anita ate one piece of chicken breast and a few bites of her macaroni and cheese and then gulped down two whole glasses of tap water that he had gotten for her. She instantly felt recharged, and knew that she would have to force herself to eat and drink a little bit every day in order to stay oriented enough to eventually outsmart her captor. As soon as he let his guard down and trusted her more, she would try to escape. She had to. She realized earlier that he could easily kill her at any time. Today had been a close call, and she could never make the mistake of angering him again.

"You feel any better now that you've eaten?" the mole asked.

"Yeah, I do," Anita replied. "Thanks. Um, I'm really sorry for what I said to you earlier. It won't happen again."

"Damn right it won't. I won't put up with it again." He paused for a moment and then added, "I'm glad you ate, but don't make a habit of eating so much. I like you just the way you are, and I don't want you getting fat on me." His comment reminded Anita why this creep had never had a willing girlfriend before. The man next to her had no skills when it came to communication and considering someone else's feelings. She felt sorry for the first girl he had done this to and wondered how she had gotten away from him. It gave her hope that maybe she would be able to escape as well.

Anita's comfort from the food was short-lived. The mole sat down on the couch and ordered Anita, "Pull your pants down, and bend over for me. I want to see how good your ass looks again. Take your shirt off too, so I can squeeze your tits. You might as well get used to them being sore, because I love boobs." She cringed at these vulgar words, but slowly lifted herself off the floor. Moaning from the pain in her ribs, Anita did as she was told and bent over naked in front of him. He grabbed her by her hips and backed her bottom close enough so that he could touch and smack it. He glided his rough, calloused hands over her soft skin and then rammed one of his fingers inside her anally. Startled, she jumped from the impact.

After rubbing Anita's body more, the mole then stood up next to her and started fondling her breasts. He was gentle at first, but got rough, twisting her nipples and saying crude things to her, like, "You like it rough, don't you? You bad girl. What am I going to do with such a nasty whore?"

It was growing harder for Anita to like herself anymore after all the sick things that her captor had made her do. She was becoming beaten down like a kicked dog.

"Okay," the mole demanded. "You know what I need now. Get to it." When Anita hesitated, he pointed down to his exposed penis. She got down on her knees and began to perform. He still had not ejaculated after about twenty minutes. Frustrated, he said, "I guess I just can't come tonight after all the action you gave me earlier. We'll try again tomorrow, hon. Get some sleep now." Anita was again exhausted, sore, and ready to be back in the box and away from this animal. She gladly put her damp clothes back on and stepped into the box.

The mole latched the box, put the quarter on top of it, and called to her as he was leaving the room, "Goodnight, sweetheart. I'll wake you up in the morning. I had fun tonight with you." Anita closed her eyes and covered her ears with her hands to block him out completely. She begged God in a whisper, "Please forgive me for what he is making me do, God. Please forgive me for hating him. Please get this animal away from me. I need you to stay with me, dear Lord. Please stay with me and help me to sleep. Please help the police to find me and be with my family. I know that they have to be in so much pain not knowing where I am. Amen."

Anita felt the Holy Spirit wash over her like a blanket to provide her with both the warmth and strength she needed to endure another night of torture. Meanwhile, the mole stayed up late into the night in the next room masturbating to several pornos that he had brought along with him.

DAY FOUR
SUNDAY, JUNE 28, 1998

CHAPTER 24

Gasping for air, Anita came to the next morning around eight o'clock. She went to sit up, momentarily forgetting that she was in a metal box, and once again banged her head on top of it. It created a loud boom, which made the mole beside her jolt out from under the blankets and jump to his feet. "What the hell? You scared me," he yelled. "You weren't trying to get out, were you?"

Anita replied desperately from inside the box, "No! I swear. I just woke up and tried to sit up and hit my head. I didn't mean to scare you." Anita was writhing in pain already from yesterday's beating. The last thing that she wanted was another beating to start off the day.

The mole sat by the box and toyed with his victim by letting the wooden dowel he used to keep the box's double doors locked slide through his hands over and over again. It was a habit of his that he often did when he was in deep thought. Most of the time, he had no idea that he was even doing it, but today he was trying to make Anita worry about what he was going to do next. It was an annoying sound that she had become all too familiar with. The constant *swoosh* sound for nearly thirty minutes was pure torture. The mole was having fun and refused to say anything even when Anita informed him, "I have to go to the bathroom really bad. Please, let me out!" He took his own sweet time this morning. When he was done with his game, he opened up the doors to let her out and led her down to the old, dingy basement.

Anita relieved herself under the scrutiny of his beady eyes and was led back upstairs. She happened to catch a glimpse of herself in the mirror on the wall and did not even recognize the person that stared back at her. Her once beautiful, shiny auburn hair was matted to her face in greasy strands. She had not showered since Friday and felt so disgusting, especially when she would occasionally get a strong whiff of her own body odor. She also noticed big, purple bruises all over her arms, legs, wrists, and ankles. She was beaten up for sure; she felt like she had been run over by a Mack truck. She dreaded what would come next in their typical morning routine. The mole asked her his usual question, "Do you want anything to eat? I'm having some cereal and toast."

"I'll just have some Sunny Delight if you have any," Anita responded. "I'm not hungry right now, though."

"Okay, but don't say I didn't offer," he spat out at her.

The mole sat down beside Anita on the dirty couch, eating his breakfast like a pig eating from a trough, while she sipped her Sunny Delight quietly. Her stomach was in knots knowing what was to come next. The mole threw his paper plate on the floor and set his empty cereal bowl on the couch. He was not one for cleaning up after he ate. The house was now filled with sandwich wrappers and tubs of uneaten chicken lying on the floor. It was starting to create a foul stench in the already stifling corridors of the cramped house. It reminded her of the smell of her garage at home the night before trash day when the garbage was full and had been sitting there rotting for days.

The mole, keeping to his newfound daily routine, made her suck his penis and then raped Anita again on the dirty carpet right next to a bucket of rotting chicken. In her mind, Anita was in a boat on the lake during all this torture. She blocked all of it out as best as she could and went through the motions of pleasing him to get it over with quickly.

The mole had not showered for several days either, and the smell of his skin near her almost made her vomit. She quickly put her clothes back on when it was finally over and tried to make conversation with him. "So, what is the plan for today?" she asked her captor. "Maybe we could go somewhere. I've been cooped up in here for so long. I want to go with you the next time you leave."

The mole chuckled. "Good try, hon. I wasn't born yesterday. You're definitely not ready to leave the house. I don't trust you enough yet. The pigs are probably still hard at work looking for you. Give it a few more weeks and then you will be yesterday's news. They'll give up looking and just assume that you're dead. I'll feel safer letting you out then. Just be patient, girl." He kissed the top of her head and smacked her rear as he went into the kitchen to get a drink for himself. The vile man let out a loud, disgusting belch and stretched his arms over his head, exposing his bulging belly that hung over his shorts in rolls of fat. Anita noticed his balding head had tiny wisps of sparse hair sticking out in all directions. She had to turn her head in disgust so that he would not see her disdain for him written all over her face.

Anita's plan to get out of the house had failed this time, but she would try to get along with him today no matter what he did to her. She knew that, in order to stay alive and increase her chances of escaping, she had to make him believe that she would never leave him. "I have to go out for a while to get some more supplies to build my bookshelves," the mole announced. "I won't be gone long, but you need to get back in the box again." Anita, glad to have a short reprieve from him, did as she was told. As usual, he tried to trick her by leaving and returning several times to see if she would attempt to get out. He even yelled from the other room, "This is the police. Are you in here, Anita?" She did not make a peep: she knew the mole's twisted mind games by now. When he was finally satisfied that Anita would not try to escape, he left for good in his old, red truck.

CHAPTER 25

Investigator Chuck Wilson had not slept a wink the night before in this strange home he had been forced to stake out. He refused to take the risk of this Snake character waking up through the night and taking off. No, not on his watch. Chuck looked down at the shiny Seiko watch he had worn daily for the past ten years. It was now seven on Sunday morning, and he still heard the suspect snoring loudly in the next room. Chuck had searched the entire house for any evidence that could link Snake to the crime but had come up empty-handed. This Snake guy was a shady character, but he needed rehab, not prison. Chuck had conducted many investigations in the past and had a gut feeling that this was not their man. Nonetheless, he had invested a whole evening of his time away from his new girlfriend, whom he was supposed to have taken out to dinner last night, on this drug addict, and so, he was determined to talk to this comatose man as soon as he was able to wake him up.

Chuck had unsuccessfully attempted to awaken Snake several times throughout the long night. He poured water on him, shouted in his ear, and even shook him as hard as he could. He finally accepted that it was no use; he would just have to wait. Chuck had killed the time by talking to his girlfriend, Cindy, on the phone. He was jealous that she had gone out with her girlfriends last night without him. He understood, but he really liked her and did not want to take the chance of her meeting someone else at the bars. It had been rough for him over the years to keep relationships going as his work required him to be on call for days at a time. Most women he met wanted someone with a normal, nine-to-five work schedule. That just was not his life. Chuck was pulled out of his thoughts when he heard loud footsteps running from the suspect's room, down the short hallway and into the adjacent bathroom.

Chuck jumped up off the sofa in response to the sudden sounds. He ran over to the bathroom and peered in through the open doorway, just in time to see Snake vomiting violently into the already-stained toilet bowl. Apparently, Snake did not believe in cleaning supplies of any sort. The sight of the reddish brown chunks swirling around in the bowl, drool hanging off Snake's open mouth, and the foul odor that drifted up to Chuck's own nostrils was enough to make him want to vomit as well. But he was able to turn away and get it together before that happened. Snake saw the detective out of the corner of his eye and wiped the drool from his face as he yelled in a raspy voice, "Who the hell are you?"

Chuck was unshaven and looking rather scruffy in street clothes. Snake was worried that Chuck was some dealer that had shown up to collect from him, and he could not even remember if he had any money left over after his weekend binge. Chuck responded by showing Snake his badge, saying, "I'm a detective, and I need your information regarding a case we're working on. I would suggest that you cooperate fully with me as I've already found enough evidence in here to put you behind bars for years." Snake couldn't believe that this was happening. He may have a tough exterior, but he was a softie in reality. He wondered several times if he might be in a nightmare. He struggled to lift himself up from the bathroom floor and onto his feet.

"I'll be out here in the hall," Chuck said. "Go into your room and get dressed, and then we can have a talk. Oh, and don't shut the door. I can't take the chance of you escaping out your window."

Snake shook his head and ran his clammy fingers through his wild hair. "Man, this is a trip! I'm not gonna run. Just give me a minute." He returned wearing a Green Day T-shirt and jean shorts. "Is it all right if I have a smoke while we talk?" Snake asked the rather laid-back detective. "I don't know how long I was sleepin', but I really need a nicotine fix!"

Chuck smiled. "Sure. We thought you were dead when we first found you yesterday. I was beginning to think you'd never wake up." He began to explain to the young man that Anita had been kidnapped on Thursday morning of this week and that today was Sunday morning.

Snake's jaw dropped in shock. "B-B-But who'd want to hurt a sweet girl like Anita? I just went out with her and a group of friends on Wednesday night, I think it was. She and her boyfriend Scott looked real happy."

"Where have you been since you last saw Anita that night?" Chuck asked.

Snake shook his head in disbelief, "Oh, I get it now. You can't possibly think I did anything to her!"

Oh, this is going to take all day, Chuck thought. *He's a little slow.* But he remained calm as he explained to the boy, "Well, it did appear odd that you came up MIA. at the same time as Anita. You were one of the last people to see her. We at least need to question you and see whether you have a tight enough alibi before we dismiss you as a suspect. Just answer my questions, and if you tell me the truth, we can get this over with quickly. Okay?"

Snake sat down and lit his cigarette. "Yeah, okay. I'll tell ya anything. I don't have anything to hide at this point, since you guys already know about the drugs. I just want you to find Anita. She's one of my best friends. You know, she's one of the few people that I can trust, because she's never judged me for my piercings or my lifestyle. She's just always been there for me as a friend, no matter what."

Snake proceeded to tell Chuck that his real name was Douglas Carter. "I'm sorry," he added, "but I don't really remember much since Thursday afternoon. I can recall going to Applebee's Wednesday night with Anita and our friends, and then Scott took Anita home, and I stayed out with my girlfriend, Stacy, and a few guys. We went over to our buddy Jake's place and crashed there that night. He lives with his mom still, so you can call and ask her to verify that we were there. The next morning, his mom made us a big breakfast with waffles, eggs, and bacon, and then she left for work. There were still four of us there when she left, and we all decided to drop some acid since no one had work for a few days. The next forty-eight hours after that are a blur to me. I do remember going to Muncie to visit some of our buddies at Ball State University on what must have been Thursday night and all day Friday. On Thursday night, we stayed at my friend Mike's apartment that he lives in with three other guys. We just crashed on the floor."

Snake put out his cigarette butt in the ashtray on the table and continued, "I know we took a lot of shots of alcohol, and at one point, I remember just sitting back and staring at a blue TV screen for a few hours while we were still trippin'. Friday night we drove back to Kokomo and hooked up with different buddies of mine. We went back to their place and snorted lines of cocaine and then smoked lots of weed to come down some. I just remember doing crazy stuff like going in his backyard and climbing a tall willow tree.

"Then, I think we went over to Denny's around three in the morning and vegged out. I got into a fight with another drunk guy talking trash to me and my girlfriend in there. Good thing they didn't call you guys on me, but I bet the staff there would remember me being there that night. I don't remember anything else. I don't even know how I made it home yesterday or where my girlfriend and friends are now, but I can promise you that I didn't take Anita."

"Well, I thank you for being so honest," Chuck said, "because you really have been a pain in the ass to hunt down and babysit until you woke up. I've already searched your house and found no evidence to link you to Anita's disappearance. We did get a search warrant first if you'd like to see it." He put it on the glass table for Snake to look over, but Snake was not interested.

"Do you think she's still alive? I mean, she's been gone for a few days now." he asked Chuck.

The veteran investigator replied truthfully, "All I can tell you is that the odds are against her at this point. But we won't give up looking for her. I'll verify your alibi with your friend's mom, the staff at Denny's restaurant, and your girlfriend. Just give me their numbers, and I'll be on my way." Snake wrote the numbers down on a piece of wadded up, crinkled paper that he pulled out of the pocket of the jeans he had worn for the past four days.

Snake handed the information over to the detective. "You mean you aren't going to charge me for possession of drugs?" he asked, disbelieving.

Chuck paused and looked Snake square in the eyes, "Look, kid, if you keep living this way, you won't make it to thirty. You need to go to rehab and get clean. Consider this your one and only warning. After all, you did cooperate with my questions, and as long as your alibi checks out like I think it will, you'll be free to leave the state again. We might need to call you in for further questioning regarding your statements, so don't leave town until you hear from me, or else you *will* be charged. Are we clear?"

Snake sighed. "Yeah. No more drugs, at least until I know Anita's safe. Just call me if you need anything else. Thanks for not turning me in, man."

Chuck left the young man's drug-infested house and hoped that this had been a wake-up call for the lost kid. Maybe he would turn his life around now. He seemed like a nice enough guy if you could look past all the piercings and tattoos, like Anita had. Chuck did not leave the driveway until he had called and verified his alibis. Snake was also cleared as a suspect. Chuck called Captain Roberts to notify him immediately.

———

Deputy Don Howell had done his job as promised to Captain Roberts the day prior. He had called their prime suspect,

Scott Miller, his parents, and his lawyer into the precinct this morning to conduct the lie detector proceedings. The kid was shaky again but did not stray from his original story. Scott maintained that he knew nothing about Anita's disappearance or who had abducted her. Don started off with standard questions, like how long Scott had known Anita, and then began to grill him on more serious matters, like what time he had shown up at the Wooldridge house on the day of her disappearance and whether or not he had been involved with kidnapping her or knew information as to who did. The questioning only took half an hour, but the poor kid broke down several times during it. Don began questioning whether they would be able to make it through all the vital questions he needed to ask.

"I can't do this anymore! I did not hurt Anita!" Scott stammered at the end. "You guys are wasting your time on me while the person that did this is out there! Please, just let me go home!" Don looked at the young man. Deep down, he had a gut feeling that Scott was telling the truth, but he had to continue and wait for the results of the test to rule the kid out as a suspect.

Finally, Don looked up and said, "Thanks for your cooperation today. We will be in touch with the results soon. You are free to go for now, but do not leave the county. We might need you to come back in." They all stood up to leave.

"My client has been through enough," the lawyer stated. "He has fully cooperated, so don't even think of calling him back in for further questions without me present. You'll have a lawsuit against this station if you try to harass my client." With his idle threats out in the open, the family and local attorney turned to leave solemnly. Don scratched his forehead and sighed. He knew he was only doing his job, but he still hated being the bad guy. He would have the results in a few hours if he was lucky. He sent the polygraph technician away to get them the findings as soon as possible.

CHAPTER 26

The mole entered the nearest hardware store, Menards, and put stacks of wood and nails into an available cart. As he walked around the store, he noticed that people avoided eye contact with him even in this town. *Fuck 'em all*, he thought angrily. *I don't need anyone but Anita now. They won't look down on me when they all come to buy the books I've written. Then it'll be my turn to look down on these losers.* He paid for the items in his cart and threw it all in the back of his truck. He peeled out of the parking lot like an idiot and nearly ran over a kid riding his Schwinn bike on the road. "Get off the fucking road!" he yelled out to the poor kid. "You almost made me wreck, you little shit!" The twelve-year-old boy nearly fell off his bike from fear. The mole sped past the boy and over to the nearest payphone where he called his voicemail to retrieve his messages. He had ten just from his overbearing, meddling mother.

The mole listened to his mother's raspy voice grow louder and angrier with each message. In each one, she asked, "Where the hell are you? Call me back as soon as you get this message." By the final call, she threatened her son with, "Tom, now I'm pissed. If you don't call me back today, then I'm gonna throw the rest of your things outside and just consider you dead to me. Call me back!" *That bitch is just going to have to wait,* he thought. *I told her I'd call her when I was good and ready. I was going to call her today, but not now. Screw her. I'm not some kid she can just order around anymore. Never again.* He slammed the phone back on the receiver as an act of defiance and got back into his truck. Stopping to pick up some McDonald's Big Macs, he headed back home to start building his bookshelves. He could feel his dreams in reach.

While the mole was gone, Anita lay uncomfortably in her box, wrestling with her overwhelming emotions. Often in the past, she had had persistent thoughts come to her that she knew must be from God. He had talked to her in this manner a few minutes earlier, and she could not even fathom what she knew he must be asking her to do. The annoying thought that kept creeping back in her mind, like a command, was shockingly, *You need to witness to Tom today. He is lost and needs to hear the gospel if he is ever going to be saved.*

Anita cried out loud, "No! I can't do it. I can't witness to this monster that has ruined my life. I'm not the one to do it, God. Please, let someone else do it. I hate him!" But the thought kept overriding her many pleas and refusals. In the end, after half an hour of trying to argue her point, she accepted the fact that she had to be obedient to God's plan. He was the only one that she had left to rely on, and she would do whatever he asked of her. She believed that God would reward her for this act of obedience and allow her to be rescued.

When the mole returned, he swung open the metal doors of the storage cabinet. "Okay. I got all my supplies, so I'm going to start building the bookshelves now." He lifted Anita out of the box. She could smell the strong odor of onions and greasy food on his breath. She still had no appetite at this point. "Hey. What do you think of this being a young adult bookstore?" he asked her. "That's typically the crowd that likes reading sci-fi books. Don't you think?"

Anita nodded her head yes. "I think that's a good idea. The more people you get in here the better." She was hoping it would be a success so that she would have a better opportunity to escape. "Why do you love sci-fi shows so much?" she asked her captor out of curiosity. "I just never could get into them."

The mole chuckled. "I grew up watching every episode of *Star Trek* in the '60s," he answered. "The show gave me hope that there could be life outside this awful planet I call Hell. Everyone else looked to that faggot, pretty boy Captain Kirk as their hero, but I never felt like he earned the right to be the leader of the Enterprise. His first officer in command, Mr. Spock, and his cohort, Dr. McCoy, were the real brains in running the ship and keeping it from being attacked by aliens. They were my heroes. I'll be a true Trekkie until the day I die." Anita could tell that the mole was very passionate about the show and that a part of him believed it to be real. She dropped the subject; she would never understand him.

"You've got to sit on the couch and watch TV while I build," the mole ordered his hostage. "I'm coming to check on you every five minutes, so no funny business." Anita did as she was told. She watched an old *I Love Lucy* rerun where Lucy and Ethel were stomping on grapes at the vineyard. It was actually funny but was not a show she would have chosen on her own. They were only able to get a few channels, and her options were limited. It was a nice break from her thoughts and the mole, though. She actually caught herself on the verge of a laugh once during the show. It was the first time she had smiled in days.

Every five minutes or so, Anita could feel the mole watching her from behind the couch. She could feel his stare and sensed his presence, even though she could not see him. After about an hour, the mole yelled to her, "Hey. Come in here. I need some help." She walked into the next room submissively. "Hold this board while I hammer the nail in," the mole ordered his girl. "I need this one to be straight, and I can't seem to do it by myself, hon." Anita gripped the board tightly. His next question shocked her. "Hey. I remember when we used to talk at the gym, and you'd always try to get me to come to your church and all. Do you actually still believe in God?" he asked her casually. Anita was now convinced that God had prepared her for this question all morning.

Still holding up the board for him while he hammered nails in, Anita answered, "Yes, I do. I have a relationship with God through Jesus Christ, our Savior. It's the only way to have peace and eternal life. I pray every day and read the Bible as much as I can. I still go to the same church I went to when we used to talk at the gym. Well, at least I did before you brought me here."

The mole laughed quietly. "What kind of God would let you go through something like this?"

"Well, I think God allows us to suffer on earth to teach us things," Anita responded, "or maybe he wanted me to reach out to you and plant a seed in you to let you know that God is real."

The mole smirked as he said confidently to Anita, "Honey, I could never believe in a God. If he were real, he could prove himself right now, if he is as powerful and all-knowing as he claims to be."

"But it says in the Bible that he wants his children to go by faith, not evidence," Anita countered quickly. "The evidence is found when you have a relationship with him. If you invite him in and start repenting, you'll feel it in your heart and be able to start seeing his truths through the Holy Spirit. I know it may sound weird, but it's an amazing gift to know that all your burdens are lifted off your shoulders. When you believe in Christ and are saved, things here on earth seem more tolerable, because you know that it's all just temporary and that God is with you at all times. Even now, I feel that he is with me."

"Well, you'll never convince me of any of this shit," the mole said, still unbelieving. "If there really were a God, he would've given me a burning bush to talk to me through."

Anita was shocked that he even knew about the burning bush that God had spoken to Moses through. It convinced her even more that the mole felt superior to everyone: he had the audacity to compare himself to such a godly, Old-Testament patriarch. The mole's grandiose thoughts kept coming out in his unusual statements, and Anita was growing more aware each day with him of just how delusional he must in fact be. She tried again, despite all his rejections, by saying, "Well, you don't need a burning bush to talk to him. You can go to him in prayer anytime. He's always there to listen and hopes that you'll knock on his door. In fact, he laid on my heart this morning that he wanted me to tell you about the gospel."

The mole shrugged this off. "Don't waste your breath. I'm not interested. There's no God, and that's final. You're going to feel real dumb when you die and find out there's no Heaven up there. You're wasting your time praying to no one." The debate went on for the rest of the afternoon, until Anita finally gave up. She felt like she had at least obeyed God and had tried her best to witness to him. Maybe someday it would all sink into that tiny little brain of his and turn his life around, but for now, her captor would remain the rotten pig that she had come to know these past few days.

During their talk, the mole finished everything he had wanted to accomplish on the bookshelves for the day. He stood up and brushed his shorts off in triumph. The sawdust and dirt fell onto the carpet, adding to all the preexisting filth that covered it. He went into the kitchen and made himself a dinner of a peanut butter and jelly sandwich, chips, and a can of Coke to wash it all down. He skipped washing his hands, of course. The mole made Anita sit on the couch with him and eat a piece of toast and drink some water. "I've got to keep you alive, girl," he said. "You have to eat."

Anita ate slowly, but had a hard time doing so as she dreaded what might be coming next in their typical evening routine. *Maybe I can talk him into just playing some games or watching a movie,* she thought earnestly. *Maybe he'll be too tired to want sex again today.* In the back of her mind, she knew she was just fooling herself. She knew that he would want her again before bed, and she was right.

Twenty minutes later, the mole threw his paper plate onto the floor and walked over to the VCR to push in one of his many selections of pornos. He turned back to her and dropped his shorts and underwear to the floor. He pointed to his penis and once again ordered, "Suck it." She did it as the girl in the porno was screaming, "Yeah! Harder! Oh Baby. Deeper. Fuck me hard!" When the mole was hard, he bent Anita over the side of the couch and pulled off her shorts. He tried once again to ram his penis inside her anally, but was unable to keep his erection. Still, the searing pain was torturous. It felt like he was ripping her open, and she screamed out in pain.

Anita desperately tried to block all of this out, to get to her happy place in her mind, but the pain and obscene noises coming from the TV made it impossible. "Stop! No!" she yelled. But the mole covered her mouth and kept right on. When he finally decided to give up on the anal sex, he picked her up and sat her on his lap to ride him. Anita wept silently with every sharp thrust until he finally came inside her while groaning in delight. As he was ejaculating, he yelled to her, "You're going to worship *me* now, girl. I'm the only God you need. Yeah. I know how much you want me! Just like that whore on TV." He was deranged enough to think she wanted this torture; he believed it in his fantasy world.

Anita lifted herself off the mole as the girl on the video was still moaning loudly in ecstasy. Anita felt so dirty and disgusting. She wanted to wash all his filth off her but did not dare take a shower in front of him, having his eyes on her exposed body. She had not brushed her teeth all week and had not seen him do so either. So when he came over and thrust his tongue inside her mouth to kiss her passionately, Anita wanted to die. It was more degrading and intrusive to her than any sexual act. It was more personal, something that you only did with someone you loved.

The mole's kisses were like bullets going into her chest, and she wanted this nightmare to stop. He backed away from her, and she put her shorts back on quickly. "Goodnight, sweetheart," the mole said cheerfully. "I hope you sleep well tonight. I'll see you in the morning. I had a good day with you today. Thanks for your help on the bookshelves." Anita did not say a word as she climbed into her cramped safe haven once again. The mole latched the double doors with the wooden dowel and butter knife behind her.

Anita did not even have the strength to pray again that night. She just whispered these few words to her God, who she still knew was real, "Please help me, God. Help the police to find me soon. I can't take much more!" She blacked out soon after and did not wake up until the next morning.

CHAPTER 27

Deputy Don Howell received word from the lie detector technician that their prime suspect, Scott, had failed the mostly accurate, yet controversial, polygraph test. Don was more than surprised at the news. He gasped and said, "Are you sure, Steve? A young man's life is on the line here."

"Yes, I'm sure," Steve responded. "I've gone over the results a number of times, and I keep coming up with the same answer. Mr. Miller failed almost all the questions regarding Anita, and his voice test came back more stressed than usual. That's all I can tell you, buddy."

"Okay," Don said. "Thanks for your promptness. Talk to you soon. Please send over a copy today if you can. We'll need the results in front of us when we confront the suspect and his family."

"Sure thing. I can drop it off at the station today if you want," Steve said.

"That'd be great, Steve," Don answered. "Have a good evening." Don got off the phone and slowly dialed Captain Roberts's cell phone number to fill him in on the newest details.

Jack answered his phone almost immediately, "This is Jack."

"Hey, Jack. It's Don. Wanted to let you know that I just got word that Scott Miller failed the polygraph test he took. I'm shocked. Especially after we got the lead about that Tom suspect. I thought for sure Scott would be cleared. I don't know what to think about this. I guess Scott knows more than what he's willing to share about Anita's whereabouts. I still have a gut feeling he's not our man, though. What do you think?"

Jack cleared his throat. "Well, I guess we have to get him back in here for more questioning then. It's unfortunate because I've got a feeling we're on the right track with this new Tom character too. Maybe Scott knows something about him. Who knows. We'll just have to wait and see. Hey, I did get the results back from Tom's criminal background check just now. It seems that our guy was convicted in 1985 for raping an employee of Indiana University in Bloomington in December of 1984. He received a twenty-year sentence to serve in the Indiana State Prison, but he only served ten years before being released to his mother in Kokomo in 1995. Says in here that he was released early for good behavior and so that he could care for his mother who was in bad health. He later sued the Indiana State Prison for unfair treatment while he was incarcerated and won five thousand dollars to boot. Sounds like we're dealing with a smart criminal here. He knows his rights and how to work the legal system."

Don smiled. "Yeah. Lucky us. Well, have you spoken with the Indiana University Police Department yet to get all the particulars on this guy and his prior charges?"

"Yeah. I put a call in as soon as I got this information," Jack answered. "I spoke with an Officer Kolosky that was familiar with the details of the case. He remembered Tom well and said that the similarities between the two cases were high. Unfortunately, it's Sunday, and the only way to get a hard copy of the information without sending it through the mail is to do a pony express at each county line. It'll be passed from each county officer until it reaches Howard County sometime this evening. Damn! I wish we had all this in a computer database to access more quickly! Time is of the essence here. We need to get moving on this guy in case he's the one. He could be getting further and further away with Anita as we speak."

Don tried to console Jack. "We're doing the best we can with limited resources, Jack. I'll wait until tomorrow to interrogate Scott again so I can pick up the hard copy at our end of this pony express delivery. I'll bring it over to you at the station as soon as it gets here, and then we can sort through all of it and formulate a plan as to where to go from here. Sound good?"

Jack felt relieved to have such a dedicated staff behind him on this case. He answered wholeheartedly, "Sounds perfect, Don. I'll wait here at the station until you get here. I better call Dorothy and let her know not to wait up. It's going to be a long night. Thanks for all your hard work, Don. It means a lot that I can count on you. We just need to make sure that none of the information about our new suspect is revealed to the press yet. They'd have a field day with this, and I'm afraid that'd put Anita further at risk if she's still alive."

"I understand, Jack," Don said knowingly. "You don't have to worry about me talking to the media. I don't know a thing. See you later."

They got off the phone, and Don headed over to the county line to wait for the important package of information while Jack made his phone call to his anxiously awaiting wife.

Dorothy was empathetic on the phone, but her eagerness to have Jack back at home with her was becoming more evident. They had attended their local church service together this morning and were overwhelmed by the community support and prayers for Anita and her family. It was amazing to Jack to know just how many people truly cared about this girl and her dire circumstances. The whole city seemed to fear that the same thing could now happen to their own daughters. Anita was put on their church prayer list that morning.

Jack had prayed earnestly on his own, "Please God, give me the strength, wisdom, and patience needed to bring Anita back home safely. Nothing is too large for you. Please guide me in the right direction and lead me to the person that did this unthinkable crime. Amen." Jack had felt a sense of peace and confidence flow over him when he was done praying, and he at once felt like he was going to be able to crack the case under the supervision of his all-powerful, all-knowing master in heaven. This confidence overwhelmed Jack again as he prepared to go over the Bloomington case files with Don this evening.

Don Howell proved true to his word: he walked into the station around seven carrying a rather large manila folder with papers threatening to spill out of it. The folder contained the information Jack needed to start building a case against the suspect, Victor Thomas Steele. The two men spread the contents of the folder out onto the large conference room table and began sorting through it in a timely, organized fashion. They worked mainly in silence, except for the occasional grunt or exclamation, as they uncovered the folder's contents.

"Well," Jack said, "this is what we know about this man's prior conviction in 1984. It says here that the rape victim, Maggie

Thompson, was a thirty-two-year-old mother of two. Her children resided with her ex-husband at the time. The victim met our suspect in the laundry room of an apartment complex where they both resided in May of 1984. A few days later, Ms. Thompson agreed to meet Mr. Steele at his new residence across town to watch the sci-fi movie, *V: The Final Battle.* They sat in separate chairs during the movie, and when it was over, Ms. Thompson alleged that she and Mr. Steele played cards. During the game, Mr. Steele told her that he often liked to pretend to be different people for days at a time, like in the popular Dungeons and Dragons role-play game.

"He then allegedly propositioned Ms. Thompson to play this game with him, and she refused. She alleges that he then tried to kiss her, and since she thought that several of his comments were strange, she refused his kiss and quickly left his residence. She also refused to take his persistent phone calls after this first meeting." Jack lifted his head up briefly and commented, "Smart girl."

Don nodded his head in full agreement as Jack went on, "In July, a couple months after this strange encounter, Ms. Thompson states that Mr. Steele dropped in on her at the office she worked at on campus and announced to her, 'Well, I've decided to give you a second chance to go out with me.' She claims that she refused to go out with him again and told him to stay away from her and her work, or they would have him escorted off the premises. She did not see or hear from him again until the evening of the assault."

Jack continued, "Ms. Thompson then claims that on December 18, 1984, at approximately 9:30 p.m., her new boyfriend left her trailer. She sat down to read her mail after he left and soon heard a knock on the door. When she opened the door, thinking that her boyfriend had returned, Mr. Steele forced his way inside. First, he inspected her residence, room by room, to make sure they were alone and then sat down on a sofa next to Ms. Thompson. He forced her backwards onto a couch and put a knife to her throat, telling her that she had better cooperate with him or else he'd kill her. She screamed for help, so he gagged her with a T-shirt that she reports he had brought with him in his gray backpack. He also tied her hands behind her back with a rope that he'd brought with him as well. So, we know that he brought a rape toolkit with him in this backpack. Fred Taylor also saw a suspect approach Anita's home with a gray backpack. That's too large a similarity to ignore."

Don agreed, and Jack continued reading, "Okay, so after he had her bound and gagged, he walked Ms. Thompson back to her bedroom with the knife still clearly visible. He used the knife to cut her shirt off and then removed her pants and under-wear. He placed her on the bed. Then he went out to make sure that the front door was locked. All this seems so thought out and methodical, doesn't it? This guy is obviously some sort of perverse sociopath. He proceeded to take off all his clothes but kept his T-shirt on. He then made some filthy remarks about the victim's breasts and then removed the gag from her mouth and warned her not to scream. He laid her across the bed and attempted to have vaginal sex with her. He couldn't become erect, so he turned her over and tried unsuccessfully to have anal intercourse with her.

"Mr. Steele then asked Ms. Thompson if she had ever given a blow job and forced her to perform fellatio on him. He finally became erect enough to penetrate her both vaginally and anally. According to Ms. Thompson, he was extremely rough in his actions. He ejaculated inside of her and then quickly dragged her over to the attached bathroom to clean her up to destroy all forensic evidence of the rape. He showered her, scrubbing her with soap, and then cleansed her with a sixteen-ounce bottle of Coke to further destroy any evidence that remained.

"This guy must have done his research on forensics before the crime. He poured about one-third of the bottle of Coke into her rectum and another third into her vagina. He then took her back into her bedroom and informed her casually that they were going to go on a walk together into town, acting like lovers. He put jeans and a cardigan sweater on Ms. Thompson so that she would not be cold. Well, that was so thoughtful of him, wasn't it?"

"He definitely sounds like a sick, twisted creep to me!" Don answered.

"We at least know that for sure," Jack said. "They then left the trailer together and headed south. He untied her arms during the walk. He was wearing a long black trench coat and had his backpack with him. He put his arm around her, keeping the knife up against her side and threatening to use it if he had to. During their walk, he informed her that he was now done with her unless she went to the police, and then he'd either kill her or pay someone to do it for him. He also threatened to find her daughters and kill them if she ever messed with him.

"He then indicated to her that he was good at staking out houses and people and that he'd watch her for some time to see if she attempted to talk to the police. He then walked her back home and told her to have a nice evening. Can you believe this guy? Luckily, the victim went straight to the police, and they were at Mr. Steele's door within minutes of his return home. He was still in the trench coat and had the backpack just lying out on the sofa. Sounds like it never even occurred to him that she might be brave enough to rat him out.

"Mr. Steele tried to claim that the two had been an item and that she was just making these accusations because she was angry with him for breaking up with her after they had had consensual sex. He might have gotten away with it if his backpack hadn't been found as evidence. Says here that he later blamed the police for setting him up and vowed that he would never speak with the police again without an attorney present. When he was incarcerated for the crime and was awaiting trial, he had the audacity to call the victim on the phone and ask how she was doing. This guy is unbelievable! All right, let's go over all the similarities between the two cases. We need to figure out if we've got enough to conclude that Tom Steele is our prime suspect."

"Okay, but I need a bathroom break first. Give me just a sec," Don said.

They got back to business a few minutes later, after they had stretched and gotten themselves two boiling-hot cups of caffeinated coffee to keep them awake. The two men began brainstorming, throwing out various observations or ideas. "We still don't know where Anita and her car are," Don began, "but I think we're getting closer to finding who may have abducted her. Tom Steele sure sounds like he could be our guy. Sarah told us that Tom used to ride his Schwinn bicycle everywhere, and we just happened to find an old Schwinn bicycle abandoned by the road about half a mile from the Center Road crime scene. And Fred Taylor says he witnessed a stocky male approach Anita's front door carrying a gray backpack…could be the same one used in the '84 incident."

"Yeah," Jack chimed in, "and when you add in the fact that this Mr. Steele knew Anita a couple years ago, it makes it hard to believe he's not our man. We do still have to keep our eyes on her boyfriend for now, though. With him failing the polygraph test and all, we just can't rule him out as a prime suspect yet."

Don agreed, "I'll get him in here tomorrow for sure. I'll have to take a harsher approach this time so that if he does know anything, he'll crack and tell us. He has to start talking."

"If anyone can get it out of him, it's you," Jack stated. "He'll have to explain why he failed the test. And if you focus on Scott tomorrow, it'll give me the opportunity to talk with the FBI profiler from Quantico about the case in detail. I plan on contacting my old friend, Todd McCain, about it as well. He was an FBI agent for twenty-six years, and now that he's retired, he helps local law enforcement agencies off the record on psychological profiling. It'll make me much more confident if both profilers are telling me the same thing. Of course, I can't tell either of them that I'm discussing the case with the other. The Quantico guys hate getting their toes stepped on, but at this point, my only concern is bringing Anita home. I trust Todd's experience and opinion more than anyone else's, and he's close. He works as a professor at the Indiana University Kokomo campus. I'll give him a call now and try to set up a meeting with him here tomorrow afternoon."

"Sounds like a good plan," Don replied. "We're lucky to have two profilers as resources on this one. We're going to need all the help we can get."

Jack and Don left all the information lying out on the table. Jack quickly set up a meeting with Todd McCain for tomorrow at noon. Todd had been surprised to hear from him but was more than willing to help out in any way possible. Jack had always looked up to Todd as a mentor and was looking forward to hearing his take on all the leads they had gathered thus far. It would also be nice seeing him again and catching up. Before Jack left the station for the night, he placed a graduation photo of Anita at the top of his dry-erase board to keep the team focused on her. He was struck by Anita's look of both radiance and innocence. Her gaze seemed to be pleading with him to please find her. The picture haunted Jack and made him even more dedicated to finding this young woman and bringing her home alive.

DAY FIVE
MONDAY, JUNE 29, 1998

CHAPTER 28

Anita awoke to the grating, yet familiar sound of *swoosh, swoosh, swoosh,* the wooden dowel slipping through her annoying captor's hands. It repeated incessantly until she could not take it anymore. She did not want to get up and go through the torture again, but her bladder felt like it was going to burst. She knocked tentatively on the top of the metal box and heard the mole ask, "You awake now? I thought you were never going to get up. I've already been to the grocery store and everything." Anita reminded herself once again that she must be nice to this monster if she wanted to remain alive.

"You missed breakfast," the mole said sternly. "I couldn't wait any longer. I'll take you down to the bathroom, and then you need to start cleaning all this shit up around here. That's a woman's job to pick up after her man. I'm the one working hard around here to get our business up and running. You've had a free ride up until now. No more laziness." Anita was appalled that he actually expected her to clean up *His* filth, but what choice did she have? At least it kept her from having contact with him for a while. She was grateful for that.

Anita was again led down to the bathroom in the dirty basement to relieve herself and then led back upstairs to start throwing all of the mole's trash into a large bag he had thrown at her. The mole sat back down on the couch, only wearing his dirty shorts and socks, and watched his girl clean. His belly hung over his shorts, and it sickened Anita to even glance at him. He did not even seem to notice her disdain for him. In fact, he looked like he was proud of his physique, and she caught him flexing his arm muscles several times, trying to show them off to her. She finished picking up the last bits of his trash and washed off a few dishes in the sink. "I think I'm all done," she said. "Is there anything else you want me to clean?"

The mole smirked. "Yeah, baby. You can clean me off now. I'm real dirty." He dropped his shorts and made her give him oral sex again. He then took her into the bedroom and raped her for what seemed like an eternity. Anita was able to go to the peaceful place in her mind this time and blocked out all his grunts and thrusts completely. Her rapist got off her and stood up. He gazed down at her naked body and said, "Damn, that was real good. Did you enjoy it?" She was surprised that he was asking her. He never seemed to care before how she felt about anything.

Anita answered him truthfully, "I don't really like sex, and I hate being naked in front of people. I've always been pretty self-conscious about my body."

"Well," the mole said, "if you hate me staring at you, then just think how awful it'd be if they ever find you and run all those tests on you and check out your whole body. It'd be a whole group of people there. Here, it's only me. So, don't worry.

I like what I see when I look at you. Oh, and thanks for cleaning the house up. It looks much better now. I'll expect you to do that at least every other day. Okay, hon?"

Anita answered through gritted teeth again, "Sure. Whatever you say."

The mole rewarded her by throwing a piece of Juicy Fruit in her direction. Anita chewed the gum desperately to get the nasty taste of her disgusting captor out of her mouth. The mole put her back in the box for a few hours so he could go to the hardware store for more nails and lumber. Anita lay inside the box in total darkness, unable to sleep or rest at all. Her mind raced, thinking of ways she could possibly escape. She would ask him when he returned if she could help him set up his computer. He had been complaining for days that he needed to get that done and that the damn phone company still hadn't hooked up his phone system yet. She hoped that his computer had the date and time on it: she needed to know how long she had been gone, and she wanted to count down the days until Sarah's wedding. She had to make it home by then. She just had to.

CHAPTER 29

Deputy Don Howell met with Scott Miller and his lawyer on Monday at nine in the morning. Don had been ready to play hardball if needed. He could tell that Scott was filled with apprehension about this interrogation, as he seemed jumpy. Beads of perspiration made his light brown hair appear damp around the edges. Don had only told the boy that he had more questions for him and would not answer when Scott had asked him about the results of the test. Scott apparently had taken that as a bad sign. Don asked Scott and his lawyer to join him in the tiny interrogation room that was lined with video cameras and informed them that this conversation would be recorded and was admissible as evidence in court. The attorney grew impatient, demanding, "What is this all about? What more can my client tell you guys? He's already devastated by the loss of his girlfriend, and now he has to deal with daily harassment from your department."

Don dismissed the lawyer's comments and instead turned his attention solely on Scott. He gave the boy a penetrating stare as he announced, "I have bad news for you, Scott. It seems that you haven't been telling us the whole truth in our prior discussions regarding Anita's disappearance. You failed several parts of the polygraph test." For emphasis, Don slammed the polygraph results down on the table in front of Scott as he spoke. Scott's lawyer grabbed the papers and began reading through them. His confident countenance began to fall the further he read on.

"I did not lie!" Scott responded adamantly. "I don't know what in the hell happened to Anita! I swear! The results are wrong."

"This test has high accuracy, and we have to go by the results here," Don replied. "Now tell me what you know!"

Scott put his head down in his hands and said repeatedly, "I know nothing more than I've told you."

"Does Anita have a friend that carries a backpack and rides a bicycle around?" Don asked.

Scott thought a minute. "No. Not that I ever met. Why? Is that who took her?"

"We don't know yet. It's just a lead that we need to look into. You're our number one suspect right now, though, so you better start talking if you know anything about this other person."

"I told you," Scott said in exasperation. "I don't know anything about this person or Anita's disappearance. I came over to pick her up for lunch and she wasn't there. I don't have any idea what happened to her between the time that I left her in her bed the night before and when she came up missing. Maybe I fibbed about the time that I actually left her house that night, but that was just because I wasn't allowed to be there that late.

We just made out a little in her bed before I left that night. I swear, that was all I lied about. I'm just so scared. I don't know what else to tell you."

Don felt sorry for this tearful young kid and his latest admission. Scott had just lied about what any normal teenage couple would lie about, and by doing this had made himself a top suspect. Don did not believe that Scott committed this crime, but he still had to pump him for more information, as he might know more than he had told them. Don's last attempt to get Scott to give him more information was to threaten him. "Okay. Have it your way. You are to be here at 1:00 p.m. daily until Anita is found. You'll eventually talk to us and tell us what you know. See you tomorrow."

Scott looked at his lawyer. "Can they do this?"

"They have the right to call you in for questioning whenever and however many times they like," his lawyer answered. "Sorry."

"Please find her!" Scott desperately begged Don before he left the station. "I swear I didn't do it! Please keep looking for the real suspect. I love Anita and her family! I just want our life to go back to normal again!" Scott broke down sobbing right in front of Don. Tears splashed onto Scott's new Converse high-top tennis shoes. *He's really a mess!* Don thought. *Maybe he doesn't know anything.* Don knew, though, that he had to keep this kid nearby until he was positive he wasn't lying. He headed over to Jack's office to brief him on his meeting with Scott before Jack met with retired FBI profiler Todd McCain.

In Kokomo, Anita's family struggled to make it through each and every long hour of the endless days and sleepless nights.

It had been five days now, and the distraught Wooldridge family still had no word from the authorities on any leads as to where Anita or her car might be. They were all worried sick about her and were beginning to fear the worst—that she was dead. It was Monday, and it just so happened to be Anita's older sister, Melanie's, thirtieth birthday.

Birthdays were always a big deal in the Wooldridge family. They typically had a family barbecue where the entire extended family came together to celebrate. They made a futile attempt on this miserably hot day to celebrate Melanie's birthday with a hot dog roast at the family home that Anita had been abducted from. They thought it might help them get their minds off their misery even for a few hours; it did not work. Every time the phone rang, they all leapt to their feet and prayed it was the police telling them Anita had been found alive. No such luck. It was always friends or family instead, calling to see how they were holding up.

The gathered family had just seen a photo of a smiling Anita pop up on the Indianapolis TV station on the television in their family room. The broadcast included numbers for people to contact if they saw Anita or knew any details about her disappearance. They had all tried to stay busy and remain positive by posting her picture all over town. Anita's brother, Daniel, was an attorney and had flown back early from a business trip in Detroit as soon as he had heard the news of his little sister's disappearance. They had always been close, and he was very protective of her. He could hardly stand not knowing anything in this nightmare. *How does someone just disappear off the face of the earth in broad daylight, and no one sees or knows anything?* Daniel thought.

Daniel just could not fathom this. He had always relied on facts, and none of this made any sense. He started to feel like the police knew more than they were telling them. They had to. He had half a mind to march up there right now and demand to know everything. But that was not his nature. Instead, Daniel kept himself busy by fielding all the media inquiries. He became the family spokesperson, which took the added pressure off his devastated parents and sister.

Melanie had tried to remain strong, but her emotions and the fact that her sister was not there to celebrate her birthday with her got the best of her. It would never be the same again if Anita was gone. She burst into tears after seeing Anita's beautiful face posted on the broadcast, and seeing Melanie, the whole room of family members began crying for the loss of their precious Anita. They all formed a circle and hugged one another for support. Anita's grandmother said a prayer for Anita to be returned home safely, and soon. Melanie's five-year-old daughter, Natalie, innocently asked, "What happens when someone dies, Mommy?" Anita's young niece had obviously heard the grown-ups talking about their worst fear that Anita could be dead by now.

The room got very quiet as Melanie bent down to respond to her daughter's shocking question. She answered her in simple terms, "Well, honey, they go to be with Jesus." Melanie was trying to hold back her tears as she continued, "We'll all be together again one day either here or in Heaven. I promise that you'll see your auntie again one day, one way or another. Okay, sweetie?"

"Okay, Mommy," Natalie said sweetly. Her mother's comforting response seemed to satisfy the previously sad little girl.

She ran off to swing on her grandparents' playset in the backyard with her toddler brother, Colton. Melanie stood up and fell into her husband Ben's arms. She was completely worn down, both mentally and physically, at this point. All she wanted was her little sister back home for good. Natalie looked just like Anita had as a young girl when she used to run off and play. Natalie favored her aunt's looks more than her own mother's, and it made Melanie miss Anita even more. She wanted Anita as a birthday gift today. No other gift would even matter to her right now.

The extended family, consisting of grandparents, aunts, uncles, and cousins, stuck around for another hour, and they all did their best to console the family and wish Melanie a happy birthday. "Keep your heads up! We're all praying for you guys!" they encouraged the family as they were leaving. It did feel good to have all their support, but the words of hope and celebration felt contrary to the way the family currently felt. They were all beginning to feel the desperation creep in. Each one of them felt like they might go insane from the constant, obsessive worries about what Anita might be going through and all the terrible nightmares that ensued if they ever did miraculously reach one of the initial stages of sleep. It was pure torture for the Wooldridge parents, Daniel, Melanie, and her husband, Ben.

Twenty minutes after the last car had pulled out of the Wooldridge home driveway, the five adults were sitting at the kitchen table in complete silence. The two children, Natalie and Colton, were in the backyard playing in the sandbox with their joyful laughter floating in through the kitchen window. Anita's mother, Carrie Ann, thought wishfully, *Oh, to be a kid again. They don't have a worry in the world! They are just so sweet and innocent.* She could see the children from the window while sitting at the kitchen table, and it reminded her of when Anita, so happy and carefree, used to play out back when she was a little girl. That thought brought new tears to her eyes; she tried to shield them from the others at the table by putting her head in her hands. She did not want to further upset any of them. She needed to be strong, but she was beginning to wonder how she could take any more of this.

With the sight of his mother and sister crying again, Daniel lost control of his emotions for the first time in his life. He had always been the mild-mannered, calm, and collected one in the family. He was like his father in that sense. Daniel never got too emotional, and none of them had ever seen him cry, at least not like this. It was as if a dam broke, and the river started crashing over the banks. As if the scene of Daniel crying were not enough to scare them, the family then suddenly heard a muffled groaning sound within the room that soon amplified to a loud screeching. They all turned their heads to the left and saw that the noise was coming from Gerald, Anita's father. He could not take seeing his only son break down and the sight of his daughter and wife bawling and inconsolable for another moment.

Gerald pushed his chair out from under the table rather forcefully, and it made a loud scooting sound on the linoleum floor. He stood up with his full six-foot frame and started pacing the floors as he moaned and started babbling jibberish to himself. Carrie Ann tried to put her hand gently on his shoulder to calm him down, but he shook her hand off and announced in desperation, "I'll be back! I've got to get out of here, and do something to help my little girl! They have to find her! They have to! I'll find her myself if the police aren't going to! It's been five hellish days now, and still no word or leads! I just can't sit around here feeling helpless anymore!"

Despite his family's protests that he should not drive in this condition and all their persistent offers to drive him wherever he needed to go, Gerald hopped into his car in the driveway and sped off toward the sheriff's department located where Markland and Berkeley roads intersect. It was about a ten to fifteen minute drive over, and the grieving father tried to prepare himself for what he would say to the deputies on the case. *I have to make them understand that they have to find my baby girl!* he thought wildly. *They just have to find her!*

Gerald glanced over at the local Top Banana Farm Market sign that was located right across the street from the sheriff's station. He had fond memories of taking the kids to buy their Halloween pumpkins there and found himself bawling again. He wiped the tears away as he turned his truck left into the parking lot and drove straight up to the circle drop-off space directly in front of the dark-tinted glass doors of the precinct. He knew that it was a no-parking zone, but this was an emergency! He frantically got out of his car and headed for the double doors to enter the building.

As he approached the doors, Don Howell, whom Gerald had known for years, was coming out of the building to go home for the evening. Don walked out the front door of the station and stepped out into the bright sunshine. He was more than ready to head home for the evening after briefing Jack about his meeting with Scott that had been useless, making several necessary calls that he could not put off any longer, and then finally completing paperwork that had been piling up on his desk this entire week due to his frequent absence. He started to take in a breath of the fragrant summer breeze and nearby lilac tree when his thoughts were abruptly cut short.

Anita's father met Don at the door, and Don was immediately struck by Gerald's deteriorated appearance and state of mind. Don had never seen Gerald shed even a tear. He was always very private and unemotional with a stellar reputation in the community as a hardworking, strong, and sensible man. It hit the deputy hard to see the pure anguish written all over this grieving father's face. He was breaking down in front of Don's very eyes. Don's children had grown up with Gerald's kids over the years. He could not imagine being in Gerald's shoes, not knowing where his daughter might be. As soon as Gerald saw Don, he rushed up to him and began his desperate pleas. Gerald was sobbing and could barely utter the words that he so desperately needed to say.

"Don!" Gerald pleaded. "You have to help us! Please, bring my baby girl back home! Bring her back home! I can't go on another day without her!" All the officers had tried to remain emotionally distant from the family so that it would not cloud their vision of the facts of the case. But today, seeing this broken father and remembering fond memories that he had of Anita growing up was enough to bring tears to his eyes as well. The veteran deputy investigator embraced Gerald as a friend and patted his back. A single tear rolled down Don's cheek, and he quickly wiped it away. He stood back and said the only words that he could think of to console Anita's father. He put his hands forcefully on Gerald's shoulders and looked him directly in the eyes, trying to snap him out of his state of shock.

Don spoke in a pressured tone, "Gerald, don't you give up hope on us! We're all working day and night on this case. We *will* find your baby girl! You just have to try to be patient. Give us a few more days. All right? I give you my word. We'll do whatever it takes to get her back home safely!" Don felt an awful pang of guilt that he could not share with Gerald that they finally had a prime suspect and that the case was now looking up. Don could not risk letting this information get out to the media and jeopardize their investigation.

Don offered to drive Gerald home, but Gerald would not hear of it. He seemed to have calmed down and said in an exhausted voice, "I'll be okay. I'm sorry. I just can't take any more of this!"

"I understand, buddy," Don said. "Just try to get some rest." Don got into his squad car and headed for home, bawling like a baby the whole way there. The sight of a grown man so distraught on top of his own lack of sleep had really gotten the best of him. But this incident gave him the extra resolve and determination he had needed to push even harder to find the suspect in question. The next day during a debriefing meeting with the rest of the investigation team, he would share with the other officers the moving scene he had encountered with Anita's father. It would inspire them to work harder as well, even if they had to give up sleep altogether until Anita was found. They would sacrifice it all to bring Anita home. They had to. She had become, to all the officers, the symbolic daughter or sister that each one of them had at home. For the rest of the investigation, the authorities would refer to Anita's case over the scanner by the code name "Bring My Baby Girl Back Home!"

CHAPTER 30

Anita was still lying in the metal box, cramped in her usual position on her side, when the mole returned, whistling a cheerful tune. He came in, yelling to his girl, "I'm back. You ready to get out?"

"Yes!" she yelled to him. "Please. I'm really sore and need to stretch out." He grabbed her arm to help her out of the box. "Hey, do you still need your computer set up?" Anita asked immediately.

"Yeah," he said. "Can you do it while I work on my bookshelves?"

"Sure. What do you need done?"

"Well, it's an old computer from the eighties that my old boss gave me for doing undercover work for him," the mole replied. "We had to erase everything off the hard drive when we were done, so I need you to reformat everything and reload it. You know how to do all that?"

"You're in luck," Anita answered. "I just graduated in May with an associate's degree in computer technology. It might take a few days, but I know I can do it."

"Well, all right. We make quite a team, don't we?"

Anita fought back the instinct to gag. "Yeah. We do," she said politely.

Anita started working right away. She was thrilled when she finally got the date and time running. It was Monday! She could not believe she had been gone for five days now. She had to make it back by this coming Saturday. The time read 3:16 p.m., and Anita's stomach was growling fiercely at this point. "Can I get a piece of toast?" she asked. "I'm starving!"

"Yeah. Give me a sec," the mole answered her. "I need to finish up this board first. Hey, how's it coming on the computer?"

"Good. I'm almost halfway done already. It was easier than I expected."

"Great. I'm going to need it soon to run my business on." The mole brought Anita a piece of dry, slightly buttered toast and a glass of the putrid water. She was so famished and thirsty that, despite the appearance, it was the best food that Anita had ever tasted. "Thank you. I feel much better now," she said to her captor.

"Well," the mole said. "I'm done with my work for the day. You can wrap things up on the computer, and then we'll play a game of Life." Anita would do anything to avoid having sex with him again.

"Yeah, that sounds like fun," she said. "I haven't played that game in years."

"Don't worry," he said cockily, "you'll never beat me anyway. I never lose in games." They played the game for almost an hour, and when they had finished, Anita cleaned it all up by herself while the mole ate a frozen dinner. He ate the fried chicken and mashed potatoes with his fingers and drank a whole two liter of coke right out of the bottle. He burped loudly when he was done. "Okay. You know what time it is now. I told you I have a very high sex drive, and I need it now."

Anita cringed and looked down at her feet; they looked huge in his large socks, which hung from her and often caused her to trip. She could not look at him in the face and considered fighting him off. But she had to fight her urges so he would not hurt her again. The mole led Anita over to the couch and again turned on a porno with the volume blaring. The sounds must have helped him get off in some way. He pulled her damp T-shirt off over her head and began squeezing her sore breasts. He then put what felt like all his fingers inside her and told her gruffly, "Turn over now. I think I'm going to be able to do this tonight, baby." When she resisted, he threw her over the side of the couch and again starting trying to thrust his hard penis inside her anally.

"No! It hurts! Stop! Please!" she screamed, but the mole just kept right on going. Her pleas seemed to excite him even more.

"Yeah, you like that, don't you? You want it harder? Yeah. I know you do. All girls do." He was ramming himself inside her so violently that she became dizzy from the searing pain. It felt like her insides were being ripped open. The loud noise from the TV and the panic that was setting in fast were enough to make Anita fall over onto the floor. Everything went black. The last sound that she heard was the *thump* when her head hit the dirty carpet floor.

The mole had just climaxed when Anita hit the floor hard. *My God!* he thought. *I think I killed her!* He knelt down to see if she was breathing. Thankfully, she still was, so he picked her up and placed her onto the couch and dressed her. He wiped the sweat off her with a washcloth and placed her snugly into her box for the night.

He noticed as he was walking back into the other room that his t-shirt was drenched in blood. "Shit! I must have been too rough!" he said out loud to himself. The mole felt a tiny ounce of remorse for causing the girl such pain. *I'll have to give her a break tomorrow, he thought. She'll probably be sore, and she's been good to me so far. She deserves a day off. That was just her first time doing that. She'll come to like it soon, and it won't be so painful next time. I'll go easier on her.* Thinking of someone else's feelings was a new twist for the mole. He did not quite know how to deal with guilt. But the mole justified his actions by assuring himself that she had wanted it and that she would forgive him tomorrow when he was nice to her. He walked back into the dark bedroom and whispered to her as he hugged the box, "Have sweet dreams. I love you." Luckily, Anita was still out cold and would remain unaware of anything until the next dreadful morning with her insane captor.

CHAPTER 31

It was noon on Monday, and Captain Jack Roberts was feeling hopeful about his meeting with Todd. Jack and Don both had gut feelings that they were on the right track with this Tom suspect, and Jack was hopeful that Todd could confirm that they had enough to go on. He wanted to make Tom Steele their prime suspect. Jack poured himself another searing-hot cup of coffee and sat back in the conference room chair, waiting for Todd to arrive. He absentmindedly rubbed his chin and was startled when he felt the stubble on his normally clean-shaven face. Jack was growing wearier by the minute with his inability to get a good night's rest, and his grooming skills had been put on the back burner for now. His gaze immediately settled on Anita's picture, and he felt like he could hear her cries for help. It was almost more than Jack could stand. He looked down at his watch and tried to keep his eyes averted from the photo on the dry-erase board, at least for now.

Todd came through the door minutes later and distracted Jack from the desperate thoughts that were building up deep inside his mind. Jack knew that he must remain positive and not let his emotions get the best of him. Todd walked in with an air of confidence, and his mere presence immediately filled Jack with a sense of relief. Todd came over to him, and the two men shared a manly embrace, giving each other a pat on the back. They had not seen each other in several years but had managed to stay in contact over the phone. Todd stepped back and exclaimed, "It's good to see you, Jack. It's been too long! You haven't changed at all, but you do look like you could use a good night's sleep. I remember those days."

Jack shrugged his shoulders. "You know how it goes in a case like this. I can't seem to sleep when there's so much to do. I appreciate you coming over on such short notice. I know that you're a busy man."

"This is true, but you sounded desperate on the phone. I'll do whatever I can to help you out on this one, but of course, it'll have to be off the record for now."

"Of course. How's Jan doing?"

Todd answered sincerely, "She's great. She's my better half. She wishes I'd retire completely so we can travel and enjoy our grandkids more, but I keep assuring her it'll all come in time. I just can't seem to break away completely yet. My passion has always been my work, and I still enjoy educating my students on the criminal justice system and organizational management. I'll know when it's time to wrap things up."

Jack could identify with this. "Well, I'm sure you're good at it," he said. "You helped me so much when I was just starting out as a wet-behind-the-ears officer."

The two reminisced about the good old days when they were both in their prime years of their career in law enforcement.

Jack recalled fondly how he had completed his training and entered the law enforcement field at the ripe age of twenty years old. He was twenty-six, already working as a captain for the Kokomo Police Department, when he had met Todd. Jack was aspiring to promote his career to the next level, and Todd, at the time, was working with the FBI. Todd worked with local law enforcement agencies in training their officers to utilize basic hostage negotiation techniques. Kokomo happened to be part of Todd's territory, so he had gotten to know Jack through the training and developed a connection with the young officer.

Todd was impressed with Jack's professionalism, persistence, and willingness to go above and beyond to solve cases and learn as much as he could. He saw something in Jack that reminded him of himself when he had first started out. Todd was already a veteran FBI agent at the time and had worked on hundreds of cases of abduction and murder. It was not standard practice, but Todd had been able to persuade the FBI Academy to admit Jack into their training program, despite his young age and lack of crime scene experience. Jack would always be grateful to Todd for going out on a limb for him and giving him the opportunity to learn from the best of the best.

The knowledge and skills that he had learned at the Academy had remained with him all these years. It allowed him to think outside the box on various cases when needed. Jack had worked on several bank robbery cases and homicides and had been able to locate three fugitives that escaped from the jail within eight months' time. Now nearing the age of fifty, Jack had twenty-eight years of experience in law enforcement, but he had never worked as the lead investigator on an abduction case of this magnitude, until now.

Todd was quite a talker, and the old friends enjoyed themselves while rehashing old stories and catching up on each other's lives for a while. But their conversation quickly turned to the real reason Jack had called Todd over for this meeting. Jack questioned whether Todd felt like they had enough to go on to focus primarily on this new suspect, Mr. Steele. He called out to his secretary, Ethel, and asked her to bring them another pot of coffee.

Ethel, an older woman in her sixties, had been with Jack for the past twenty years and had always been fiercely loyal and trustworthy in his book. She arrived with the coffee minutes later, and the two men got right down to business. Jack spent the next thirty minutes getting Todd up to speed on the particulars of the Wooldridge abduction case. Jack was sure to fill him in on every lead, every piece of evidence, and every witness or potential suspect until now. He wanted Todd to have all the details, even if seemingly minute, so that he could make an informed decision in the end.

Jack saved the most important details for last. "Anita's been missing for five days now, and we've managed to narrow our suspect list down to two potential males. The first one is her boyfriend, Scott, who just failed his polygraph test regarding Anita's abduction. Despite that, he isn't talking much. But in his defense, he did admit to lying about the time that he had left Anita's home the night before her disappearance, because they had been making out. I just have a gut feeling that the twenty-year-old kid didn't do it. He may know who did, but he just does not seem capable of this crime."

Todd paused to think. "Well, you know that I always taught you to go with your gut feelings," he said as a mentor would. "It's always worked for me."

"The suspect that I have a strong feeling about is a guy by the name of Victor Thomas Steele," Jack continued. "He goes by Tom for short. Anita's boss from two years ago, Linda Noll, came forward and told us that we may want to look at Tom as a suspect. Anita worked at Linda's fitness center at the same time that Tom was a gym member. Linda indicated that she began to have problems with Tom in the fall of 1996 when he asked three of her female gym employees out repeatedly and was rejected by all of them. The three girls were Anita, her best friend Sarah, and another female named Danielle. Tom apparently took offense when Danielle turned him down, and Linda alleges that Tom would disappear in the gym when Danielle was working there alone.

"Linda did a background check on Tom and found that he was a convicted rapist. So this news, and the fact that Tom had been harassing her female employees, led Linda to terminate his membership, and she never heard from him again. Linda wasn't sure whether Anita had seen Tom since his termination, but she stated that Anita had a soft heart and felt sorry for him when he'd been a member. She was nice to him, and Tom had even given Anita a book he'd written that he wanted her to give him feedback on. Linda felt guilty that she'd never told the employees of Tom's criminal background, but she'd just thought he was gone for good. She never even gave him a second thought until she read in the papers about Anita's mysterious disappearance."

Jack ruffled through some papers and continued on, "We then interviewed Anita's best friend Sarah, and she confirmed that she remembered Tom as a loner. She says that Tom did ask them out multiple times, but that they would just ignore him or start talking about their boyfriends with him. Sarah describes

Tom as a male in his forties with balding, light-colored hair, approximately five feet eight inches with a medium build and a large gut.

"The most crucial things Sarah told us are that Tom would ride his Schwinn bicycle everywhere he went, just like the bike we found abandoned by the side of the road near the crime scene, and that he always carried a gray backpack with him whenever he entered the gym. The neighbor witness claims that he saw a man of Tom's description, wearing a dark backpack on his back, approach the Wooldridge's front door right before Anita's disappearance. We also just received the NCIC records of Tom's criminal history, and in the '84 rape, Tom had carried a gray backpack that contained his rape tools in it."

Jack took a sip of his coffee and paused before he went on, "On top of all that to link this creep to this crime, Sarah also informed us that she was sure Anita hadn't had any contact with Tom since he was kicked out of the gym, but that she and Anita had sent him an invitation to Sarah's upcoming wedding about a month ago. This invitation could've put Anita back into his thoughts, even though he hadn't seen her in years. What do you think, Todd? Am I way off base here? I know there's been no contact between them in years. That's the only piece I question: would she have even been a target for him? I keep wondering whether or not all this is just a coincidence."

"I always begin profiling a case taking the known facts to search for the unknown," Todd responded. "You've provided me with a large amount of facts here to start compiling a profile for the man in question. The more organized and complex behavior Mr. Steele has demonstrated tells me that we're dealing with an intelligent criminal and that, if he is the guy, he took his sweet time in sophisticating his skills and in his planning. It sounds to me like he had years during his incarceration to develop new strategies. He was patient and probably took his time in sorting through multiple female prospects to abduct. He probably had several in mind to ensure that one way or the other he would find at least one woman to take with him that day.

"Mr. Steele's rape tools and backpack are so unique to the '84 charges, and it links him to Anita's abduction now. Think about it, Jack, he used a rope and a knife in the '84 case. My guess is that he moved up to using a gun as a weapon this time and a more secure means of keeping this victim subdued. These perpetrators tend to get braver with each crime. He only raped the first victim and then let her go. I don't believe he'll be willing to let this one go alive."

Todd's honest statement hit Jack like a punch to his gut. He did not want to believe that Anita was dead. Todd saw Jack's look of despair written all over his typically stoic face. "You do know, Jack," Todd said gently, "that you can't get your hopes up that you'll find this girl alive. She's been missing for five days now. The probability that she's still alive is probably about a 1 percent chance. He won't want to get caught again, so he'll dispose of his victim whenever necessary by whatever means available. I don't want you to give up hope, though, or lose focus. This guy needs to be found and brought to justice, regardless of whether Anita is dead or alive. He'll continue victimizing women until he's caught. You're on the right track, and I think you need to put all your efforts and manpower into locating Mr. Steele."

Jack leaned back in his chair and gazed up at Anita's picture, which continued to haunt him. "How can you be so sure,

Todd?" he asked skeptically, still looking perplexed. "They hadn't seen each other in years."

Todd nodded his head in understanding and got up out of his swivel chair. He knew Jack well enough to grasp that Jack had always been a visual learner. That was why Jack had written all the case facts on the dry-erase board; it helped him see it all clearly. Knowing this, Todd picked up a black marker and drew a large Venn diagram on the blank part of the board, which was sitting right in front of the conference table. Todd set the marker down when he was done. He picked up a pointer stick and announced to Jack as a professor would, "These two circles represent Anita's and the sexual predator's lives. The two circles don't have to fully overlap. It only takes one interaction, one glance or conversation, one chance meeting that allowed this psychopath to see this woman as a target or potential victim. We already know that their paths did cross, on multiple occasions. That makes him the prime suspect for sure. He might have taken those few years to simply watch Anita and wait. He knew that he had to be extra careful this time around, especially in a rural setting like Kokomo, where it's harder for him to blend in and remain unnoticed. He probably knew Anita's routines and planned to execute this crime at just the right time."

Jack jumped up out of his chair, looking as if a light bulb had just turned on in his head. "You're absolutely right," he exclaimed. "We need to move fast and get as much information on this guy as possible. We have to find him immediately!"

Todd put a hand on Jack's muscular shoulder. "You're right, Jack," he said in a serious tone. "You have to locate this suspect, but complete discretion is necessary right now. If you start asking his friends or family where he is, they'll certainly let him know. If the media gets wind of this, Anita's 1 percent chance of coming home alive will decrease to zero. The first inkling Mr. Steele gets that the police or feds are after him, he'll kill her to get rid of any evidence. You need to talk to the chief sheriff's deputy and persuade him to keep this prime suspect knowledge under wraps. There's no room for leaks.

"Then you've got to start brainstorming and decide which officers are trustworthy enough to join forces with you on this case. It's imperative that you choose wisely here. Don't be swayed by people who think you should bring them on the team out of loyalty. Instead, take some time, and be very selective as you form your dream team. You'll have to step on some toes, and you'll be criticized along the way, but I trust that you'll be able to pull together at least three or four fellow officers to get the job done. Never lose sight that finding Anita is the goal here, not to be politically correct or make friends."

Jack was full of gratitude for Todd's help. He was glad he had called him over and now felt confident in focusing the investigation solely on Tom Steele. Jack took a deep breath in and slowly exhaled before asking one last question, "So, with this type of predator, are there any other behaviors or patterns that I should be aware of at this early stage in the investigation?"

"Typically, the predator will first take his victim to a place where he has maximum control and familiarity, possibly his home or garage. Now, if he decided to keep her for a period of time, he might have had to take her elsewhere to keep her hidden. You did say that he lives with his mother, right?"

"The last anyone heard," Jack answered.

"Okay. Then, wherever he hides her, he'll probably have at least two locked doors between the outside world and her physical body. That'd give him enough of a sense of security that she'd be unable to escape to allow him to leave the premises without her if needed. That's all I can tell you for now, Jack. Keep me posted as you get more information on this guy. I'd be more than willing to give you more profiling tips along the way. I hope you catch this creep!"

Jack smiled genuinely at Todd. "Thank you so much for your advice today. I feel like I have some stamina again. I'd felt like I was one of those rats in a maze, just running around hitting my damn head on the wall over and over. But now I can see with some clarity and know what direction I need to go in to find the prize at the end. I'll get in touch with you as soon as I learn more about this guy's whereabouts."

The two men stood up in unison and said their good-byes in the hallway. This day marked a positive turn of events in the case. Jack was now on a mission to form an investigative team, and to talk to his boss, the chief sheriff's deputy, and to the Quantico FBI profiler to see if his opinions differed any from Todd's.

CHAPTER 32

Jack's mind was still reeling from the overload of information he had digested over the course of this long day. After Todd left, Jack had called the Quantico FBI profiler, Bob Thorton, to get his assistance in the crime scene analysis and in developing a profile of the sex offender's criminal motivation and behaviors. After learning the particulars of the case, Bob agreed that Mr. Steele should be their prime suspect. Bob informed Jack that typically in a sex crime, 70 percent of the sexual gratification for the perpetrator is mental, or fantasy based, and the other 30 percent is the physical gratification. The violence involved is stimulating and makes the perpetrator feel a sense of power and control.

Bob added that sex offenders and murderers are generally characterized by an egocentric personality filled with narcissism. They are often control freaks who have learned through their life experiences to link sex and violence together. The fantasy and their elements of power, or rape tools, will go further with each crime that they commit. There is no rehabilitation for this type of sociopath, and if they are let out of prison, they will reoffend whenever an opportunity presents itself.

Bob felt like the backpack, bicycle, and familiarity with the abducted victim were enough to tie this convicted rapist to Anita's crime. He further advised Jack that in cases of crimes of interpersonal violence like this one, it is not uncommon for offenders to hold on to items from their victims, including photographs of the victim and articles of the victim's clothing, from which the offender will receive gratification from their possession. These articles are of extreme importance to the offender and are typically found in his possession; they often take extreme measures to hide these articles from others. Offenders may also have in their possession journals that reveal their fantasies and might include identities of potential victims. Bob expressed to Jack the importance of searching for such items once they were able to attain a search warrant for the suspect's mother's home.

"We're just not ready to let Mr. Steele's mother become aware that we're looking for him yet. We'll just have to find a way to enter the family home under false pretenses so that we don't alert our suspect that we're on his trail. I believe he'd immediately kill Anita and then escape," Jack warned Bob.

Bob understood and told Jack, "I'm here to assist you in this investigation whenever you need my help or resources. I'm just a phone call away." Jack felt relieved that Bob was willing to give him the time needed to conduct the investigation, instead of just calling in the FBI squad to take over.

"Thanks for all the profiling tips you've given me, and I'll stay in touch with you as any incoming evidence surfaces. It helps me to get inside my opponent's head by learning from you how a serial rapist thinks and operates," Jack responded with sincere gratitude in his voice.

As soon as Jack hung up with Bob, he dialed the number of his superior, Chief Sheriff's Deputy Tim Madison. "Hello," Tim answered.

"Hey, Tim. It's Jack. Could you come over to the station now? I've got a great deal to tell you about the Wooldridge case. We have some new leads that look very promising."

"I'll be right over," Tim quickly answered. "Just give me a few minutes to wrap up this meeting with the mayor. Jack, I'm telling you, I have had to take some heat for this one! I can't believe how many calls we get every day regarding Anita's disappearance and whether we have any leads. We have to start answering questions soon. My boss and I are going to have hell to pay if we don't give the media something. I'll be there in a few. Bye, Jack."

Jack hung up the receiver and had to go outside for some fresh air.

He noticed that the sky was turning shades of crimson and gold as the bright sun began to set. Dark gray hues were beginning to appear as a backsplash to the radiant colors. In just minutes, the darkness would envelop him. It marked another day gone and Anita was still missing, but Jack's prior despair was replaced by a new excitement and hope. The fact that they had found their suspect today made adrenaline pump through his veins and gave him the strength and stamina to run the last leg of the race. He had been starting to drag, but this lead supplied him with the boost that he needed to reach victory.

Jack stretched his arms up over his head and cracked his neck a few times to get out the kinks from sitting down most of the day. He ran his fingers across his chin and noticed with astonishment that he now had nearly a full beard. He had not allowed himself any time for his typical grooming regime; he would make time for that once this case was solved.

Jack went back inside the station to wait for Tim's arrival. He made a call home to Dorothy to apologize that he would not be home again tonight. Jack told her how much he loved and missed her and even shed a few tears that he quickly brushed away. Jack desperately missed his wife, but he had to stay focused on forming a team to bring Anita home. The entire Kokomo community was counting on them to do this, and he did not plan to let them down.

Chief Sheriff's Deputy Tim Madison walked into the sheriff's department station around eight in the evening and looked as ragged as Jack felt. Jack knew that he had his work cut out for him in convincing Tim to keep all these new details quiet for now. Jack took in a deep breath and prepared to give the most effective sales pitch that he could muster this late in the day. Jack was already keenly aware that Tim trusted his judgment, yet he also was aware that Tim was going to have to go in front of the firing squad if their plan failed. It was a huge risk for both of their careers, but one that Jack was more than willing to take. Tim walked into the conference room and greeted Jack with a weary smile. "So, what do you have for me, Jack?" He got right down to business. "I've already heard that Scott Miller failed his polygraph test. Did he finally confess to what he knows?"

Jack shook his head, "No. He did fail the test, and we still plan to bring him in daily for questioning to see if he does know anything, but we ruled him out as our prime suspect today."

"Well," Tim said, shaking his head in bewilderment, "you need to fill me in on why you aren't looking seriously at him, and this better be good! Do you know how much heat I have on me right now?"

"Of course I do. I'd never try to make you or our department look bad, believe me. I'm feeling the heat just as bad as you are. We received information on a different suspect that appears much more plausible at this point in the case. His name is Victor Thomas Steele. He's a forty-two-year-old convicted rapist that was familiar with Anita. He lives with his mother in close proximity to the Wooldridge home. The unique facts of his prior charges in 1984 are strikingly similar to the evidence that we have in this case. I've spoken to two FBI profilers that believe that we need to put all our efforts into finding this suspect. I believe he's our man, Tim. I can feel it. We're moving in on him, and it's just a matter of time before we find him."

Tim looked over all the piles of paperwork strewn out in front of him; Jack had looked over them numerous times already.

He stood up and started pacing back and forth as he began formulating a plan in his head. He stopped suddenly and turned to face Jack. "Okay. I'm with you on this. So, what is your plan of action here? Are you going to his house to bring him in for questioning now?"

Jack sighed, "We can't do that yet. Both profilers have warned me that if this guy finds out we're looking for him, he'll kill Anita if he hasn't already. We can't jeopardize the case by asking around for him or letting the media know yet. I'm planning to form an investigative team of five men, including myself, by tomorrow morning. Then we'll set up surveillance of the suspect's residence and try to devise a plan to approach the home without letting them know that we're law enforcement. If the suspect isn't home, then maybe we can get his mother to tell us where he might be."

Jack continued, "I also plan on obtaining the suspect's phone and credit card records tomorrow. If he left town, then those records should give us some clues as to where he might have headed. We'll just go from there, but I'm confident that we'll come up with some information that'll quickly lead us to him and, with any luck, to Anita. What I need from you, Tim, is a commitment that none of these details will be leaked to the press. For now, just let everyone know that we have some promising leads that we're unable to comment on at this point. And keep urging everyone to keep their eyes out for Anita's car. That'd help a great deal to find some DNA evidence on her vehicle."

Tim slapped Jack on the back and stated confidently, "It's a done deal, Jack. You know you can count on me. I trust your judgment, and if you feel this strongly about the guy, then I'll back you up 100 percent. Just find Anita soon. I'm too old for this type of stress, you know?"

"I know all too well," Jack answered. "I've found out this week that I'm really not as young as I thought I was. Thanks for supporting me, Tim. I'll work on this day and night until we find her. I won't let you down after everything you've done for me over the years."

After Tim left for the evening, Jack felt a sense of relief wash over his tired body. *Well, that's over with,* he thought. *Now I just have to pick the right players for my dream team. This is a game we cannot lose!*

Jack went into his office. Mountains of paperwork that he had not had time to look over this week were scattered all over his typically neat desk. He started piling all the papers into a neat stack in the corner of his already cramped office: he needed room to work at his desk, the same one he had used for the past twenty years. Jack had to decide who would make the team. He hoped it would not take all night, but either way, he would have a roster made up by morning. Jack wanted to call in the selected candidates as soon as possible to get started on finding what seemed, to his weary brain, like a needle in a haystack.

Jack could feel God's presence guiding him through this process and knew that God would surely lead him to that needle, like a light shining down into the dark crevices, exposing what the human eye is incapable of finding on its own. Jack knelt down and prayed, "Please, dear God, give me the wisdom to choose the right men for my team, and please let us find Anita alive. Only you have the power to make this happen. I give you all the glory. Amen."

Jack's faith gave him the will to keep going that night in search of the best men for his team. He had played multiple sports in his lifetime, even coached a few basketball teams when his children had played, so he knew the fundamentals of assembling a team that could work together and gain success. Jack began sorting through the credentials of his staff at the sheriff's department, the police department staff, and then the regional drug task force special investigators. Jack wanted to look at all potential candidates so as not to base his decision on any biases he may hold for those he was closest to. Jack wanted the most qualified team possible, even if that meant bringing in someone he disliked.

Jack chose his first team member rather easily. He knew that Curtis Hoover, the captain of the Kokomo Police Department, was the polar opposite of himself, and Jack wanted diversity within the team. He did not want five clones of himself. Jack was smart enough to realize that he needed all types of characters within the team to win. While he and Curtis had disagreed on numerous occasions and did not always see eye to eye, Jack still valued Curtis's opinion, and their differences often gave Jack a fresh look at things, giving him ideas he never would have thought of otherwise.

Curtis had numerous connections on the street and within the department and city government. His strength was that he was a good talker and could connect with anyone to get the information that he needed from them. Jack knew that, in this investigation, he would have to think outside the box and that the standard practices typically adhered to would not cut it. Curtis's communication skills, connections, and charisma would be essential in helping Jack implement this new way of thinking among the team players.

Jack's second choice did not come so easily. He debated for nearly an hour on whether or not one of his most trusted sheriff deputies, Ron Eastwood, would be a good fit for the team. The only doubt Jack had about Ron's capabilities was that this case might hit too close to home for him. Jack knew that Ron was a strong, wise man with good morals, integrity, and a strong faith in God, and he never attempted to hide these facets of his personality and character. Still, Ron had a ten-year-old daughter of his own and was familiar with the Wooldridge family. He had grown up in a house adjacent to Center Road, the street where Anita was abducted.

Jack sensed that Ron was struggling with holding back his emotions in this investigation, but he also wanted to keep an open mind and not rule Ron out as a member of the team until he got a chance to talk to him about these reservations. So, Ron was put second on the list with a question mark beside his name. Jack would have to replace this veteran detective with another candidate if he did not hear the right answers from Ron in the morning.

The next addition to the team was actually Jack's superior at the sheriff's department, Deputy Major Phil Lyons. Jack needed Phil to supply him with a steady supply of encouragement and wisdom. Phil looked like a big, tough guy on the outside, but he had a soft side as well. He had the same core values as Jack and was also a family man. They shared the same old-school philosophies when it came to solving criminal cases, yet they were also both willing to work around the red-tape bureaucratic policies that tended to limit an investigation and lead to poor results. The two buddies complemented each other, and Jack knew that Phil would have the respect from the rest of the team as a father figure. This might be a good calming factor for some of the younger members of the investigative team Jack was forming.

Jack felt a little apprehensive about his last selection, but knew that Investigator Chuck Wilson could not be left off this team. Jack knew he would take some heat by bringing in an outsider from the regional drug task force. Other officers within both the sheriff's department and the police department would feel like they had their toes stepped on due to politics and turf issues. But Jack was willing to stand his ground and ignore politics here to build the most qualified team possible. Chuck had already demonstrated from the beginning of the investigation that he could be counted on to find out information from the public. He was reliable, a remarkable undercover agent, and a necessity to the team due to his willingness to go above and beyond. Jack needed his young energy, optimism, and street smarts to unify and complete the team roster.

Jack glanced down at his watch and was not surprised to find that it was nearly three in the morning. He was confident in his choices and had zero difficulties falling into a deep sleep right on the floor of his office. He had brought over a sleeping bag a few days before in case he had to pull another all-nighter. Jack lived by the Boy Scout motto: Always be prepared. He set the alarm on his watch for five in the morning so that he could call the candidates in early to offer them positions on the team. They needed to get started on locating this Mr. Steele. For a brief few hours, Jack found reprieve in a sound sleep, where he finally could escape the chase.

Anita as a child

Anita's high school graduation, 1995

Victor Steele's mugshot

Steele's bike

Steele's mother's detached garage in Kokomo

Steele's attic bedroom at Kokomo home

The note found at Steele's mother's home in Kokomo

Anita's car found in Indian Heights

Steele's red truck

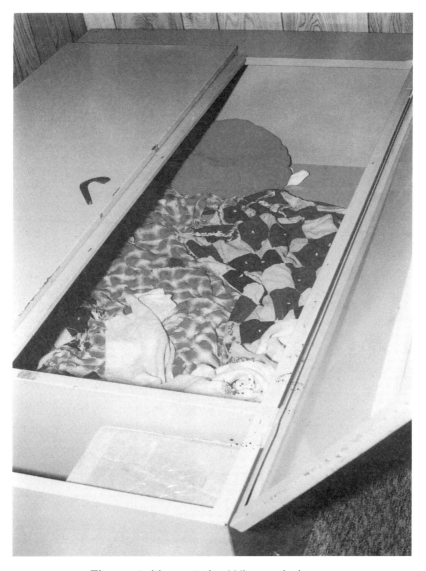

The metal box at the Wisconsin home

The wooden dowel and butter knife used to secure
the metal box

■ Details about Anita Wooldridge's abduction were released Monday.

By Kokomo Tribune staff

Wooldridge   Steele

The search for Anita Wooldridge ended when Howard County Sheriff Det. Don England opened the metal box she was in. A tearful Wooldridge grabbed him and said, " 'Thank God! Take me home.' "

It was a box England said "was made so she would have air."

During a press conference Monday, Howard County Sheriff Department and Kokomo Police Department officers released other details about Wooldridge's abduction.

Wooldridge, 21, 2813 E. Center Road, was reported missing June 25, was found July 2 in LaCrosse, Wis., and returned to Kokomo July 3. Victor Thomas Steele, 42, formerly of 236 E. Road 400 South, Kokomo, was arrested and faces charges in connection with Wooldridge's abduction.

In Wisconsin, he faces first degree sexual battery and kidnapping charges, according to Howard County Sheriff Jerry Marr. In Howard County, police have arrested Steele on a charge of criminal confinement, a Class B felony carrying a prison term of six to 20 years, Howard County Sheriff Maj. Dave McKinney said.

Steele had lived at the Howard County address with his mother, but Howard County Sheriff Det. Steve Rogers said police have "no reason to believe she knew anything about this."

Marr, Rogers, McKinney and Kokomo Police Capt. Michael Holsapple spoke during the press conference.

When asked why Wooldridge was targeted, Rogers said "We can only assume (Steele had) been watching her and stalking her."

Neighbors reported seeing a man with a green backpack in the area near Wooldridge's home on June 25. When asked if women's clothing and a wig were in the backpack, McKinney said, "I can neither confirm nor deny that."

According to Marr, Steele had recently rented a house at 812 Clinton St. in LaCrosse. On June 25, Steele rode a bicycle to the vicinity of Wooldridge's house, the sheriff said.

Steele let the air out of a tire and proceeded to the Wooldridge home, Marr said. He said Steele knocked on the door and asked for help. Wooldridge had previously met Steele. She worked at Celebrity Fitness Center, and he had a membership there. She agreed to help Steele.

Once inside the home, Steele allegedly used a stun gun to immobilize Wooldridge, Marr said. Steele then allegedly taped and otherwise "secured" Wooldridge, put her in her car and drove her to 236 S. Road 400 South. There, he allegedly "secured" her again, Marr said. When asked how Wooldridge was secured, Rogers said there was "something tied around her. She was either tied up or secured somehow the entire time she was with (Steele)."

Steele then allegedly proceeded to abandon Wooldridge's vehicle on Buckskin Court in Indian Heights

▶ Turn to **HOME** / A2

Kokomo Tribune, Tuesday, July 7, 1998

Their little girl is now home

By Kokomo Tribune staff

Not only were details of Anita Wooldridge's abduction released Monday, but so was what police are calling "the real story."

Kokomo Police Capt. Michael

▶ Turn to **REAL STORY** / A2

Howard County Sheriff Det. Steve Rogers, middle, speaks at a press conference about the abduction of Anita Wooldridge and the apprehension of Victor Steele, her alleged captor. To his left is Howard County Sheriff Jerry Marr. To his right is Kokomo Police Capt. Michael Holsapple. (KT photo by Tim Bath)

Steele faces federal charges

Victor Thomas Steele now faces a federal charge in connection with the abduction of Anita Wooldridge.

According to a news release from the U.S. attorney for the Southern District of Indiana, in U.S. District Court in Indianapolis on Monday Steele was charged with kidnapping, punishable by a maximum term of imprisonment for life; however, any actual sentence will be determined if he is convicted of the charge and pursuant to the federal sentencing guidelines.

Steele is in custody in Wisconsin and will be returned to Indianapolis following his initial appearance before a United States Magistrate judge in Wisconsin. He will face indictment by a federal grand jury within 30 days of his return to the Southern District of Indiana.

This is the house at 812 Clinton St. in LaCrosse, Wis., where Anita Wooldridge allegedly was held captive by Victor Steele. (Photo provided)

Kokomo Tribune, Tuesday, July 7, 1998

Howard County Sheriff Deputies Don England,
Steve Rogers, and Roger Smith outside of the front
entrance to the Wisconsin home on the day of the
rescue

Photo of Anita just days after her rescue at her best friend's wedding

Anita and her brother Daryl at FBI headquarters
in Quantico

Anita with the Kokomo "Dream Team" that
rescued her: (from left to right) Don England, Michael
Holsapple, Roger Smith, Doug Mason, Anita, Steve
Rogers, Mike Wheeler, and Rick Nutt
Photo taken in 2007

DAY SIX

TUESDAY, JUNE 30, 1998

CHAPTER 33

Anita awoke once again with the terrifying realization that she was still in this nightmare. She heard the mole rustling around in what sounded like the next room. Slowly, the horrific details of last night's events began creeping back to her in bits and pieces. The brutality of it all crashed over her like waves slamming into the shore during a heavy storm. A frantic Anita banged urgently on the top of the box to get the mole's attention. He came scurrying in and asked, "You okay? What do you need?"

"Let me out!" she cried out. "I'm gonna get sick! I'm gonna puke!" The mole rushed over to lift her out by her arms. He led her over to the kitchen sink, which was filled with dirty dishes from the day before. Anita had to walk slowly, despite her urgency, because she was so sore from the waist down.

Anita dry heaved into the sink: she did not have enough in her stomach to actually vomit anything of substance. Her stomach was turning over in waves of nausea, and she kept trying to hurl up anything still left in her empty stomach. She finally collapsed on the dirty linoleum floor in exhaustion and defeat.

The mole stood over her, clueless on how to help her or what to say. After a few moments, Anita stood up slowly while holding her stomach. "I have to get down to the toilet quickly!" she said. Her captor lifted her off her feet and took her down the steep basement steps one by one. Anita saw, out of the corner of her eye, cobwebs hanging from the walls and ceiling. Somehow, she had never noticed before how run down and dirty it was down here. With the lights on bright, it illuminated the filth; it looked like an old dungeon.

The mole placed his captive girl on the toilet and turned his head as diarrhea immediately filled the bowl along with a great deal of blood. Anita, doubled over in pain and agony, started whimpering. "Are you done yet?" he asked impatiently.

After a few more minutes, she wiped and was alarmed at how much blood she had lost. The damage to her body from last night was more severe than she had thought. She could tell that it even surprised the mole. He helped her back upstairs and laid her down on the couch. "Look," he said. "I know I hurt you pretty bad last night, but I thought you were into it too. I guess if you keep me busy by talking, playing some games, and watching some movies, I won't touch you today. You can have the whole day off to recuperate. How's that sound?"

"Good," Anita answered. "But I don't know how much company I'll be. I still feel really sick, and I might need to go back down to the toilet a lot today."

"Well," said the heartless creep, "you better do your best to entertain me, or I just might change my mind." The mole obviously thought he was being more than nice to his woman and that she should greatly appreciate all his generosity.

He pulled out his old Monopoly board game, and Anita attempted to get as comfortable as possible on the floor to play. Her legs fell asleep several times, and she had to take a break to slowly walk around and shake it off. The mole was oblivious to her pain at this point: he had Park Place and Boardwalk and had just put hotels on both of them. He was rubbing it in, as if she cared in the least. At one point, he even yelled, "Yeah! I told you I'm the champioooon of all games, didn't I?" The mole drawled out the vowels in *champion* to stress just how great he really was.

Anita was sick of him and how arrogantly he behaved, but she had to hide her feelings. "Yeah," she responded. "You told me, but I never guessed you'd be this good. I'm usually pretty good at board games, but not against you." The mole seemed satisfied by her acknowledgement and took a bow for grand gesture. He went on to beat her, because she never made any attempt to defeat and anger him.

While a battered Anita was left to clean up the game, her captor sat on the couch, looking perplexed. Out of the blue, he said, "You know, I could never understand why girls never wanted to date me. I mean, of course, they were always attracted to me in the beginning because of my looks, but after the first date or so, that was always it. They just wanted to be friends, they all said. I guess they're just intimidated by how smart I am. What do you think?"

Anita was inclined to tell him that the other girls had been smart to run when they found out how crazy he was, but instead, she chose her words carefully. "Well, maybe you just came on too strong in the beginning. I remember a few girls from the gym thought you were nice but kind of clingy."

"Those bitches got me kicked out of that gym," the mole said defensively, "'cause they all said I was harassing them. They wish! They were all teases. They made me think they wanted me, and then when I kept asking them out, they'd always say they were busy. A couple of times, I even hid in the locker room after closing time so I could listen to them talking and watch them clean up the room. I've got to admit they both looked real good. I thought of taking one of them home with me one night when she was finally alone.

"I was going to show her what a real man would feel like, but I'd only been home from prison about a year then, and I needed more time to plan things out. I vowed I'd never go back to prison. It's not a fun place. Anyway, enough about those stupid sluts. I remember every date that I ever took a girl on. I would always bring her flowers and open her car door and stuff. What more could you ask for? I think girls are just spoiled, and they need a man to lay down the law and tell them what to do. That's what they really want, anyway."

Anita let the subject drop: she knew not to say anything further to correct him. He obviously had it all figured out in his mind. Besides, she had to make another trip down to the toilet. Anita eased herself back onto her feet and said, "I have to go again." This seemed to snap the mole out of his trip down memory lane.

"Already? Man, you must be allergic to the tap water or something." Anita's captor would never admit out loud that it was his fault she was so torn up. The mole took her back down to the basement bathroom and let her stay there for five whole minutes alone. When she was done, Anita staggered over to the dusty mirror and stared back at a complete stranger. *What has this animal done to me?* she thought. *How will I ever be the same girl I was again?* Her once vibrant curls were matted and tangled so deeply that it looked like she was trying to grow them into dreadlocks. Her disheveled appearance and blank eyes scared her. She heard his loud, clunking footsteps descending the stairs, and panicked, she reluctantly turned to head up on her own.

"Well, I don't know about you, but I'm starving," the mole said at noon. He made himself a big ham sandwich, dripping with mayonnaise and, of course, onions. He also shoveled in a whole bag of potato chips with it and washed it down with a Dr. Pepper. She knew by now that nutrition was not in his vocabulary. That would explain why, during the years that she knew him at the gym, she would see him come in daily and do strenuous workouts without ever losing a pound. He had always remained overweight. He obviously could not give up all the fattening junk food he loved to devour. The mole made Anita a piece of toast and poured her a glass of Dr. Pepper. "Drink this and eat the whole piece of toast," he ordered. "It'll make you feel much better."

But he was wrong. As soon as Anita got it all down, she quickly limped over to the kitchen sink and vomited. The mole just shook his head and said coldly, "Don't you think you've played this whole 'I'm hurt' thing to the hilt now?" Anita just continued vomiting and ignored him.

The mole walked away without consoling her. Anita felt so alone and unloved at that moment. Her mother or boyfriend would hold her hair back or ask her if she needed anything when she was sick. A wave of overwhelming homesickness washed over her, and it made her feel even worse. She longed for her dad to bust down the door, carry her out of here, and return her safely back home. She yearned to sleep in her comfy queen-sized bed tonight like she always had. She had always sprawled herself out during the night, never sleeping in a ball like she currently was forced to do. Be strong, she reminded herself. *I know they're looking for me. Just stay alive another day, and they might find me soon. I know God will lead them to me. I've been faithful, and he'll allow me to be rescued. It just has to be on his time.*

Anita forced herself to stop thinking of the luxuries of home and trudged back to the living room where the mole was waiting for her. He was sitting at the computer and checking the progress that she had made. "All better now?" he asked.

"Yeah. I feel all right now. It just hit me hard. I couldn't hold it back."

"Well, at least you're okay now. No more food for you the rest of the day." He paused and then added, "And since you're feeling better, do you think you could finish up reformatting my computer? I'm going to need to start sending out fliers to the community real soon. I'm almost done with the bookshelves. They're coming out even better than I expected."

"Yeah. They look really good. You've done a nice job on them."

The mole beamed with pride, basking in the compliment and in his admiration for himself. "I can work on it right now if you want me to," Anita offered. The thought of sitting on the hard, unpadded computer chair sounded almost intolerable today, but the reprieve from the mole, and her own thoughts, had enticed her to offer her services.

He quickly accepted. "Go ahead and get started then. I'll be reading one of my books in the next room. I'm going to come check on you every now and then to keep you honest." The mole squeezed Anita's shoulder rather hard when he said this and then left the room quietly. She patiently waited until her captor was not in sight and she could hear him whistling in the next room. Anita quickly checked the date and time and found that it was now Tuesday at 1:15 p.m. It seemed like she had lost so much time when she had blacked out last night. She could not grasp that another whole night and day had passed and she was still trapped.

Anita had searched for any way out of the small box of a house. She still had not found a single way to escape. The windows were barred, and the back door was barricaded. The only way out was the front entrance, but he kept it locked and bolted and had a chair up against it at all times. He only opened it to leave or when the landlord or mailman came a few times. In Anita's current physical state, she could never make it over to the door, unlock everything, and escape from him. The mole would pounce on her within seconds, and she knew that he would not hesitate to kill her if she tried to leave him. She would just be another girl that was rejecting him, and he would never tolerate that. He had repeatedly told her over her first few days of captivity with him, "Learn to love me or I *will* kill you!"

The mole would probably get off by actually killing someone. The power and control of it all would be ecstasy for him. But for now he was okay with the knowledge that he had the power to take her life if he wanted to. He was fully in control for once in his, up until now, dreadful existence.

Anita returned from her thoughts and began loading files back onto the computer and reformatting everything. She feared that he would come in at any second to peer at her and make sure that she was doing what she was supposed to. The mole did pop his head in several times over the course of the next hour.

"I'm really close to being done," she informed him. "I can finish it up tomorrow. I just can't sit down on this chair any longer. I've got to get up for a while."

"Okay. You've worked hard. Just give me a few more minutes to finish this chapter. I'm at a really good part. The aliens are taking over this town. Then we can play a game of Life."

"Okay. Is it all right if I go down to the basement to use the bathroom again while you finish up? I promise I'll be back up in a few minutes."

The mole thought about it and said hesitantly, "Okay. I guess. But you better be back up soon, or I'm coming down."

Anita descended the basement steps one by one and stepped down onto the concrete slab floor in the mole's socks, which she was still wearing for warmth. As she relieved herself once again, she tried to find any weapon or way out. There were no windows or doors in sight, and the mole had made sure to keep it as bare as possible, never leaving a tool or sharp object out. He did not want the girl to get any ideas. Anita's hopes were dashed. She went back upstairs to where he was already setting up the board game on the living room floor. She was sick of playing board games and wanted desperately to go outside and get some fresh air. She knew deep down that that would be out of the question. Her heart sank as she knelt down to the carpet to be defeated once more by this vile man.

As they played, Anita built up a family of five and got the vacation card; the mole had a family of three and had just lost his job. He became visibly upset and spat out like a baby, "I hate this game. I'm bored. Let's do something else." *What a sore loser he is!* she thought. *I didn't even try to start winning. It's all just luck of the draw anyway.* But the mole got up off the floor, knocking all the pieces off the board with a sweep of his arm.

"Clean this shit up," he said coldly, "and then I'm putting you back in your box for a while. I have to go out to check my messages, and I need to call my mom to let her know I'm still alive." The mole's mood swings were so unpredictable and aggravating. One minute he was laughing and carrying on a conversation, and then she could see a cloud come over his face and he would fly into a fit of rage about absolutely nothing.

It was around three thirty in the afternoon, and it sounded nice to have a break from him to rest her weary, broken body and spirit briefly. She did not know whether she could believe the mole's promise not touch her for the whole day while she recovered, but she had to cling to those words to have any sort of peace. Anita picked up the game pieces quietly and then climbed back into her box. Her captor shut her in the metal cabinet and called over his shoulder, "I'll be back." *Take your time!* she thought to herself.

Hearing the door slam shut, Anita took the opportunity to pray again for peace for her family and friends that must be losing hope by now that she was still alive. She also recited one of her favorite Bible passages for when she was feeling tired or discouraged. She took comfort in repeating the consoling words of Matthew 11:28 several times. "Come unto me, all ye that labour and are heavy laden, and I will give you rest." With God's grace, the beaten down girl was able to fall asleep until the mole returned.

CHAPTER 34

Captain Jack Roberts awoke with a start to the annoying beep of his alarm on his watch. He felt like he had just fallen asleep, and it took him several minutes to figure out why he was still lying on his office floor. It was five in the morning, and the staff was not in yet. Jack took the opportunity to shower in the station locker room. He had brought with him a clean set of clothes and quickly threw those on. He was now fully awake and anxious to call in the four candidates he had chosen last night. Jack returned to his tiny office and began making the necessary calls. He knew that most of the men were probably still asleep, but he did not want to waste any time today.

Luckily, Jack was able to reach all of them and asked them to meet him at seven this morning at the station gym for a workout and a meeting. Jack was evasive about what the meeting would entail, but made it clear that he needed all of them present. They had all groggily accepted his invitation, so Jack headed into the conference room to get the coffee started. He would need as much energy today as possible.

In his excitement, Jack tripped over the cord to the coffee machine and nearly fell flat on his face; the mishap humbled him, forcing him to slow down and take his time. His gaze once again fell on Anita's photograph on his dry-erase board, and he thought, *Just be patient, Anita. We're getting closer, hon.* Jack spent the next hour refreshing his memory on all the newest discoveries made yesterday. He would need to fill his prospective team members in on the case as quickly as possible this morning so they could get started right away.

Jack, running on pure adrenaline and caffeine, could not lose sight of the mission at hand. He had to convince all these men to drop their busy lives and join him in the crucial task of finding Anita. He was almost positive they would all feel honored to be asked, but Jack was somewhat unsure whether they would be willing to jump into such a time-consuming, high-profile investigation. It could either make or break their careers, and he needed all of them to commit to giving him 100 percent of their time and focus. Jack knew that this was a great deal to ask of anyone.

He finished up his mental preparations and headed over to the gym that was located inside the station. He was wearing his gym shorts and T-shirt and felt ready to work out a few of the kinks that had formed in his neck and lower back from sleeping on the floor last night. Jack's routine workout regime was one that he had religiously adhered to since he was a teenager. He had always tried to keep up his strength and stamina, and he was in excellent shape at his age. Though small in stature, his commanding presence and confidence made him look a few feet taller. Jack was well built, and his muscles were transparent even through his baggy T-shirt. He opened the gym doors and turned on the lights to begin some stretches and weight lifting while he waited for his men to arrive.

Luckily, as if he knew that Jack needed to speak with him before the others arrived, Deputy Ron Eastwood walked through the gym doors about twenty minutes early. Jack sat up from the bench press and wiped the sweat off his brow with the back of his arm. He greeted Ron as enthusiastically as he could at this early hour, "Hey, Ron. I'm glad you came early. I have a few things to talk with you about before the other guys get here."

Ron looked perplexed. "Okay, sure. What is it, Jack?"

"Well, I called you guys here to offer you all a position on the Wooldridge investigative team. We have a new lead, and we need to get started today if everyone accepts. But my reservation with you is that you might be too emotionally tied to this case. I'm aware that you know the family, and I can't allow emotions to cloud your judgment."

Ron was a man in his forties with a stocky frame and a permanent smile on his face. He was extremely likeable and down-to-earth. He did not take Jack's reservations personally, but Jack could sense that Ron disagreed with the assumption that he might not be able to put his emotions aside. Ron pleaded his case to Jack, "I see what you're saying, Jack. It's true that I know of Anita's family and grew up in the same area, but if anything, I think it'll make me a more determined investigator on the case. I'll put 110 percent into finding Anita and bringing her home alive. Whoever took her took a piece of our community with her as well, and I feel like I need to bring her back to calm the fears of our entire community."

Jack knew one thing about Ron for sure. He had always been honest to a fault, and he took his job as an officer very seriously. Ron's main objective in life was to ensure the safety of the people in his community. Jack slapped Ron on the back. "Good to hear, Ron. I just needed to be sure. You've convinced me. We do need you on this team. So, I take it you're accepting the position?"

"You can count on that. I'm honored you would ask me. Thanks, Jack."

"You deserve it. Now, let's get in a workout before our real work begins!"

The two men worked up quite a sweat before the three others sauntered into the gym about a half hour later. They were all loudly discussing their plans for the Fourth of July weekend and jeering each other in a friendly manner. They quieted down when they walked into the room and saw Jack and Ron waiting for them. None of them knew what to expect in this meeting. They had no idea whether they were in trouble for something or if Jack just needed some advice on the case.

They all greeted Jack and Ron, and Jack, acting as the leader, asked them all to listen up for a few minutes. Jack's voice seemed to echo within the gym walls, and it gave him an air of authority. The men were all ears as Jack spoke. "Okay. Thanks for coming in so early. I called you all in to offer you positions on the Wooldridge abduction investigative team. The investigation is well under way, and many of you have already become a part of the process over the course of the past week. I stayed up all night trying to decide who'd be best for the team, and I feel strongly like each one of us would bring different strengths, skills, and perspectives needed to solve this case."

Jack was pacing back and forth in front of the men, who leaned up against the gym wall, listening intently as he spoke.

Jack stopped and faced the men. "I realize that most of the department thinks I should just hand the case over to the FBI, but I still believe that it needs to be our team of officers to bring Anita home. I just don't believe that the FBI would be as committed to putting forward so much effort since they have no ties to her…and since she's been missing for so long now.

"I'm also aware that I'll catch hell from various departments for breaking rank and not making politically correct choices as far as my team members. I'm willing to take the heat as long as we can all commit to working together as a close team on this case. I can't risk any leaks to the press. We all have to be committed and unified in our task of bringing Anita back home, dead or alive. Despite all our differences, I believe we can work well together and complement each other. For instance, Phil, you'll be our voice of reason. You're the most experienced member here, and I think you'll act as a good sounding board to the younger officers that might need to slow down and listen to some constructive criticism at times."

In his late fifties, Phil was the oldest candidate in the room. He was torn because he knew he would have to sacrifice time away from his wife, kids, and grandkids until the case was solved, but he quickly dismissed his selfish thoughts and stepped forward to address Jack. "Jack, I respect your choices for the team. I'll gladly accept the role and will do my best to bring Anita home. Whatever it takes, count me in."

Jack was grateful for Phil's enthusiasm, which seemed to spread to the other men in the room. "Thanks for your approval. It means a lot. Now, Ron has already accepted the position, so that just leaves the two of you, Curtis and Chuck, my two street-smart officers. I desperately need the two of you for undercover work and to follow up on leads by asking your contacts for information. Time is of the essence here, so I need your answer today."

Chuck Wilson was by far the biggest and most intimidating man in the room. In appearance, he looked like he could take on the role of team bodyguard. Chuck was shocked he had been chosen as a candidate for the team. He knew he was at the top of his game as an undercover agent on the drug task force, but to be asked to join this elite team was quite an unexpected honor. He stopped briefly to consider the likelihood that his girlfriend would leave him this time. She already felt like he never had any time for her as it was. But he decided right then and there that she would have to accept him and his work schedule if she truly cared for him. He could not turn this incredible position down just to appease a woman that might not stick around regardless. Chuck stepped forward and shook Jack's hand graciously to let him know that he appreciated Jack's willingness to go out on a limb for him. "I'm all in, Jack. I'll go above and beyond whatever is asked of me. Thanks for your confidence in me. I won't let you down."

Last to agree was the always comical bachelor of the team, Curtis Hoover. Even in his workout clothes, he was able to look cool and confident. Curtis reminded Jack of Robert DeNiro with his looks and charm. People looked up to Curtis, and he would be essential to their team morale and ability to achieve success. Curtis stepped forward with zero reservations; he had no family to consider or to tie him down. He gave Jack a playful punch in the arm as he joked, "I'm all in too, Jack, you know that, but why in the hell did you have to call us in here so early? I do need my beauty rest, you know." The whole group chuckled. Jack was relieved that all the men had accepted his offer and seemed more than up for the large task at hand.

Jack called the whole team into a circle for a pep talk that ended with them all putting their hands in and yelling together in unison, "Let's bring Anita home!" They were all pumped up and ready to get started. Jack ended the meeting with, "Let's put our all into this, say our prayers, and try our best to win this game as a team. For the next few days, we will eat, sleep, and breathe together. You need to completely clear your schedules so we can work around the clock." Jack asked the team to finish their workouts and then join him in the conference room. It was time to tell them about their new prime suspect.

CHAPTER 35

The mole headed his truck toward the nearest gas station and payphone in town. He got out, walked over to the payphone, and put the change in required to call his voicemail. He dreaded hearing more of his mother's threatening messages in her nagging tone, but he knew that it was time to just deal with her. That was the reason for his latest mood swing at the house just minutes before. He took a swig from the Mountain Dew can he had brought with him as he waited to hear the incoming calls.

"You have two messages. To listen to your messages, press one now." He pushed the button, and his mother's voiced filled the warm afternoon air with, "Tom, this is your mom. This is the last damn message I'm leavin' you. You better call me back today and let me know if you're comin' back for your stuff or what. Bye." Well, that wasn't too bad. Surprisingly, the next message was from an old buddy he had grown up and joined the navy with.

"Hey, Tom. It's me, Jimmy. I haven't heard from ya in a while and I wanted to know if ya wanted to come over to my parents' house for the Fourth this Saturday. We're havin' a cook-out. Your mom can come too, if she wants. Well, take care, buddy. Call me soon to let me know if you guys can make it or not. Bye."

Jimmy was the one person the mole would actually miss from Kokomo. Their lifelong friendship worked for both of them because they were both loners that still lived with their parents. They typically only saw each other once or twice a year, but they both knew that they had each other's backs if needed. The mole had never fully opened up to Jimmy about his inner thoughts, though. They tended to stick to more casual talks about old times growing up together. Jimmy was the one person the mole thought he could trust enough to tell about Anita. They had been through so much together over the years; he did not think Jimmy would rat him out.

The mole decided to invite Jimmy over to their new house one day to let him see that Anita no longer wanted to go home. That would help his friend keep his secret quiet. He thought Jimmy would even be happy for him that he had finally found someone to settle down with.

The mole put in enough change to call his friend back. Jimmy was not home, so the mole declined the invitation to Jimmy's mom. "Tell Jimmy I'd come if I was in town, but I just moved over here to Wisconsin. Tell him thanks anyway, and I'll call him soon."

"Okay then, Tom," Jimmy's mother, Elaine, replied. "You take care of yourself, honey." The mole had known her since he was in elementary school, and she still treated him like a kid.

The mole had almost lived at Jimmy's house during their elementary years to escape the wrath of his father on the weekends when he cruised into town. Jimmy's house made him realize just how dysfunctional and abusive his own household was. The mole had never heard any yelling at Jimmy's house, and it was always clean and peaceful. He would return home from these reprieves and get hit at the door with his mother's criticisms, drilling him about where he had been and how she needed him to do this and that for her immediately. She was usually black and blue when his father had been home for a visit.

Jimmy had only visited the mole's house once, and that was enough for him. He had ridden his bike over one summer day when they were about ten to see if the mole wanted to go for a ride. He had shown up unannounced that Saturday morning and had been appalled by their filthy house, with trash and clothes strewn everywhere. When the mole had entered the room to see Jimmy standing there with a look of disgust on his face, he had been so humiliated that he had quickly dragged Jimmy outside by the arm, saying tersely, "What are you doing over here? I told you never to come here. My dad's home, and if he catches you, I'll never hear the end of it."

"Sorry, Tom," Jimmy had said apologetically, "I just wanted to see if you could come out for a while."

"No, Jimmy," the mole had snapped back, "not everyone has it as good as you do! I'll see you Monday, if I can make it through the weekend without him killing me."

Even as a young boy, the mole knew that he had to be in survival mode at all times. He never doubted that his father would kill him if he thought he could get away with it. His mom knew that his dad would kill her too if she defended the kids in any way. In high school, the mole had rarely hung out with Jimmy as they had both become more isolative.

They had caught up with each other in the navy and had gotten together a few times since the mole had been let out of prison early.

The mole dialed the numbers to call his mother collect, just to irritate her further. She answered on the first ring and accepted the charges. She screamed into the phone in her loud, raspy voice, "Tom, that you? Well, it's about time!"

He took a breath and answered, "Hey, Mom. I was just calling to tell you to stop leaving me all those damn messages. I have to pay for each incoming call, you know."

"Well, you could've at least had the decency to let me know where you were and when you'd be back," she snapped.

"I told you I was moving, Mom," the mole countered. "Why do you have to make a federal case out of everything? I moved most of my things with me already in the U-Haul, and I'll be back next week sometime to get the rest of it. Okay?"

"That's fine now that I know you're plannin' on comin' back for it all. So, where you at?"

"I told you I was moving to Wisconsin. It's about eight hours from Kokomo. I'll call you back with my address and phone number if the damn phone people ever get over here to hook it up."

"Okay. Just call me tomorrow and let me know what day you're comin' next week, 'cause I might be goin' on another gamblin' trip with my friend Dottie soon. I won a hundred bucks last week. Got me some luck goin'. Have to get back over there before it runs out."

The mole could take no more of this idle chitchat and got down to his real motive for returning her calls. "Oh, I need you to sell the old '81 Datsun I have sitting out in the front yard there. I put a For Sale sign on it before I left. I need you to sell it for me for seven hundred dollars or better offer if anyone calls about it. I need the extra money to start my bookstore. I almost have the bookshelves built and all. You'd be impressed."

"Why do you always put everything on me, Tom?" she whined. "I'm livin' alone now, and you want to put something else on me to do. You should be here sellin' this car. Not me. You're just like your father sometimes!"

Her last comment was like a stab to his heart. "Look, I told you to sell it. If I get back there and the sign's not still out, then I'll beat the living shit out of you like my father used to. You better not take any of the money, either. I'll only go as low as four hundred. Okay?"

"Well, I guess it'll have to be okay. I got no choice, do I? Well, call me tomorrow. Don't forget."

"Okay, fine. And let me know if anyone calls about the car. Bye."

Furious, the mole screamed as soon as he hung the phone back on the receiver. His mother made him want to strangle her, but at least it was over with for now.

CHAPTER 36

A half hour after their early morning workout, the newly formed investigative team congregated in the conference room. Jack was able to quickly fill them in on Victor Thomas Steele's criminal history. He added, "Don Howell also informed me that one of his buddies graduated with Tom Steele and had mentioned to Don a few years ago that at his ten-year high school reunion, Mr. Steele threatened to murder his entire graduating class if they ever held another reunion. Apparently, he was never even questioned by the authorities after this incident. Everyone just chalked it up to idle threats."

The team members took a few minutes to digest all this new information. Phil Lyons was the first to break the silence. "Looks like we have a true sociopath on our hands, Jack. This guy had several years after his early release from prison to sit back and devise his next plan of attack. We have to find out as much information about him as possible. We need to get inside his mind and try to think like he would. That's the only way to outsmart a lunatic like him."

Jack agreed with Phil. "Our two FBI profilers are a great help with that whole process. What we do know is that he lives with his mother, Daphne Steele, here in Kokomo," he said.

"Have you called to see if he's home?" Curtis asked.

Jack shook his head. "No," he said. "I was waiting until we all had the chance to strategize our next move. It's crucial that his mother doesn't figure out that we're looking for him." Jack asked Ron to retrieve the Steele residence phone number. They had to devise a plan to call the house and ask for him under an alias. Ron headed out the door immediately, returning within a few minutes with the number scrawled on the piece of paper in his hand. Ron handed it over to Jack.

"Do you want me to make the call?" Ron asked.

"No. Let's let Chuck do this one. Just ask for Mr. Victor Steele, and if his mother asks who's calling, tell her you're selling a home security system." Chuck obligingly went over to the phone with the piece of paper and dialed the number.

The room was completely silent: all eyes were on Chuck. He cleared his voice and waited as the phone rang five times before he heard a raspy female voice on the other end.

"Hello," Daphne Steele answered.

Chuck put on a business-like voice and stated, "Hello, ma'am. Could I please speak with Mr. Victor Steele?"

"He ain't here."

"Do you have any idea when he'll be back?"

"Who the hell wants to know?" Mrs. Steele asked gruffly.

Chuck could hear the blaring TV in the background and could sense that the woman was irritated by the disruption of this call. "My name is William, and I'm with Integrity Alarm

Systems. I'd like to speak with Mr. Steele about our products and see if he might be interested."

"Well, he won't even return his mother's calls, so you're out of luck. I don't know when he's comin' back. He says he moved to Wisconsin somewhere, but if he's not back by the end of this week, I'm gonna throw out the rest of his stuff."

"Okay, ma'am. I'll just call back at a later time. Bye."

Chuck hung up the receiver and informed the team, "His mom claims he's not home and she has no idea when he'll be back. She said he rarely returns her phone calls, and it sounds like he already took most of his belongings with him, to somewhere in Wisconsin."

Jack was not surprised by the news. It just further convinced him that they were on the right track. "Okay. We do know that a red pickup truck is registered to Mr. Steele. We need to set up surveillance of his mother's home and see if his truck's there. Once we have confirmation on whether or not the truck is present, we need to find a way to get in and talk more with his mother. It'll have to be an undercover operation. At least we now know he's possibly across state lines in Wisconsin with Anita, if she's even still alive." Those last few words seemed to linger in the room, and several of the officers frowned to even think of the possibility that she might be dead.

Curtis stood up, wasting no time. "Chuck and I can head over there right now and check out the situation. We'll call you as soon as we know anything." With that, they flew out the station doors to head for Curtis's squad car parked right out front.

That left the other three men to strategize alternative ways to find information on their suspect. "We need to pull up Mr. Steele's phone and credit card records for the past few months to see where he's been lately," Jack stated. "That could lead us right to him as long as he's made some mistakes in covering his tracks." Ron left the room to retrieve the records in question while Jack and Phil went over the details of the case once more to make sure that they had not missed any leads.

Ethel, Jack's secretary, walked into the conference room to let Jack know Curtis was on line one, waiting for him to answer his call. Jack walked over to the phone and said, "What do you have for me, Curtis?"

"Well, no red truck. But Chuck plans to stick around here for the rest of the day to see if Tom returns. But we hit the jackpot! We have a perfect alibi to get in to talk to his mom. There's an old beater car parked in the driveway with a For Sale sign on it. If it's okay with you, Chuck wants to call a few of his undercover investigative buddies and ask them to help him keep the house under surveillance around the clock tonight. A few of them could go inside and speak with his mom to get information on the car and her son's whereabouts. She seemed like quite a talker, so maybe she'll tell us about her son before we even start probing for answers. She seemed to need to vent to someone about him. We may get real lucky here, who knows?"

Jack could not believe their sudden luck in a case that had started off so slowly. It had to be by the grace of God that so many doors were finally opening and they were narrowing in on this guy. Jack only had one question. "Is Chuck positive that his investigator friends can keep all this undercover work under wraps? He has to be for sure before I can okay this."

"I know," Curtis answered. "I was skeptical about that initially as well, but I just met the guys. They're highly qualified and used to working on these types of cases. They were more than willing to keep it all top secret. I trust Chuck's judgment on this, Jack."

"Okay. That's all I needed to hear. Hey, could you come back to the station soon? Ron is having a harder time gaining access to those phone and credit card records than we expected. We need you to call some of your contacts and make it happen by this evening if possible."

"Sure thing," Curtis replied. "I'll be right over after I let the office know I'm going to be on a leave of absence from there for a few days. See you soon."

Jack could not wait to unveil the records and see just where their prime suspect had been recently. While he waited for Curtis to return, Jack stayed busy making phone calls to the department heads to inform them of his team member selections and to once again stress the importance of not leaking information to the press.

CHAPTER 37

Kokomo Police Captain Curtis Hoover strode confidently into Jack's office wearing a triumphant smile on his typically cool and collected face. He carried in his hands a binder that contained pertinent information about their suspect's whereabouts over the few weeks leading up to Anita's disappearance. "I've been working on this for hours, but I think I have Mr. Steele's location narrowed down to a nearly exact radius in the Wisconsin area now."

Curtis laid out the papers on Jack's newly cleaned off desk and pointed down to a map of Wisconsin with a section highlighted in red. "Mr. Steele's credit card records indicate that, on June 23, he used his credit card to buy gas at a convenience store in Onalaska, Wisconsin. Onalaska's a little suburb north of a town called La Crosse. Most people just travel through it to get to La Crosse. It's kind of the equivalent of the Greentown area for Kokomo, right outside the city limits. On June 22, Mr. Steele had rented a U-Haul truck in Kokomo and then returned it the following day. The log shows that he put 941 miles on the truck. That's only sixty-one miles more than a round trip between Onalaska and Kokomo."

Curtis put down a map of Indiana and Wisconsin and stuck a pin on the Kokomo area and attached a string to it. He pulled the string across the map to what equaled half of the 941 miles travelled, allowing for the few extra miles that their suspect may have travelled elsewhere, and it landed the string right in the center of the La Crosse area. "Now, these calculations won't be as exact if he happened to drive around more than we think, but my guess is that he didn't. The records also confirm that he owns a red Ford Ranger pickup truck. He's been smart enough to not use a credit card or an ATM since the abduction date. But my gut's telling me Mr. Steele's somewhere in or around La Crosse, Wisconsin."

Jack took all of this in and stared down at the map on his own for several minutes before he nodded his head in agreement, "I'm with you 100 percent on this. You're amazing, Curtis. Good work. We'll just have to wait and see what Chuck's men are able to find at the suspect's mother's residence. Then we can decide how to proceed as far as getting over to La Crosse and establishing an investigation command post there. It'll be tricky with all the red tape that comes with crossing state lines, especially with the limited evidence we have thus far. I agree with you, though. I have a feeling we've narrowed in on the right location. It just makes sense. Let's call it a night and try to get some rest for tomorrow's events. I bet we'll be travelling by tomorrow, and we'll need to be able to think clearly." Curtis agreed fully and headed out the door for home.

Jack decided to call Todd McCain to see what he thought about the new evidence. "Well," Todd said after Jack filled him in, "the timing of his trip to Wisconsin and the fact that he was driving a U-Haul to take his belongings there indicate to me that he was making preparations for the kidnapping. I'd bet he took Anita to that location after he abducted her."

Todd provided Jack with profiling details regarding the suspect in question. "Psychologically speaking, men who commit such crimes are very self-centered, and yet they don't fit in. They can't compete with the rest of us for a lady's affections, but they're convinced that if they can control and manipulate her mind, she'll come to find out that she's attracted to them after all. The dark side is that this type of criminal builds his dream around winning the victim's love and will keep her alive only as long as that goal seems attainable. I just hope Anita's been able to play along with him so that he's kept her alive."

Jack was relieved that Todd felt like they were on the right track. "That's good to hear. Wanted to make sure it all sounded plausible to you too, so we don't go off on some wild goose chase. We'll make a trip there soon if I can talk my bosses into letting our team go."

"Good luck with that. Crossing state lines to complete an investigation typically falls on the FBI. You'll run into some turf issues, but if anyone can do this, it's you, Jack. I've always been amazed by your ability to pull things off. Keep me posted, buddy."

"Sure thing. Thanks." Jack hung up the phone and, when he left for the evening, was in good spirits from the promising steps they were taking to reach Anita. He was even able to notice the beautiful sunset in the sky and take a deep breath of fresh air as he walked briskly to his car. But Jack sensed that this could be the last night he would spend at home with his wife for some time.

CHAPTER 38

His phone call to his mother now out of the way, the mole went inside the gas station to pick up a *La Crosse Tribune*. He flipped straight to the national news headlines and saw just a tiny blurb about a girl from Indiana missing. There was no picture of Anita or anything. Beautiful! He chugged down the last of his Mountain Dew and was amazed at how beautiful the scenery here in La Crosse was. It had turned out to be another beautiful summer day, and the weather forecaster on the radio predicted the same ideal temperatures for this holiday weekend. There was a summer breeze that whipped through the mole's rather greasy and thinning hair. He inhaled the breeze deeply and, with a slow exhale, let go of all the stress from talking to his mother.

The mole was in better spirits now and ready to get back home to watch TV with his girl. He had put about five episodes of his favorite sci-fi show, *V*, onto a VCR tape. His plan was to get her interested in the show so that they could watch episodes together and act the scenes out in real life for the days that followed. He loved to go into different characters. He and Jimmy had played Dungeons and Dragons for years and acted out scenes in Jimmy's basement. He thought that he and Anita would have to give that a try as well when she got to feeling better.

The mole sped home in the truck with the radio on. The announcer gave the weather predictions and then went on to the top stories. The mole turned it up, eager to hear whether Anita's kidnapping would reach national news or not. He had not heard anything on the radio about her thus far. "On a tragic note, a twenty-one-year-old girl was taken from her parents' home in broad daylight last week in Kokomo, Indiana. She has been missing for six days now, and the police have no leads at this point. If you know any details regarding Anita Wooldridge's disappearance, please call the police hotline immediately."

The announcer moved onto talking about the exciting events going on locally this weekend. Tom snorted and thought with delight, *Even more beautiful! I knew those pigs would give up looking for her after the first few days. They're all out golfing or getting hammered for the holiday weekend. They could care less about one girl missing, and there's no way for them to catch me. I'm too good!* When the mole returned to the white box of a house on Clinton Street, all was well. He went inside and made himself a frozen pizza and chips. He scarfed it all down in no time flat and went over to let the girl out of the box again. Anita was awake by the time he returned. She had had a dream of her and her best childhood friend, Maggie, walking down Center Road on a summer day to a convenience store just a mile or so down the road. They would often gather up all their change to play some video games and buy candy there. In the dream, the once-safe trip turned into a nightmare when a man on a bike began chasing them on their way home. They were running at top speed, scared to death. They finally made it to Anita's house and ran in to tell her dad about the scary man. They made it to safety in her dream. In reality, Anita was still scared to death and longed for her dad's protection from this evil man.

The mole opened up the box with a goofy grin on his face. His mood had changed again. At least this time, it was for the better. Anita had done a term paper in high school on rape. She knew the research showed that rape is more about the rapist having complete power and control over their victim than the sexual act itself. She knew that she had to keep talking to him and listening to him as a friend would: she needed him to see her as a human being, not just an object or possession. She could tell that several times he had to catch himself when he became sympathetic to her or started caring about her in any way. It appeared to startle him when he would have these emotions, like it scared him to actually care. It also proved to her that her plan must be working; she had better keep him talking to stay alive.

"Hello, beautiful!" the mole said cheerfully. "Did you get some sleep?"

"Yeah, I did. Thanks. Maybe we could watch a movie now, and I could stretch out again."

"I was just coming in to ask if you wanted to do that. I'll take you down to the bathroom first, so we don't have to be interrupted during the episodes. I think you're really going to like this TV series. My buddy Jimmy and I love the show." This was the first Anita had heard of him having a friend. The mole took the girl down to the toilet and stood on the steps to wait for her.

She was glad to see that she had stopped bleeding and was not as sore now. When she finished, he led her back upstairs, and they began watching *V*. It was so boring that Anita had to fight back yawns. She had never been a sci-fi fan. It all seemed so far-fetched to her. But she knew she had to mask her true feelings and pretend to be engrossed in the shows. The deranged mole was on the edge of his seat and could hardly contain his excitement from all the action on the screen.

Two long hours later, he turned away from the TV. "What do we do now?" he asked her.

"We could talk for a while. I want to know more about you and your family."

The mole quickly dismissed this. "There's nothing more to tell you about us. As far as I'm concerned, I don't really have a family. My mom is a pain in the ass, my dad's dead, and I haven't seen my sister in about a decade. I rarely see my brother. End of story."

"Okay. Well, what do you want to talk about?"

"I did hear on the radio that the pigs don't have any leads as to where you might be. That's great news!" he said with excitement.

Anita saw it as good and bad news. At least now she knew that they were still looking for her on a national level. But she did not want to hear they had no leads.

"I wonder what my family must be going through, not knowing what happened to me," she said aloud to herself.

"Oh, if they're like my family, they'll get over it. You're an adult now. It was more than time for you to leave the nest."

"My family isn't like that at all. We're all pretty close, and they'll never stop looking for me until I'm found dead or alive. I'm sure of that."

"Well, they'll have to give up eventually," he retaliated. "The pigs obviously aren't working too hard to find you if they have no leads at all."

"Who do you think their prime suspect is?"

"I don't know. Did you have any enemies?"

She thought a minute and said, "No. I can't think of anyone."

"Well, I'd never even be considered a suspect, since we hadn't talked since I was kicked out of the gym a couple years ago," the mole said smugly. "Did you ever talk about me to anyone?"

"No. Not that I remember. Just Sarah when we talked about inviting you to her wedding."

"Then I think the main suspects will be your boyfriend and your ex-fiancé, the one I used to see you with at the gym all the time. Maybe they'll think Mitch wanted you back and was jealous of you and your new boy toy. If you ask me, they're both losers."

"You've never even met Scott," Anita said defensively, "and Mitch was always nice to you at the gym."

"I don't have to meet Scott," he shot back. "I know your type, and Mitch was never nice to me if you weren't around."

The mole talked on, and she listened for the next hour about his unrealistic plans for their future together. It was around ten at night, and she prayed that he would just let her go back to the box to sleep. She wanted no part of him touching her in any way. She was just starting to feel somewhat better physically.

The mole surprised her by saying, "Well, you better get to bed now, so you feel better in the morning. I might need your help on my bookshelves, and you can finish up on the computer for me."

Anita was so thankful. She stepped down into the box and scrunched up in a ball as he shut her in. "Goodnight," she said.

"'Night. Sweet dreams," he said back. The mole stayed up for the next few hours reading his book on ways to draft a business plan. It was going to be harder than he thought to attain a loan, but he knew he could pull it off. He had managed to orchestrate this whole plan successfully. In his mind, everything else would just fall into place.

Anita lay there restless for several hours, but was more than happy to be in that box. She had made it through another whole day, and she was shocked that he had not hurt her at all. She had hope for the first time in days that she could make him trust her just enough that he would slip up in some way to allow her an opportunity to escape. She fell asleep thinking of all the different scenarios. She knew she had to eat tomorrow and get enough sleep tonight in order to remain coherent. Tomorrow would be another day in survival mode. She was ready for combat. She had to get back home by this weekend. Anita was confident that God would make it all happen.

CHAPTER 39

On Wednesday morning, Detective Rick Monroe of the Ko-komo Police Department Special Investigations Unit walked up cautiously to the front door of the old farmhouse the suspect had allegedly lived in with his mother. Rick had been more than up for the challenge of staking out the residence and watching for the red truck to arrive. As the hours had rolled by, he and his investigator buddies had formulated the plan to approach the home by pretending to be potential buyers of the vehicle for sale in the front yard. Rick's trained eyes darted from the old windows of the house to the unattached garage and around the perimeter of the property in search of any signs of the man in question. Rick did not see any signs of life as he strolled up the front walk, except for a dim light in the front room and the background noise of a TV.

Rick was wired and his team sat in the car across the street, just waiting for a signal from him. They were all on alert and ready to jump out in pursuit of the suspect if needed. Rick knocked on the front door several times and heard a woman yelling, "What do you want? I'm busy." The old woman answered the door and looked Rick up and down before she asked, "Who the hell are you?"

Rick answered politely, trying to charm her, "I'm sorry, ma'am, but I was driving by and noticed the car for sale in your yard. Do you own it?"

Daphne Steele, Tom's mother, looked like a beat-up, bitter woman that you did not want to mess with. She appeared to be at least ten years older than her real age of sixty-four. You could sense that she had lived a hard life, and her voice sounded as hoarse as a man's. In her hand, she was holding the culprit. Her unfiltered cigarette dangled from her fingertips, and she took a long drag before she answered in irritation, "No. It's my deadbeat son's. He ain't here, but he ordered me to sell the thing for him. Can you believe him? He's supposed to be helping me out at my age, and instead I'm still picking up the pieces for him."

Rick jumped at the topic of her son and said coyly, "Oh yeah. Well, he should be more respectful to such a fine mom like you. Do you know when he'll be back so I can talk to him about the car? I'm sorry, what's his name?"

"His name's Victor," Mrs. Steele replied, "but everyone calls him Tom. He told me he was moving to Wisconsin, but I thought he was leaving next week. I came home from my gambling boat trip, and he had already packed up most of his things and left in his truck. He left this old junker here for me to deal with. He made a trip up about a week ago and took all the heavy stuff in a U-Haul. He should have gotten all of it the first time. That boy is so secretive, though, so he hasn't told me yet where in Wisconsin he moved to, and he still don't have a phone set up. He just calls me when he feels like it. He did tell me he'll probably come back to get his other stuff, but I don't have any idea when."

Rick took all this information in and continued, "Well, how much does he want to sell the car for?"

Mrs. Steele replied with a chuckle, "He says seven hundred dollars. Hey, let me get your name so I can tell him you asked about the car."

Rick had already decided on an alias and told her convincingly, "Oh, sorry, my name's Eric Tanner. That price seems pretty high to me. Ask him if he'll come down on the price and to give me a call."

Mrs. Steele replied quickly, "Yeah. He won't call you back. He wants me to do all the work here. I'll ask him to lower the price, though."

Rick extended his hand to give her a handshake, "Thanks. I think I'll come back tomorrow if that's okay and bring my mechanic buddy with me to check out the car's engine and all."

"Fine by me. As far as I know, it runs just fine. Maybe I'll hear from him by then. I'll go and leave him a message to call me back again."

Rick thanked the woman for her time and walked slowly back to his car. He had to drive off, but he returned several minutes later in a different unmarked vehicle so as not to arouse any suspicions from the lady. Rick had hoped for further information but felt confident that she was telling the truth and that their man was still somewhere in Wisconsin. He felt like it was a game of cat and mouse, and they were getting closer to catching their prey every minute. Rick called Chuck to tell him the details of his conversation with Mrs. Steele. The rest of the team needed to know immediately.

CHAPTER 40

Anita woke up on this bright, beautiful summer morning, still trapped like a caged animal. She had been hoping again that the past few hellish days had been just one long nightmare. Anita felt waves of desperation and panic start to roll over her, and her breathing became irregular. She heard a noise coming from outside the box.

Swoosh, swoosh, swoosh. Anita knew that her captor must be waiting for her to wake up as he was absentmindedly letting the wooden dowel slide through his hands to kill the time. She wanted to shout, "shut up!" but wisely chose to keep her lips sealed. She dreaded seeing his beady eyes, and the thought of him raping her again made her want to curl up and die. He had given her the reprieve from sex all day and night yesterday, but how long would that last? Anita decided that she would have to try keeping him busy by talking and playing games. Maybe that would distract him and keep his filthy hands off her for another day.

"Can I get up now?" Anita called out to the mole. "I have to go to the bathroom."

"Sure!" he answered cheerfully. "Did you sleep okay?"

"Yeah, I feel a little bit better today. Thanks."

The mole took out the butter knife and wooden dowel to unlatch the doors and swung them open. He let Anita out and took her down to the basement bathroom. He sat on the stairs and talked to her as she took her time on the toilet. "I went to the store this morning and bought you a toothbrush and hairbrush," he said. "It looked like you really needed to comb your hair. I also put a wash rag by the toilet so you can wash yourself off at the sink if you want to."

Anita was somewhat skeptical of her captor's uncharacteristic generosity this morning. She did not know what he expected from her in return, and she was on pins and needles that whole morning, just waiting for the bomb to drop. Oddly enough, when the mole wasn't raping or threatening her, he treated her like his fantasy girlfriend and attempted to be the ideal boyfriend. "Thanks," she called back to him. "That was thoughtful of you. Just give me a few minutes to wash up and try to get this brush through all of these darn tangles in my hair."

Anita took her time, stalling as long as she could. The mole was very patient and quietly waited for her to finish. When she came into his view, he exclaimed, "Wow! You look much better. Ready to eat some toast or something now?"

"Yes. I'm starving," Anita replied. They walked together up the stairs, and the mole made her buttered toast and poured her a glass of Sunny Delight. He whistled as he made himself a large bowl of Cocoa Puffs and four pieces of peanut butter toast. He scarfed it all down and then brought her meal in to her. She ate it quietly on the couch while the mole read the *La Crosse Tribune* and commented on world events. Anita listened quietly; it felt good to hear what she had missed over the past week.

"I love President Clinton," the mole said. "He's the only president that likes eating fast food like me. You always see him eating fries and checking out hot women. I would too if I had that ice princess Hilary as a wife. She looks like the type of woman that doesn't know her place as a wife. She's probably the one calling all the shots in the White House while Bill just sits back and enjoys the women and food. Yeah, I like him."

The mole read on in silence for a few minutes and then stated, "It says here that, so far, this has been the warmest and wettest year in the U.S. since 1934, and this damn crazy weather is all related to El Niño. Wildfires in Florida and Texas are running rampant. The South is experiencing a drought while we're being flooded with rain and tornadoes. I think it's funny! Do you think Americans give a damn about what all our pollution is doing to the Earth? Hell no, they don't! We're destroying the world, and no one seems to care. I saw this coming a long time ago, but the stupid fucking leaders around the world are just now starting to debate it. I don't even associate myself with the human race. I see things you humans can't. Soon, it'll be too late, though. These natural disasters are going to become more frequent and more devastating. Just wait and see."

Anita had seen the devastation with her own eyes just weeks prior. The tornado had ripped the roof off her high school and had taken several lives around the county. She was perturbed by her captor's callousness in assuming that all Americans did not care about the intense storms and damage spreading across the nation. She did care. He was the one that could not care less about the plight of others.

The mole broke the momentary silence, saying, "Good thing we weren't in Wisconsin about three weeks ago. A squall line packing one-hundred-mile-per-hour winds plowed down thousands of trees and took several lives in western Wisconsin on June 7," he read as he began to laugh. "Oh, and the summer floods in China and India have taken over six thousand lives," he continued. "What? Am I supposed to care about them? These fatal floods, landslides, tornadoes, hurricanes, and wildfires are a blessing, I think. I'd wipe out the whole world's population if I could. These natural disasters are just doing me a favor."

Again, Anita held her tongue. Instead of yelling at him, she said, "All people aren't as bad as you think. Some of us really do care about the world and try to make a difference. It's just a problem that's bigger than us. The world has to come together to make any of the real changes necessary to cut back on all the pollution and global warming."

"Ah, you're one of those idealists! Give it up! The world will never come together and fix things! Everyone's too damn selfish and used to their comfortable lives."

Her captor was growing angry again, so Anita wisely dropped the subject.

She wanted to see what time it was, but there were no clocks anywhere in the small house. "I could get back on the computer and finish it all up for you today if you want me to," she offered.

"Okay. It'd be nice to have all that ready soon."

Anita logged on to the old, outdated computer and found that it was 11:26 a.m. It was almost afternoon, and he still had not touched her. She was amazed. She was able to finish up the reformatting within the next few hours while he used the last of the plywood materials to build the bookshelves. Like everything else he did, the bookshelves were assembled shoddily. The boards were uneven and mismatched, but he viewed his work as a one-of-a-kind masterpiece.

"I'm finished," she called to him. "You're all set up now."

The mole walked over to her and put his hand on her shoulder. "Thanks, hon. You've done a great job. I just have to cut a few more of these boards, and then we can spend some time together. We can play another game. I need you to get back in the box now, though, because I've got to cut them out on our front lawn. It won't take me but a few minutes, I promise."

Anita got back into the stifling hot box and closed her eyes as he swung the doors shut and latched her in. The mole unlocked the securely bolted front door and slipped outside. He immediately started working up a sweat in the afternoon heat. He had not been working long when a woman came by delivering Foxxy Shopper fliers. She delivered the papers monthly to every residence in that area. The woman looked at him as she handed him the paper. "Hello. What're you building there?"

The mole hated making casual talk with strangers, but he humored her. "I'm opening up my own used bookstore from the house here. I'm building the bookshelves for all my books. You'll have to come check it out when it opens soon."

"Good luck with that," she said cheerfully. "I come by here every month, so I just might stop in to see what you have." She walked on to the next house and called over her shoulder to him, "See you around."

"Yeah. See ya."

The conversation gave the mole hope that people would come to his business, but it also scared him: he still felt unprepared to keep his girl hidden. He was not sure that he could fully trust her yet. He had not felt the need to threaten her lately; in fact, he had been feeling more confident that she was falling in love with him and wanted to stick around. But he decided that he needed to let her know who was boss just one more time. He would do it before they sat down to play the game together.

The mole finished up outside and carried the pieces of plywood inside, leaving the mess out in the yard. He did not even consider tidying it up. He let the girl out of the box and ordered her to read a book on the couch while he put the last few pieces of plywood together. Anita had immediately noticed that another one of his mood swings had come over the mole. He was no longer Mr. Cheerful. *Oh great! What did I do now?* she thought.

Anita was sitting, reading another suspense novel on the couch as she was told to do, when suddenly the mole came up behind her and put her in a choke hold. He had her pinned down and spoke in a pressured, agitated tone right into her ear, "I don't mean to scare you, but I just want you to understand that this is a serious situation, and I will hurt you badly if you ever try to leave me." He placed one of the broken boards he had removed from the wall during the renovation in front of Anita's alarmed face. The old board had nails poking out of it. "I could use this as a torture board, you know?" he warned her. The mole let one of the nails graze her throat as he eased his grip on her neck.

Anita gasped for air. "Where is all of this coming from? I'm not trying to escape. I've done everything you've asked of me."

"I know that you have, hon," he said patiently. "I just wanted to make sure you still knew not to mess around at all. Pretty soon we're going to have lots of people in and out of the house, buying my books, and I'll kill you if you ever try to alert one of my customers." The mole stood up and came around the couch to sit down beside Anita. He squeezed her shoulder and said, "I just have to keep you on your toes is all. I know you're a good girl. That's why I chose you."

The mole kissed the top of Anita's head and went back to building the bookshelves like nothing had ever happened. He was even whistling the tune to "My Heart Will Go On" by Celine Dion. He had mentioned to Anita that he loved the movie *Titanic* and felt like he would be heroic like the character, Jack, if he were ever put in those dire circumstances. He told her that he knew how Jack must have felt being looked down upon by socialites and that he had often felt like Jack did while trying to conform to society's standards.

The mole had mentioned that he had never truly fit in anywhere before and felt resentful and hateful because of the rejection. He had also told Anita that he was fond of the love story between Jack and Rose. It had made the mole yearn for a love like that, where he felt one with a woman. He was growing more and more hopeful that he had found that love with Anita.

Threatening her had obviously made the mole feel at ease again, and he cheered up instantly. He felt the power and control surging back into him, like pure adrenaline flowing through his veins. Anita, on the other hand, was still reeling from her captor's latest brutality against her. Just when she had started feeling slightly safer, he had to put the fear of death in her again. She tried to turn her attention back to her book but was too on edge, terrified that he might return and actually torture her with that board just for the pure fun of it. He was 100 percent insane, and she was trapped with him in his messed-up sense of reality for another long day. Anita dreaded what was to come next.

CHAPTER 41

Wednesday afternoon brought the police investigation some promising clues. Jack received an urgent phone call from Deputy Don Howell that afternoon. Don informed Jack that a homeowner in the Indian Heights subdivision had called in to complain about a blue Buick that had been sitting in the court in front of his home for days. Somehow, the guy had not heard about Anita's disappearance or that the police had been searching for the car all week. Don confirmed that it was Anita's 1990 Buick vehicle.

Excited by the news, Jack ordered Don and his crew not to touch anything until he could get there. As he was driving to the location in his squad car, Jack made a call to the Indiana State Police, asking for a technician to meet him at the scene. Using the white powder technique, Danny Manns, a crime scene technician, scoured the vehicle for any prints that could ultimately be used as evidence. It soon became clear that the suspect must have been wearing gloves and had wiped the car clean before disposing of it.

Danny was about to finish up when he yelled out to Jack, "Wait a minute. I think I found something. It's on the inside of the front driver's side window. It looks to me like the outline of an elbow or something." An elbow print had never been considered as evidence in an investigation before, only fingerprints. But they decided to send the elbow print to the Indiana State Police Laboratory in Fort Wayne to see if the lab could take on the challenge of linking it to a specific suspect. Of course, they would start by getting an inked elbow impression of Anita's boyfriend, Scott, since they already knew where to locate him. They would have to find Mr. Steele to get his inked impression as well. They hoped that the print would match one of their two suspects to use as evidence if the case ever made it to court.

After Danny Manns left for the lab, Jack took on the task of searching the entire vehicle and its contents. Inside the trunk, Jack found the red robe that Anita's mother had told them was missing from their home. It was apparently her favorite robe, one that her mother had given to her as a present. Jack also found cut electrical ties in the trunk. He figured out in his head that it was only about a five to ten minute walk from the Steele residence to the court where Anita's car had been abandoned. The suspect could have easily disposed of the vehicle and walked back to the house unseen. Jack allowed the other deputies that had arrived on the scene to complete the rest of the search while he made phone calls to the two FBI profilers. He needed some sound advice as to what to think about the newest evidence.

Jack called Todd McCain first and reached him on the third ring. "This is Todd."

"Hey, Todd," Jack exclaimed. "We found Anita's car." He quickly ran through all the evidence they had just uncovered. "What does all this say to you, Todd?"

Todd took a few moments before he responded, "Well, all the evidence you found in the vehicle is indicative to me that Anita was still alive when she was taken out of the vehicle. It also suggests to me that her captor took her with him to a designated site."

Jack agreed and added, "After reviewing the suspect's recent phone and credit card records, we determined that he more than likely relocated somewhere near the vicinity of La Crosse, Wisconsin. I feel like we need to get a state police aircraft to get over to La Crosse and find our guy as soon as possible. What do you think?"

Todd chuckled and replied, "I don't think anyone's going to be able to stop you from going, are they? You do know that it's typical for you to turn this investigation over to the FBI now, since you'll be crossing state lines. Even if you can convince the state to provide you with an aircraft to get over to Wisconsin, you'll still run into some turf issues with the La Crosse police. They're not going to like you coming over and stepping on their toes to complete this investigation. I just want to make sure you're aware of all the red tape you'll have to overcome."

"I'm fully aware of the battle that lies ahead," Jack responded confidently, "but our team has made it this far, and we refuse to hand the case over now. We have to keep going until we find Anita, dead or alive. We're committed to bringing her home."

Todd was amazed at Jack's determination to crack this case. "I have to tell you the only case that I've ever worked on where the victim was still alive after this many days of captivity was

Larry Bird's ex-wife's success story. She was rescued after a serial rapist/killer abducted her. There's only about a 1 percent chance that Anita is still alive, so don't get your hopes up too high. Well, can you keep me posted once you get there?"

"I will. I'm still going to need your expertise once we find the suspect's location. I'll call you soon. Thanks, Todd. Bye."

Next, Jack called the Quantico FBI profiler Bob Thorton to get his advice as well as to ask him for any contacts he may have over in La Crosse. Jack filled Bob in on the discovery of Anita's vehicle and the evidence they had found inside it. Jack also informed him that his investigative team had narrowed their prime suspect's location down to a radius near La Crosse, Wisconsin. Bob paused and then commented, "I commend you on all the hard work you and your team have done on this case, but I urge you to hand the case over to the FBI now. The evidence in the car suggests to me that Anita was still alive when she was taken to the location in Wisconsin. We need to get over there and establish a command post to find the suspect immediately. Time is crucial right now."

Jack sighed into the receiver, "I hear what you're saying and fully respect your advice, but I believe our team can conduct this investigation by working with the La Crosse police and their local FBI agency. We're ready to jump over any hurdles involved. We need to see this case through to the end, and we'll bring Anita back home to her family, one way or another. Do you have any contacts we could call in La Crosse?"

"Sure. Can you hold for a few minutes while I find that information for you?"

"Yes." Jack was able to get the numbers for the head of the City of La Crosse Police Department and the FBI agent located in La Crosse. He thanked Bob profusely and promised that he would call him if he needed the FBI to swoop in to provide the force and resources needed to locate and apprehend this sexual predator.

Now Jack just needed to speak with his boss, who he knew was taking all the heat for Jack's team choices and his unwillingness to hand the case over to the FBI. Since finding the vehicle, the press had been all over the police to give the media and public some answers. He was aware that Anita's family was devastated that they had found Anita's car but that she was still missing. The family had hoped that, by finding the car, the officers would have found Anita nearby. No such luck. Jack's main motive for meeting with his boss, Tim, was to convince him to allow the Kokomo team to continue the investigation across state lines. He also needed to ask Tim for his assistance in securing a state police aircraft so the team could fly out to La Crosse as early as this evening if at all possible.

Jack met with Tim at the station and could tell by Tim's ragged appearance that he was feeling the pressure. "I want to thank you for trusting my judgment in this case and backing me up. I realize the heat's on you to provide the media with information right now, but we still have to claim that we have no new leads right now. We're closing in on the suspect, and if he gets a tip that we're onto him, we have no doubt he'll kill Anita and run. We can't risk that, so if you can just stick with me a little longer, I promise to do everything within my power to find her. We owe it to her family and to our community to return her home."

Tim sank down into the conference room chair, leaned back, and sighed in frustration. "You know I'll back you up on this. I feel like you have the determination, skills, and man-power to follow through with cracking this case. I can only do this for so long, though, Jack. Soon, it'll be out of my hands, and the FBI is going to take over on their own. You need to find her within the next forty-eight hours, or it'll happen."

"Okay," Jack replied. "We have good reason to believe that our suspect has Anita in a location near La Crosse, Wisconsin. I have contact numbers for law enforcement agents there to assist us when we get there. I just need you to get me a state police aircraft that can carry the five of us over to La Crosse by this evening. Once we have that confirmed, I can start making calls to La Crosse to let them know we're on our way."

"Okay. Just don't let me down, Jack. Call in the FBI if you guys get over there and feel like you need more manpower. Promise me that."

Jack did not hesitate. "I promise. I don't have a problem doing that if needed. I just believe my team is equipped to com-plete this investigation without arousing the media's attention at the same time. My guys are all highly invested in receiving a positive outcome in this case."

Within minutes, Tim had given Jack the phone number for the Indiana State Police superintendant's direct line. Jack made his sales pitch to the initially skeptical Jake Miller and was able to miraculously secure an aircraft that would get the team to La Crosse by 8:20 that evening. Jack thanked Jake profusely for all of his help and then turned to look at Tim, who was again shaking his head in amazement at Jack's success.

Jack sat back in the conference room chair to ponder his thoughts after Tim had left the station. He was used to all the noises and distractions around him that filled the station's corridors. The entire staff felt the need to pop their heads in to give Jack an encouraging nod or a kind word to let him know that they were all there for him if needed. They could all see the strain that this case was putting on him—his once-polished appearance was now disheveled. He sported an almost full-grown beard by now and just did not have the time to care or even look at himself in the mirror.

Jack was completely in the zone now and could see nothing else besides the facts of the case. He could easily block out the multiple staff interruptions. He let his mind wander, briefly thinking of his fear that their suspect was not even in the Wisconsin area anymore. It could have been just a one-time trip there, in which case Anita could be anywhere. Jack knew that they could be on a wild-goose chase, but they had to at least get over to La Crosse and see if they could find any further leads. He felt like he personally owed it to Anita and her family. Again, Anita's picture on the board came into view, and he felt her eyes pleading with him to rescue her soon. Jack shook himself out of his thoughts and picked up the phone again to call his wife.

He informed her of their plan to fly to Wisconsin to set up a command post to search for the red truck. "I love you, honey," Dorothy told Jack. "Please be careful and make sure you stop to eat and sleep some. I do worry about you. Do what you have to do, and I'll take care of the house. The kids both wanted me to tell you they love you and that they will hopefully see you on the Fourth for our cookout."

Jack sighed, "I'll do my very best to get home by then. Try not to worry about me. I'll call you soon and keep you posted. Say some prayers tonight that we find Anita alive soon."

Dorothy assured Jack that she and the entire community were already praying for that.

After hanging up with his wife, Jack picked up the phone once again to notify the La Crosse authorities and local FBI agents of his team's upcoming arrival. He was hopeful that he could get their cooperation in the matter but was not naïve enough to think that they would be rolling out a welcoming mat for them. He was ready to knock down any reservations they might hold so they could all get down to the overwhelming task of finding Anita's captor among a population of around 65,000 residents.

Jack dialed the number that Bob Thorton had supplied him with earlier. He reached the voicemail of a Sergeant Dave Lipinski of the City of La Crosse Police Department and had to leave a message. Jack said he was calling about the Wooldridge abduction case and included that his investigative team had reason to believe that the abductor and the victim may possibly be in the La Crosse area. He added that his team would be flying in from Kokomo and would arrive this evening around 8:20 p.m. Jack asked the officer to return his phone call, so they could meet at landing and hold a debriefing meeting about the case details.

Jack then called the La Crosse senior resident FBI agent, John Helton, to notify him of his team's arrival and to attempt to get their department on board as well. To Jack's surprise, John picked up the phone and was willing to hear Jack out.

"This is Captain Jack Roberts from the Kokomo Sheriff's Department in Kokomo, Indiana. I'm leading an investigative team in an abduction case here in Kokomo. We have reason to believe that the victim's captor took her to La Crosse or the surrounding area and that they could still be there now. I tried to contact the La Crosse police but have not heard back from them yet. Bob Thorton, an FBI profiler at Quantico, supplied me with your contact information for assistance on this case. I know that this isn't standard practice, but my team of five investigators is flying to La Crosse this evening to attempt to find the victim. If you could notify the La Crosse police and other appropriate agencies that a kidnapping investigation is heading your way, I would greatly appreciate your help."

Agent Helton sat back in his chair, bewildered by this sudden phone call.

"You don't have any clear proof that the suspect's even in our area—you could be on a wild-goose chase here. Typically, I'd tell you this isn't a good idea since you have no jurisdiction, authority, or knowledge of the area here. But you sound so determined. Anyone with that much confidence at least deserves to be heard, so I guess I'll tell the La Crosse police officers to pick you up at the airport and bring your team to my office for a debriefing meeting this evening. This kind of case doesn't happen often in this area, so I don't want the media alerted about this yet. The word would spread to the public like wildfire and could create panic among our local residents. Until we have more evidence, they don't need to be alarmed unnecessarily."

"I understand fully. I appreciate your cooperation and look forward to meeting with you." Jack hung up the receiver and felt like he had just won the lottery. The fact that the FBI agent had been so receptive to Jack and his team coming over was absolutely amazing. He was floored that once again a door had been opened that he had thought would be a huge obstacle. Jack got down on his knees and prayed, "Thank you, Lord, for breaking down barriers and allowing your will to be done. Please help our team to humble ourselves and work diligently to bring Anita home alive. Please let the Holy Spirit guide and direct us in this investigation and give us the wisdom and insights needed to find her. Amen."

Jack could feel the peace in his heart and sensed that they were closer than ever to finding their needle in the haystack. He stood up and started calling the rest of his team members to notify them that they had a flight to catch. He then got himself ready for their departure: he packed lightly, knowing that he would more than likely wear the same street clothes for days and would have little time for grooming himself.

CHAPTER 42

It was going on two thirty in the afternoon by the time the mole finished up on the bookshelves. As usual, he just left his mess all over the floor. But he was careful to put away the hammer, saw, and hatchet, so they could not be used as weapons against him by his girl. He walked back into the living room and found Anita right where he had left her on the couch, reading one of his many books. "I know I promised you a game," he said casually, "but I'm starving. I need to go out and get some food. I'll pick you up some of that gum you like so much while I'm out. You have to get back in the box for just a little bit while I'm gone. Okay?"

Anita nodded her head yes. She walked into the bedroom and climbed back into her cramped box for what seemed like the millionth time that day. She heard the front door slam over the noise of the TV blaring in the next room.

Again, she was just thankful that he had not asked her for sex at all yet today. The evening hours were rapidly approaching, though, and she prayed that her luck would continue into the night. Anita heard a GAP commercial come on the TV from the next room, and she could picture in her mind the khaki-clad young teens jitterbugging on the screen. Anita had hated those commercials; they were played over and over again between programs. It irritated her even more now that she was stuck in this box and had to hear the joyful music play on. It reminded Anita that life was going on without her and that she was missing out on all the fun and festivities back home with the upcoming holiday weekend and her friend's wedding.

Anita missed everyone so much. She even missed the once-irritating sound of the dog next door that seemed to continuously bark on and on. She missed being busy and active. She could not stand being confined inside this house, and even worse inside this dark box. Anita felt so far away from everything that she once had known in her life to be her peaceful routine.

Anita had to remind herself that God would get her out of this predicament on his own time. She repeated Ephesians 6:10 over and over for strength and hope. She mouthed the words, "Finally, my brethren, be strong in the LORD, and in the power of his might." She felt stronger with every syllable she spoke.

The mole was ordering food from a nearby Taco Bell in the drive-through lane. He purchased five taco supremes with hot sauce and an order of nachos to go. He had brought a Mountain Dew from the house to wash it all down. He pulled over, parked, and had eaten it all within minutes. Hot sauce covered the front of his shirt, and he wiped his greasy mouth off with the back of his hand. He belched loudly and drove over to the nearest gas station for the girl's Juicy Fruit. *She should appreci-ate how considerate a boyfriend I am!* he thought. *Not many guys would be so thoughtful. I haven't even bugged her to have sex. She definitely owes me! I'll collect later. She probably wants it again by now. I did her so good last time and all.*

The mole sped his old truck with the topper on back to-ward the house on Clinton Street. He sang along to the radio, crooning the words to Elton John's hit, "Candle in the Wind." He knew that it was a song to pay tribute to that slut Mari-lyn Monroe, who had overdosed on pills, but he liked the song nonetheless. Marilyn reminded him too much of his pill-pop-ping mother; Marilyn had used her female charms to seduce men into getting whatever she wanted.

The mole was pulling up to the tiny house as the song ended. He decided to park the truck in the alley right next to the side of the house instead of out on the street where he typi-cally parked it.

The mole eagerly went inside the house and let Anita out of her confined quarters, handing her the gum. "Thanks," she said. "My mouth is so dry. Can I have some water with it?"

"I guess," he said with exasperation. "Man, you just want and want, don't you? All you girls are alike. Nothing's ever good enough."

Anita smelled the rank odor of tacos on his breath as he spoke and noticed the grease stains running all the way down his white shirt. The mole was a mess but did not seem to care at all. He brought her out a glass of water and began setting up the game Survivor.

It was an old board game that the mole had played with his siblings to kill time while they were isolated in their attic room when their father was home. Anita had never played the old game before, but she soon found out that the object of the game was to evacuate people from your team from an island before your opponent does. You had to place a whale marker on the board occasionally, and the mole thought that it was hilarious when he placed one on and exclaimed, "We're just having a whale of a time, aren't we?" Anita thought to herself, *You are such an idiot!* But she humored her captor by laughing loudly at his joke. She let him win again to keep his spirits up. The game took over an hour, and she was bored to death.

The mole triumphantly hopped to his feet, announcing, "You know the drill. Loser picks up!" Anita was used to picking up after him. She was almost done with the task when he suggested, "Let's watch one of the tapes I brought. I recorded some episodes of *Friends*. I know you probably love that show since most girls do." The mole could not stand that rich bitch Rachel, but he was drawn to the free-spirited Phoebe. He also kind of enjoyed Ross's dry humor and could identify with his awkwardness around women. He had secretly watched the sitcom since it began and imagined what it would be like to have a group of friends to hang out with. Anita was just happy that the mole wanted to engage in any activity other than sex. She therefore said rather eagerly, "Yeah! I love that show. Let's watch it!"

The mole popped the tape into the VCR and fast forwarded to the episode he liked the most, in which the spoiled brat Rachel decides to move in with Monica after she dumped her rich fiancé at the altar. The mole loved to watch Rachel's pain. He felt no sympathy for her at all and felt deep satisfaction in her character's misery. They watched several hours of the tape before he shut it off, announcing that he was starving again.

Anita had no appetite and turned down his offer to make her some food. "Suit yourself," he said. "That's just more for me."

The mole walked into the kitchen to make a large frozen pizza and ate the whole thing by himself. It was a supreme pizza, loaded with all the toppings. He grossed her out by eating with his mouth open: the sounds of his chewing made her sick to her stomach. Anita avoided looking at him and instead picked at the nail polish on her fingernails. It was starting to all chip off. She tried to focus on the bright pink polish she had applied to her short, manicured nails Wednesday night before going out with her friends.

Anita stared at the filigree bracelet she still was wearing, the one her boyfriend had bought her just a few weeks ago. It comforted her some to have something with her from home. She rubbed it until she could almost feel her boyfriend's touch on her dry skin.

When the mole finished his meal, he abruptly told Anita he had to go back out to call his mother and retrieve his messages since the damn phone company still had not hooked up their phone. It was a little after eight in the evening and was starting to grow dark. Anita was instantly afraid that he would want to have sex with her before he put her back in the box for the night. She was surprised when he led her into the bedroom and ordered her back into the box instead. "Good night," he said. "See you in the morning. Get some beauty sleep. We have a long day tomorrow."

The mole latched her in, and she breathed a long sigh of relief. But the mole had a change of heart. He felt like he at least deserved something in return for being so nice and understanding the last few days. He pulled the box back open. "Get back up," he ordered, "and take your shirt off, so I can see some tits." Overcome with fear, Anita did as she was told. The mole started fondling her breasts roughly. When he was satisfied, he said, "Okay, you can put your shirt back on and go to sleep now. I have to go." He locked her back in and left the house.

Anita was relieved that he had not violated her any further, but it hurt so badly emotionally; she felt degraded and humiliated once again. She could not stand being told what to do anymore. Her breasts were throbbing from the pain of him pulling on and pinching them to get himself excited. Filled with absolute hatred, she beat on the top of the box in anger and frustration until she was completely worn out from exhaustion and lack of oxygen. Anita tried to take in deep breaths to calm herself down and regulate her heartbeat and breathing. It took her several minutes, but she finally was able to say a quick prayer for her family and that she would be rescued soon. She fell into a deep sleep until the next dreadful morning.

CHAPTER 43

The five Kokomo investigators all showed up at the small airfield to board the tiny six-passenger Indiana State Police aircraft
by six o'clock Wednesday evening. It was not ideal conditions
for flying; it was extremely windy and storms were still passing
through the area sporadically. Yet God came through for them
once again, and they were able to get clearance to take off on
time. Before the plane left, Jack stood up in the narrow aisle to
give a pep talk to the team. All the men were already high on
adrenaline, despite being sleep deprived from the past week.
They were all pumped up and ready for this challenge.

It had been hard for Detective Ron Eastwood to leave his
wife and young daughter, but he knew he had to make sacrifices
to bring Anita home. His ten-year-old daughter, Laura, had
looked up at her dad with loving eyes full of tears when he was
leaving and said to him, "Be careful, Dad. I love you. I know
you'll be able to save that girl. You'll always be my hero." Her
words had melted his weary heart and had given him even more
determination to make his daughter proud. Ron was now able

to completely focus on the mission at hand. He quickly turned his attention back to Jack.

Jack acted like the team's coach before a big playoff game. "Okay, guys," he announced in a booming voice, "we're about to take off for La Crosse. Some are saying that we're on a wild-goose chase, but I believe they're wrong. It'd be really easy for us to just hand this case over to the FBI now, but I know we're more invested in bringing Anita home.

"If we can earn the respect and trust of the law enforcement in Wisconsin, we'll greatly increase our chances of success on this case. Our sole mission here is to find Anita and bring her back home to her family. We can't lose sight of that goal for even a second. This case could make or break our careers, guys. We have to stick together, work as a team, and leave our egos at the door. Initially, we might face a great deal of resistance from the officers and agents there, but we won't let that deter us! Now, are we all in this together?"

All five of the dedicated Kokomo offficers put their hands in to show team unity and yelled in unison, "Let's go get Anita!" Jack said a quick prayer for the team's safety and success in bringing Anita home before the plane took off. The men settled into their seats and put their safety harnesses on. They were all quite talkative and in high spirits during the two-hour flight, except for one. Jack had noticed even during his pep talk that Chuck Wilson, typically the most macho one of the group, had seemed distracted and looked a little pale.

Jack looked over at Chuck now and noticed that his enormous hand seemed to be gripping his cell phone so hard that his knuckles were white. Chuck kept wiping sweat off his forehead and flipping his phone open every few seconds. His leg was shaking; he could not seem to sit still. Jack called over to Chuck from across the aisle, "You okay over there, Chuck? Look's like you've got a hot date or something. You expecting a phone call?" All the other guys chuckled at the joke and looked over at Chuck.

"I'll just be happy to get off this damn plane and on the ground again," Chuck responded.

Deputy Major Phil Lyons was sitting next to Jack and whispered to him, "Yeah. I didn't know if Chuck was even going to agree to fly with us. He's terrified of flying...has some kind of phobia about it. He checks his cell phone over and over to look at the time. You told him that we would be landing by 8:20 p.m., and he's counting down the minutes."

Jack could not believe the irony in the fact that Chuck was known as the team bodyguard, and now he was so visibly scared. But Jack had to give him credit for facing his biggest fear in order to complete their mission. He couldn't have asked for a more dedicated team member. Still, despite his respect for Chuck, he and the other guys would never let him live this down. Seeing this brave officer so frightened was just too classic; they had to give him a hard time. Chuck took it all in good stride. He knew he must look ridiculous, but he could not help it.

The plane went through a few patches of heavy rain but was able to land at Colgan airfield in La Crosse at approximately eight thirty that evening. They were met on the ground by three La Crosse police officers, Sergeant Dave Lipinski, Captain Jim Smith, and Investigator Larry McQuiston. The Wisconsin FBI office senior resident, John Helton, and Roger Wall, an FBI agent sent over from Quantico by Bob Thorton, were also there to greet the out-of-town Kokomo officers. The men shook hands and made quick introductions before the talk became serious. Jack could sense that the La Crosse police officers were highly skeptical of them, possibly even angry that they had gone over their heads and gotten clearance from John Helton to come over to their territory.

Jack tried to clear the air. "We really don't mean to step on any toes here, guys. We just strongly believe that our prime suspect and the Kokomo female victim are close by in your area. We'd appreciate any help you can offer us in locating the suspect or his red Ford Ranger."

"You boys do understand that you're on our turf now, and we expect you to follow Wisconsin laws while you're here. We can provide you with backup and knowledge of the area, but you have no authority here," Sergeant Dave Lipinski, a large, intimidating man in his fifties, responded in a gruff tone. "You need to call us before any arrests are made, and a search warrant has to be granted before you inspect any home or vehicle. As long as you follow these rules, we'll support you 100 percent. If you cross our rules, we'll send you back to Indiana, and the FBI and our team will take over. Can you agree to this?"

Jack and his other four team members all quickly agreed to their rules. "We appreciate all your support," Jack added. "We won't let you guys down."

The men piled into several squad cars and headed over to the City of La Crosse Police Department for a debriefing meeting. Jack was able to give the men more in-depth information regarding the abduction investigation that had led them to La Crosse. The meeting lasted until almost midnight. The La Crosse team assumed that the Kokomo investigators would be ready to get to their hotels for some sleep, but to their surprise, the eager officers asked the Wisconsin team to drive them around separately to local motels, apartments, and bars. They wanted to ask local residents if they had seen anyone new around that looked like the pictures of Anita and their suspect. They also wanted to find Mr. Steele's 1991 red Ford Ranger pickup truck with the Indiana registration number 784-214B in any of those areas.

The men scoured the entire town of La Crosse, as well as the surrounding city of Onalaska, until they were ready to fall over from exhaustion around four in the morning. They had not been successful, but Captain Curtis Hoover of the Kokomo Police Department and Investigator Chuck Wilson had made some ground. They had already built a rapport with local residents and felt confident that, if the suspect came into town, they would receive a report from someone in the community. Curtis and Chuck both had a knack for hitting the streets and finding useful contacts that could provide them with tips later on. These skills were valuable on a case like this one, where they could not post pictures of the suspect or alert him in any way that they were onto him. The men decided to reconvene the next morning at John Helton's FBI office for an additional debriefing and delegation of assignments. Jack went to bed in an unfamiliar hotel room that night, discouraged by the lack of leads but still determined to find Anita. They all just needed to get some sleep first.

CHAPTER 44

The mole drove his truck to the gas station to use the payphone once again. He listened to his incoming messages first. He only had one message from his mother. "Tom, this is your mother again. I wanted to let you know that some guy came over today askin' how much you wanted for your old beater. I told him seven hundred, and he thought that was too high, but he said he'd bring his buddy by tomorrow to check the car out and that he might be willing to buy it if it all checks out okay. If I don't hear from you soon, and it sells, I'm takin' part of the money for doin' all the work you should have done on your own. I'm sick of you takin' advantage of me all the time. Anyway, call me soon and let me know your address so I can forward your mail there and send you part of the money if the car sells. I don't think you're really gonna come back and get the rest of your junk, so I'll have to just send it to you when I can. Call me back soon. Bye."

That damn bitch! She's not getting a dime of that money! I'll kill her if she even touches it. He furiously slammed the phone receiver down. He took some deep breaths, in and out, before he called his mother back; he knew that if he lost it on her, she might not sell the car for him. The mole needed that money. He only had a little under two thousand dollars left to live on and start up his business. He carried the money on him at all times. He was paranoid that someone might rob the house and take it all from him. He could not allow that to happen. He picked the receiver back up and called his mother collect. "Ma, it's me, Tom. I wish you'd stop doubting that I'm coming back next week for my stuff. Just sell the damn car and send me all of the money in the mail this week if the guy buys it. Okay?"

His mother coughed into the phone and then took a drag from her cigarette. He could hear her exhaling the smoke into the receiver. "Tom, I wasn't born yesterday. I know you're not comin' back, but I guess I can send you the money if it sells. I can't promise that it's gonna sell for what you want, though. I think you should take whatever he offers just to get the pile of junk off my property."

The mole took another deep breath, exhaled, and respond-ed to his mother calmly, "Fine. Just don't screw me over. I need the money for my bookstore. You don't want me to fail and have to come live with you again, do you?"

"No! You're way too old to still be living with your mom. Now, give me the stinkin' address already."

"You have a pen ready?"

"I'm writin' it on this dry-erase board by the fridge. The one ya left me a message on, askin' me to get that big box off the porch. As if I need to be liftin' that! Okay, go ahead."

The mole never had been able to have a good relationship with his mother, but he felt certain that she would protect him if the authorities ever showed up asking about him: she would never give his address to those pigs, so he gave it to her without any reservations. "It's 812 Clinton Street, La Crosse, Wisconsin. The zip code is 54603. Send me the money as soon as you get it." They briefly talked more about the car, and then the mole hung up the phone, relieved to be done talking with her.

As the mole drove back to Clinton Street, he looked up at the dark night sky and was amazed at the beauty of the moon. It was a full moon tonight, and the light from the moon illuminated the sky with a bright hue. A full moon had always made him feel alive and invincible. His mind, as though in a state of mania, began to race, thinking of all the things he wanted to accomplish and experience. He turned the truck around and headed toward the river banks. He got out of his car and walked over to the edge of the bank. One wrong move and he could fall into the river, but he did not care at the moment. The water would have made him feel even more alive and refreshed. The mole briefly considered jumping in and swimming until he tired out; it would help him release all his pent up frustration and newfound energy, but he decided against it.

Instead, he stood at the edge of the river bank, lifting his arms up to the sky and howling loudly at the moon. It was almost as if he were calling to his people on the moon. He believed that, somewhere, there must be someone who could understand him, and he would finally fit in. On this particular night, the mole was mentally certifiable with the full moon lighting up his husky frame and his open mouth as he shouted into the distance. Unfortunately, no one was around to notice him or to alert the authorities. When he was too hoarse to howl any longer, he got back into his red Ford Ranger and headed back home to get some rest on the couch cushions he had set up beside the box. He could hardly wait until tomorrow morning when he could finally have his way with his girl again. In his mind, he had waited long enough for her to recover. Her break was over for good.

The mole had no idea that five Kokomo investigators had just hit La Crosse soil as he was howling into the night air. The police spent the rest of the night searching for the mole's red truck that would be parked in the alley beside his house again.

THURSDAY, JULY 2, 1998

CHAPTER 45

The mole was up by ten o'clock Thursday morning, feeling refreshed and optimistic about his progress on the bookshelves. He had returned the chainsaw to the hardware store as soon as they had opened up for business and had gotten a few more supplies to finish up his work. He eagerly went over to the box on the floor and opened it. Anita was wide awake and ready to get out, stretch, and go to the bathroom. She had waited in agony for several hours for him to let her out. "Good morning," the mole greeted his victim. "Want any breakfast?"

"No thanks. Just a drink after I use the bathroom."

The mole helped her up. "I'm going to let you go down by yourself today, but if you're not back up here in five minutes, I'll come down to find you."

Anita was shocked that he was giving her this privilege. It was a good sign: he was beginning to let his guard down some. She went down to the toilet, relieved to have some privacy for once. When she came back up, he handed her a glass of tap water. "You really should eat something," he said, but she declined his offer and sat on the couch to drink her water.

As usual, the mole scarfed down his cereal and toast quickly. He sat down beside Anita when he finished. He hadn't had sex with her in two whole days, and he felt like he had given her plenty of time to recover. It was time for her to fulfill his needs again. "Take your clothes off," he said gruffly.

Inside, Anita was crying, but she did what he asked of her. He took his clothes off too and started masturbating next to her. He forced her to touch herself as well. When he was hard, he forced himself inside her there on the couch. He made her sit on top of him and ride him like he had seen the whores do in all of his porno tapes. With the fantasies playing out in his head, he was able to climax quicker this time. "Oh yeah!" he moaned. "Ride me, baby! I'm coming!" He hugged her for the first time, ordering, "Tell me you love me, baby." When she hesitated, he pulled her hair back. "Say it! I want to hear how good that was for you and how much you love me."

The words that came out of her mouth were the hardest ones that Anita would ever have to speak. "I love you, Tom," she said through gritted teeth. "You really know how to please me."

Anita could not wait for him to let her get off his lap and away from him. Her captor sickened her, and she had never told such a blatant lie to someone in all her life. It did not matter to the mole whether she was lying or not. Those words were all that he needed to hear to confirm to himself his superiority. *I knew if I just gave her time, she would want me and grow to love me. Who wouldn't?* He ignored the fact that he had instead forced this girl to have sex with him and then tell him that she loved him. In his deranged mind, Anita wanted all of this and had meant those words. She had just needed a little prodding to help her express her feelings. He appeared to be satisfied and pushed her off his lap to get his day started.

"Okay. Time for you to get back in your box now. I need a shower. Or you could take one with me. It's your choice."

Anita cringed at the idea of being near his naked body. "No," she quickly said. "You go ahead. I'll just take a little nap." She climbed back into her dark, cramped quarters and watched as he shut the doors. She heard him slide the wooden dowel through the door handles, locking her in. She was wide awake. The hum of the fan and the TV were muffled from within the box. She could hear every beat of her own thumping heart and every labored breath. The fear felt heavy on her chest, like she was trapped under debris of some sort. Anita realized with a heavy heart that she had now been gone over a week and that she would probably not make it back home in time to see her best friend's wedding.

She had often fantasized that she would be home in time for the event, and it had kept her going. But despite her best efforts, she was beginning to lose hope. Tears of anger, frustration, and deep sadness began to stream down her once-radiant face. Anita had known deep down that he would rape her again, but the two days of reprieve had been such a luxury that the rape this morning was even harder for her to deal with.

CHAPTER 46

The Kokomo law enforcement officers that had remained in town knew that they needed to make a second attempt to talk to Tom Steele's mother. They all wanted to see Anita brought safely home, but the upcoming Fourth of July weekend made the officers long to spend time with their own families as well. They all knew it was out of the question to leave town while working on such an important case, and their hopes of getting answers from Tom Steele's mother were slowly dwindling.

Nonetheless, Detective Rick Monroe, Sergeant Doug Kellar, and Lieutenant Bruce Wright from the Kokomo Police Department Special Investigation Unit found themselves at the Steele residence at 11:05 a.m. Lieutenant Wright would stay hidden in the unmarked white van the men had driven over and parked at the end of the Steeles' long driveway. Rick and Sergeant Kellar would get inside the home to talk to Daphne Steele about buying her son's 1981 Datsun, which was sitting out in the front yard. They were hopeful that she had spoken to her son since the initial contact yesterday and that he had told her where he was now living in Wisconsin. Still, they were doubtful that they would get a break like that on this particular day.

Rick and Kellar were both wired, the audio surveillance devices taped under their shirts to record the conversation. They started testing it out while in the vehicle to make sure that it was working.

"You copy me on four? Hold up four fingers," Kellar said.

"Yeah, we got ya, Kellar," Rick replied.

"All right. Did you hear me fart?"

"No."

"I didn't. That's the reason I wondered."

"Oh, real funny. Do you hear that engine noise?"

"Yep. Hey, Rick, didn't you say your boy's in town for the week?"

"Yep. Oh shit. I was supposed to call him back this morning. God, I've got too many things going on in one morning!"

"You're right about that. I don't see how you're gonna end up in Kentucky this weekend."

"I won't. Kentucky ain't gonna happen."

"I'm not gonna end up at the lake either."

Rick laughed.

"That's not gonna happen, is it?"

"No, Kellar. Ah shit, you were just dreaming."

"Well, then, I'm just gonna sit at this place the rest of the day."

"If you could just sit out here till I can get back from doing what I gotta do this evening."

"Sure, whatever you need, Rick. Just return the favor sometime."

"I will. Damn, I was lookin' forward to going down to Kentucky. Now we gotta put on our good mood faces and go say hi to this old lady. It'd be real nice if that red truck turned into her driveway right about now, huh?"

"We're not that lucky. We're gonna try to give her, what, six hundred total for the car? Three hundred now and three hundred when we pick the title up?"

"No. I'm gonna try to talk her into lowering the price. That thing ain't worth it, Kellar."

"What are you gonna try to get her down to?"

"I'll just ask her what she'll take. If she doesn't give me a suggestion, I'll probably just throw out a number."

"Just go from there?"

"Yeah. We need to feel her out. I mean, it ain't our money, but good Lord, I hate to let her rip us off."

"She's home, I think."

"Here we go, boys. Remember, Kellar, my name is Eric Tanner."

"Okay. Here we go."

Rick and Kellar exited the vehicle and walked cautiously up to the suspect's mother's front door. They knocked several times before they heard the woman's footsteps and her hacking cough as she descended the stairs loudly. When she swung the door open, she seemed rather irritated to have visitors. She was clearly a cynical, suspicious woman. She wore a shabby nightgown and old slippers that made a shuffling sound on the floor when she walked. Her gray hair was in a web of tangles and she had no makeup on. She took a drag off her freshly lit cigarette and deliberately blew the smoke right into the officers' faces.

"What do ya fellas want now?" she asked through a fit of coughing. "Did ya bring the money for the car? I gotta get back to watchin' my soap if ya didn't."

"Yeah," Rick replied. "We brought some money. How ya doing today?"

"Okay. Well, my son called."

"Did he?"

Lieutenant Wright sat upright when she said this. He had started to doze off slightly before this information came through the wires. "Hot damn!" he said out loud. "We just may get lucky today." He pushed the earphones firmly against his ears and sat on the edge of his seat, waiting to hear the rest.

"Tom said to tell you he didn't know whether those were the original miles or not. He assumed they were."

"Okay."

"He said he doesn't know anythin' about the mechanical part of the car. He drove it for a couple years and didn't have trouble with it. He bought a truck to drive. That's why he's selling this one."

"So he parked this car after he got the truck?" Kellar asked.

"Yeah. He said tell ya that was all he knew about it."

"Um, he…Okay. Did…is there, is he somewhere where I can talk to him right quick?" Rick pried.

"No."

"Well, I got some money with me, and I'd like to…"

Now he was speaking her language. Daphne Steele's demeanor instantly softened, and she invited the two men inside her home. She led them up the stairs and into the living room where the TV was blaring an episode of *Days of Our Lives*.

"How much you want to give for it?"

"How much would he take for it?" Rick asked.

"How much you got? I'll take it all."

"You'll take it? I bet you would! Let me…I'd like to talk to him. Is he somewhere that I can talk to him?"

311

"Well, I asked him, and he said that it was too much hassle. He's trying to get that business started, and he said the phone jacks are all messed up. He can't get to a payphone without driving across town, and he got the message I left him. He said, really, there wasn't anythin' more he could tell you about the car."

"Is he still in Wisconsin or…"

"Yeah. I got his address if you want to write to him, but it won't do you any good."

"Why don't you…why don't you give me that address, and I'll write to him. That way he can send me whatever he's got on it." Rick was trying hard to conceal his excitement. He just hoped that this address would be the real deal and that it was not a false lead. He'd run into many of those during his years on the force. Daphne Steele led them into her kitchen; she put her cigarette butt out in the overflowing ashtray sitting on the cluttered table. She put her hands on her large hips and told the men that it might take her some time to find the address. Every movement appeared to exhaust the frail woman.

"Okay. Let me find it over here by the fridge. I know I put it over here somewhere. Just give me a sec."

"Looks like somebody's getting ready to celebrate the Fourth here," Kellar said. "Are you going to have a little party?" He was fishing on whether or not her son would be visiting soon.

"No. Hell, I drink them all myself." She was referring to the several cans of beer that she had stacked along the kitchen wall and was planning on drinking later that evening.

"This the address right here?" Rick pointed to the dry-erase board on the side of her fridge as he spoke and about fell over trying to lean in to read the scribbles. It said in large print: "Dolly by back door. Please get big box off back porch."

312

That top part was unsigned but was clearly not the same cursive handwriting beneath it where Mrs. Steele had quickly written down Eric Tanner's pager number. Beneath that was the address the men had so desperately wanted to find: "812 Clinton, 54603."

"Yeah, that's where he lives now. 812 Clinton."

"What city is that in, ma'am?"

"I think he said La Crosse."

"Is that in Indiana?"

"No, Wisconsin."

"Let me write that down here," Kellar offered.

"He said to sell it to you, so how much you gonna give me today?"

"I'll give you three hundred dollars cash," Rick said.

"How 'bout four?"

"You trying to rob me? Okay. I'll split the difference with you. How about three fifty?"

"Sold. Wait here while I get the title."

"Okay. I'm still going to write him, so will he be there for a while?"

"Yeah. He moved there for good, he said. He said as soon as he got a phone he'd call me and give me his phone number too. All he has right now is stupid voicemail, so I have to leave him messages and then wait for him to call back."

"He called you from Wisconsin?"

"Yep. Collect. Probably from a pay phone."

"He called you collect?"

"Oh yeah. That's my children for you. They don't pay for anything. My son's gonna open up a bookstore. I think it's just an empty building he's got now, but he's gonna build the bookshelves and stuff for all those damn books he has. Might as well sell 'em all."

"That's cool."

"He just decided one day he wanted to open up this bookstore. My kids have wanderlust. They just come and go, come and go."

"Okay. Um, there's two hundred, three hundred fifty." Rick counted out the cash into her hand. "Taking all my hard-earned money."

"What are you gonna do, race the car?"

"Nah. I'm gonna fix it up and drive it."

"Okay. Well, as long as it's out of my hair."

"Hey, I'd like to call your son tomorrow. He'll have a phone by then, won't he?"

"Ha! He said there's phone jacks all over the place, but the guy that had the place before him doesn't know which jack he had hooked up, so they can't get his phone hooked up yet. Uh, where do I sign, boys?"

"Right there where it says seller, yeah," Kellar said.

"Did your son move there by himself?" Rick asked.

"Yeah. He's a loner, that boy."

"What'd he do in Kokomo? Maybe I know him. You said his name is Victor Steele, right?"

"His name is Victor Thomas Steele, but he goes by Tom for short. He worked for the community college as a dispatcher. Then he worked at, oh, that trucking place, IPS or RPS. He also worked for a while as an accountant at H&R Block here in town. He's done it all, but never stays with any of them for long. He works for International Resources now. He does have a voicemail account through them. That's how I leave him messages."

"Well, heck, give me that voicemail number. That way I don't have to write to him."

"Well, he won't call you back, because it's long distance. What is it you want to know from him, anyway?"

"I wanted to ask him if he'd charged the car battery recently or not. Also, just some general questions for him on how it ran for him. That's all."

"Oh. Well, he's not mechanically inclined, so he wouldn't know what to tell you."

"Well, all right then. I've got the signed title so I think we're all done here. Is this your pen?"

"Yep. I'll go out with you to get my For Sale sign."

"It sure is hot out here." As Rick and Kellar walked outside with her into the heat, they both spotted an old grill by the side of the house that looked like it had been used and then hastily abandoned. Rick handed the woman the sign off the newly purchased car and casually mentioned to her, "Looks like you had yourself a cookout." He motioned toward the grill. "It still has the blackened foil on it and everything. Looks all ready to go."

"Well, my lazy son put it out here before he left, and there it's still sitting. I don't know what the hell to do with it now. I don't even know how to start it."

"When's the last time he was here?" Kellar asked.

"A week ago today. Today's Thursday, right? Yeah, he left last Thursday evening, just a few hours before I got back home from my gambling trip."

"Did he have a cookout here before he left?"

"He told me on the phone it was too windy or something, and he couldn't get the damn thing lit. He said he'd just let it sit there till it wasn't windy. Then, hell, he decided to take off."

"What'd he do, go back to Wisconsin Thursday? He'd already been there and come back?"

"He'd been there two or three times already. He just came back for his TV and stuff like that. And then he just took off for good."

"How long a drive is that for him?"

"Around eight hours, I think."

"That's a long drive back and forth. Well, it's been a pleasure doing business with you, ma'am. You take care now. Bye."

"Thanks. Bye now."

Kellar and Rick walked away from the woman as she returned to the house. They walked quickly over to the junker they had just purchased. They were both shocked that they had gotten all of this vital information. "Oh my God," Kellar said. "Oh my God. He's our man."

"He left the same damn day Anita went missing," Rick stammered. "He has to be the one."

"Yes, sir. We're gonna get this psycho now. I hope he was dumb enough to give his mom the right address." They heard the door slam shut behind them and saw the mother heading toward them. Rick looked over in her direction with pure annoyance on his face. While she was still too far away to hear, he asked Kellar, "What in the hell does she want now?"

"I need to run to my bank to deposit this money."

"We were just leaving. Don't worry about us. See ya."

Mrs. Steele hobbled over to her car and backed out of the long driveway. She even managed to avoid hitting the white van; Lieutenant Wright ducked down just in time to remain unseen. After the woman left, the men began talking excitedly to each other. "These tapes are valuable evidence now," Rick said. "You know that Steele's gonna try to say he wasn't even in town on Thursday. See? But, now we have proof that he actually was in town and didn't leave until that evening." Rick walked over to the grill and removed the burnt foil from it. He took it over to the van to be placed in a sealed bag. "This is evidence as well."

"I know. It's beautiful. You think he took her with him to Wisconsin?" asked Kellar.

Rick nodded. "Yep. I think we got him." He quickly took his cell phone out of his pocket and dialed Captain Jack Roberts's number as he left in the Datsun, following the surveillance van. He knew that Jack and the other four Kokomo investigators in La Crosse could check out this address within minutes. His heartbeat quickened, and his hands began to shake as he made the call. Anita could be rescued today if they were lucky.

Captain Jack Roberts had been up until four in the morning the night before. He and the other Kokomo officers as well as the La Crosse police force and FBI agents had driven around looking for the suspect's truck at local motels, bars, and residences. They had brought with them photos of the suspect and Anita and had asked locals if they had seen either one of them around town recently. But they had had no luck all night and had gone back to their hotel to get a few hours of sleep before the eight o'clock meeting at Agent Helton's office. They were all unshaven and running on fumes. They felt like they were in the right area, but they still lacked the critical information they needed to find Anita.

Jack answered Rick's call on the third ring, speaking in a muffled voice. "I can't talk right now. I'm in the La Crosse FBI agent's office. We've set up our command post here, and we're right in the middle of contacting all the listed property renters in the La Crosse phone book yellow pages. I'll call you back."

Monroe frantically yelled into the phone, "Jack! Don't hang up! 812 Clinton Street! 812 Clinton Street! It's in La Crosse, Wisconsin. You're in the right city, buddy. Go check out this address now! His mom told us that's where Steele's currently living. Let us know as soon as you find anything out."

"Sure thing," Jack replied, after stopping to catch his breath. "Good job, guys."

All eyes in the room were now suddenly on Jack. He jumped out of his seat and pulled on Agent Helton's shirt sleeve. "Is there a Clinton Street here in La Crosse?" he asked forcefully.

"Yeah. It's just two blocks away from where we had breakfast this morning. Why?"

Jack started for the door. "Come on. My guys back home managed to get an address from Tom's mom. 812 Clinton Street. Right under our noses. Things are coming together now. I can feel it! We're going to catch him soon. I just hope it's not too late."

The Kokomo and La Crosse officers and some FBI agents piled into several unmarked vehicles and squad cars. They sped toward Clinton Street, hoping and praying to find the red Ford Ranger at the address they were given.

Agent John Helton stayed behind to man the office while the rest of the men headed out. This was only John's second official day in charge: his FBI partner that had been in charge of the office for years had retired just two days prior. He sat in silence, cradling his head in his hands, for several minutes after the officers had left. He was stunned that the Kokomo officers seemed to have pulled this one off. Until that moment, he had been sure they were fooling themselves. Agent Helton received a phone call from Curtis Hoover within minutes. "We found the suspect's truck! It's parked in an alley right beside the residence. We got him!" Curtis exclaimed.

Agent Helton could only shake his head in disbelief as he hung up the phone with Curtis. "These sons of bitches are actually going to do it!" He was extremely impressed by the whole thing. John Helton had been an agent in the FBI for over twenty years now and had worked on several abduction cases. But he had never witnessed a case like this, where local and federal authorities worked so well together to solve it. Agent Helton was hopeful that the victim was still alive and that they would be able to get her away from the suspect soon.

CHAPTER 47

It was around one in the afternoon. Anita had been in the box for about half an hour. She was starting to go crazy from boredom. Feeling like a caged animal, she wanted out. She figured the mole had left the house since he had not come back for her yet, but she was wrong. He was getting dressed to go into town after a desperately needed shower. He put on his usual drab outfit that included a pair of his favorite Open Trails blue jeans, size 38/30; a plain white Fruit of the Loom T-shirt, size XXL; a pair of white socks; and his Pro Wing tennis shoes, size 8 1/2. He had small feet for a man of his height and build. People had always made fun of him about it, joking that it meant his package was just as small. He had never found it funny. He finished putting his tennis shoes on and was about to let the girl out of the box when he heard a knock on the front door.

The mole was irritated by the interruption, but he no longer feared it would be the authorities looking for him. He was overly confident that he had gotten away with his crime this time without leaving a trace for the pigs to follow up on. He walked over to the door. "Who is it?" he yelled.

The man on the other side of the door yelled back impatiently, "I have a package for you that you need to sign for. I'm on a schedule, so I need to make this quick."

The mole had been waiting eagerly for this package from UPS. It was material he had ordered that would tell him exactly how to set up a business plan that would convince those uptight bastards at the bank to give him a loan. It was the next step in making his dream a reality. It also contained business cards for his bookstore, which he had ordered from the same company. They had the name, address, and an advertisement on the card. It read:

"Oldies But Goodies Used Bookstore. Come and check us out! The first 10 customers receive half off! Grand Opening Day is August 1, 1998! Come to 812 Clinton Street to see what everyone is talking about!"

The mole opened the door and signed his name in a scribble. He grabbed the package out of the man's hands. "Thanks. I was waiting for this."

The delivery man looked away from the mole—he suddenly had chills come over him. He was unsure why, but this guy gave him the creeps. He dashed back to his delivery truck and sped off to his next stop. Anita had heard the knocking at the door, and was surprised that the mole had been there to answer the door. She wondered who could have been at the door. She prayed that it was the police or someone looking for her, but her hopes deflated like a popped balloon when he let her out of the box.

"Who was at the door?" she asked casually.

"Oh, just your old outfit delivering my package," her captor answered maliciously.

The words filled Anita with rage. Her mind raced with fury, not wanting to accept that what he had said might be the truth. *It's not my old outfit! I am going back!* The mole did not seem to notice her anger and went back to looking over his new reading materials. At that moment, Anita knew he would never let her go. He would kill her first. The realization hit her like a ton of bricks.

In the middle of reading his book, the mole walked cautiously to the front door, opened it, and peeked outside briefly. He came right back in, saying to himself, "I thought I heard something. It must have just been a plane overhead or something." Instead of going back to his book, he picked up his hammer. "I'm going to work on my bookshelves again. I almost have them done. Pick out a book and read on the couch where I can see you for a while," he ordered.

Anita picked up a random, dusty book off the floor and began to read to escape her dreadful thoughts. It was an old Agatha Christy murder mystery novel. It was actually quite captivating, and time seemed to fly by over the next hour. Anita was so engrossed with the novel that she nearly jumped out of her skin when the mole came up silently behind her and asked, "How many pages do you have left to read? I have to get back over to Menards to pick up some more nails and a few more boards. I'll pick up some lunch for us while I'm out."

"I'm on page eighty-two," Anita informed him. "It'll take me a few more hours to finish it up."

"Well, I can't wait that long. You can finish it up when I get back."

Anita no longer put up any protests to her captor's demands. "Okay." She put the book down and walked submissively back to her box.

The mole took a few minutes to count out his money and place it in his jeans pocket. He counted 10 one-hundred-dollar bills, 14 fifty-dollar bills, 6 twenty-dollar bills, 4 tens, 4 fives, and 2 ones. That added up to 1,882 dollars. He had to buy more supplies, and the money seemed to be dwindling away fast. He locked his girl in her box and placed the quarter on top to keep her honest. "I won't be long. See ya soon. I love you!" he called out to her over his shoulder.

CHAPTER 48

The officers had already surrounded the house on Clinton Street with a surveillance team. They were now waiting patiently for their suspect to leave the premises. They wanted to apprehend him away from the residence, which would allow them to enter the house to find Anita. Jack had already talked with both of the profilers about whether or not they thought the suspect would have Anita captive inside the home. They both had concurred that from the description of the home, the odds were high that Anita was inside.

Jack had snuck around the entire home to locate all possible entrances and had discovered that the back door was boarded up. There was only one entrance, and the windows were all blacked out with steel grate over them. Bob Thorton had told Jack that this was to provide the suspect with a sense of security and privacy. Todd McCain had said firmly, "The trophy of this crime will be in that house. The suspect has obviously taken steps to keep people out for a reason. He's hiding something in there. In his mind, he had to make it safe enough to leave the premises and not worry that she could escape. That's why there's only one way in and out." Jack had taken their advice into account and made the call that if the suspect left the house, they would take the risk and arrest him on the spot. If Anita was not in the house, they would have to convince Mr. Steele to reveal where he had hidden her. The officers were all on the edge of their seats waiting for their prime suspect to walk out the front door and drive away.

Around four that afternoon, Tom Steele walked out the front door, walked down the front steps, and stopped briefly to stretch. He walked over to the side alley where his truck was parked, and starting the engine, he headed toward Menards. The blue topper on the back of his truck blocked his view behind him. His rearview mirrors also happened to be tilted at an angle that made it nearly impossible to see directly behind him. Thus, he was completely unaware that his home had been under full surveillance since noon, and he did not notice the squad car trailing him. Officers were on standby to assist in pulling the suspect over if needed. Oblivious, Tom was in good spirits, singing to himself during the whole drive to the store.

Tom passed through downtown La Crosse, where people were in the streets decorating for the annual Fourth of July parade and festivities that were to be held this coming weekend. *Maybe I can trust the girl enough now to get some sparklers. We could do them together right outside the house.* Of course, he would have to reveal to her that they did not really live out in the country, but she had been obedient enough up until now that he doubted she would try to escape. He no longer even considered it; he prided himself on pulling off such a brilliant plan. Tom was sure he hadn't left any trail or made any mistakes thus far. He had told his mother his new address, but she hadn't acted like anyone was looking for him. He knew that she would have told him if the police were after him.

Tom spotted the green Menards building and pulled his truck into the parking lot. He walked in and browsed the aisles for the final supplies he would need to finish the bookshelves up by this weekend. The store smelled like freshly cut wood and sawdust. Captain Curtis Hoover, from the Kokomo Police Department, had trailed the suspect inside Menards. When he saw Tom looking at lumber to purchase, Curtis went back out to the squad car to wait for him. It wouldn't be long now. Tom carried some small items and his lumber tag up to the counter and was greeted cheerfully by a cashier named Mindy. He instantly noticed with delight that she did not look away from his gaze. She asked him thoughtfully, "Did you find everything okay?"

"I sure did. Thanks for asking." He misread the kindness she gave to all customers and thought to himself, *Man, this chick really wants me! She has really nice tits and a great smile. She might be a lot of fun.* He made a mental note to himself that if things with Anita didn't work out, this girl could be his next option.

"Just pick up your lumber on the side of the building. They should have it all ready for you. Have a great day!"

"Oh, I intend to," Tom said. "See you around." He left the store with a bounce in his step. He felt on top of the world. Invincible.

Tom picked up his lumber, got into his truck, and headed back toward the house. He was singing along to a new pop song by Brandy and Monica called "The Boy is Mine." He loved the fantasy of having two girls fight over him like in the song. Maybe Anita and this Mindy girl would come to blows over his attention one day. He could only hope. Tom cranked open the windows to feel the warm breeze on his face. The heat wave was over now, and it was a beautiful, sunny summer day. And that's when he heard the unmistakable sound.

Tom was sure that he had heard sirens blaring over the music, and he quickly shut off the music to be positive. He adjusted his rearview mirrors and saw the red flashing lights behind his vehicle. He came to an intersection and was shocked to see that there was a squad car on every corner of the intersection. He was surrounded on all sides. Tom was forced to slam on his brakes. He had nowhere to go and absolutely no way of escaping. *Shit*, he thought. He had to surrender.

Even though he knew it was the end for him, it still excited him to see what a commotion he had caused in the streets of La Crosse. People were standing outside their vehicles in shock as they watched it all play out. This was something you saw on TV, not in real life on a busy intersection as you are heading home from work. You would have thought they were pulling over Hitler or something. They needed all this manpower to bring him down; the thought eased Tom's wounded pride some after getting caught by the pigs he hated so much.

Still, Tom's cold heart sank as he felt in his gut that his luck had finally run out. The fantasy he had managed to make into a temporary reality was now over. He could already taste the bland food they would serve him in prison. He could see the bars to his cell, which he would stare at day after day until he was able to find a way to outsmart the system and be free. He started preparing himself mentally to once again be the one taking orders, instead of being the one in control. That was the hardest part of all of this to swallow. Tom hated anyone telling him what to do. Next time, they would not catch him. They would have to kill him first.

When their suspect pulled over, Jack and Curtis walked up to the window with their weapons drawn. Tom Steele, still in shock that they had found him, put his hands up and stepped out of the vehicle slowly. He knew the drill. This was the end of his joyride. Well, at least for now. To Tom, the past week had been worth the consequences he would soon face. He had gotten what he wanted and been in complete control for the second time in his life. If everything went well, he might even get a third chance someday. That is the thought that would keep him going while he rotted away in some prison cell.

"So, what brings you to La Crosse, Mr. Steele?" Curtis asked as he began patting down the suspect to search for weapons.

"I've just been visiting the area and doing some fishing. I was planning on heading back home in a few days. Is that against the law or something?"

Curtis chuckled, "No. So, then where have you been staying this week?"

"In my truck. I don't know anyone here and just wanted some peace and quiet away from my mother."

"Is that so? That's funny because we've been tracking you down this entire week and that story doesn't add up. We talked to your new landlord, and he informed us that you rented a house from him over on Clinton Street. Does that sound familiar?"

Tom knew he had been caught in his web of lies and could only smirk.

Curtis continued his questions, "You don't happen to know Anita Wooldridge, do you?"

"Yeah, but I haven't seen her in years."

"We believe that you have, Tom. We won fair and square here. The game is over so you might as well start giving us the truth."

Jack could hold his tongue no more and as Curtis finished patting down their suspect, cuffing him, and reading him his Miranda rights, Jack took over. "Mr. Steele, my name is Captain Jack Roberts of the Howard County Sheriff's Department. It is my distinct pleasure to tell you that you are under arrest for the kidnapping of Anita Wooldridge. You have no idea how diligently my team and I have worked to find you. Now we can put you behind bars where you belong."

Tom smirked again. He could not stand the thought of admitting that the pigs had outsmarted him. Instead, he would try to convince them that he had made it easy for them. "Well. I wasn't very careful," Tom said calmly. "I made a lot of mistakes along the way. I can't believe that it took you guys this long to find me. I made it all so obvious for you."

Jack remained calm as well. "Are you willing to talk to me about the abduction? You need to tell us where Anita is now. If you do, I can work with you, maybe be more lenient."

"Are you kidding me?" Tom asked with sudden conviction. "I learned my lesson the first time I was arrested by other pigs. I tried to work with them, and they set me up. I'll never trust another pig again. I want my lawyer present before I say anything else."

"Fine by me. We couldn't trust anything you said anyway. You're in big trouble this time, though. This is now a federal case since you crossed state lines. I hope you're prepared for many years behind bars. You had better savor every last second of the outside world, because I'll do whatever it takes to get a conviction. You'll never hurt another woman again. You can take that to the bank."

With those final words, Jack led the handcuffed, silent man to the back of his squad car. They would take him over to the station until they got the word on whether or not the officers had found Anita inside the suspect's rented home. They would not take the apprehended man back to the house until they knew for sure that Anita or her remains were safely off the premises.

Jack made a phone call to Phil Lyons to let him know that they had just scored the slam dunk to win the championship game. "We got him! He's in the squad car now. Just wanted to give you guys the okay to go in and search his home now. He wouldn't give me any information on whether Anita's in the house. Call me as soon as you find out. I plan to bring him back to the house to go through his truck after you guys get Anita out of there or find that she's not there. A few of the FBI agents already took the truck away. They should be arriving at the house with it shortly. Did you guys get the search warrant for the house yet?"

"Yep. Sergeant Lipinski brought it over signed by the judge just a few minutes ago. I can't believe how this is all coming together for us, Jack. It's just amazing! Say a prayer that she's in there, buddy. Say a prayer."

"I sure will, Phil. Call me."

CHAPTER 49

At approximately 5:45 p.m, the FBI SWAT team was preparing to go into the house to search for the victim, Anita Wooldridge. A crowd of curious neighbors surrounded the Clinton Street home as the media had been alerted. Word had spread like wildfire to the community at large. Right before they went in, a squad car pulled up in front of the home, its tires screeching to a halt. Captain Smith of the City of La Crosse Police Department got out of the vehicle and shouted to the FBI agents that were already approaching the front door, "Hold on! The Kokomo police team has earned the right to go in there first! They're going in first!" The agents stopped in their tracks, shocked at his announcement. The FBI agents demanded that the two Kokomo officers, Ron Eastwood and Chuck Wilson, and the two La Crosse officers, Sergeant Lipinski and Investigator McQuiston, put on black FBI bulletproof jackets before they entered the home.

The men agreed and quickly got suited up. The crowd of people watched in awe as the officers knocked on the front door.

"This is the police. Open up. We have a search warrant." No one answered, so they used the key the landlord had supplied them with and entered the house. The four men stayed together, their pistols drawn, ready for the unexpected to happen. Upon entering the front room, Ron could see a large amount of lumber lying on the floor. The officers had to step over it to proceed cautiously into the next room to the south. As they proceeded further, they were forced to turn off the blaring TV so that they could listen for noises.

They shouted numerous times, "This is the police. We have a search warrant. Come out if anyone is in here!" None of the men heard any noises as they advanced through each room of the cluttered home. The officers would enter one room at a time in procession and quickly case it as a team. They were all on edge as they had no idea whether the suspect had acted alone or with accomplices, but they all had each other's backs. They were nervous too about the condition they would find Anita in, if she was even in the home.

The next room was also filled with a large amount of lumber, construction materials, boxes, trash, and empty bookshelves. After determining that the second room on the west side of the building was clear, Ron pointed his finger frantically toward what appeared to be a metal cabinet of some sort located near the back of the next room. It was tan and lying on the floor on its back, a position that struck the officers as unusual.

The metal cabinet had two doors that could both swing to the outside of it. A wooden dowel, which looked like a broomstick, was placed under both of the handles, essentially locking the doors closed. The dowel appeared to be about three feet in length. The secured metal box looked out of place in the room and slowly the realization sunk in that it was large enough to hold a human body.

The officers looked at each other fearfully. It was so quiet in the room that you could have heard a pin drop. Deputy Ron Eastwood stepped forward and took a position south of the metal cabinet. As he moved, the floor creaked loudly and seemed to startle a couple of the officers. McQuiston even raised his pistol in position to shoot whatever came his way. Investigator Chuck Wilson motioned for the officer to put his weapon at ease and moved forward to help Ron remove the wooden stick from the handles.

Underneath the dowel, they found a silver butter knife wedged between the two handles. Ron noticed a quarter located on top of the metal cabinet as well. He removed the butter knife and slowly opened the right-hand door of the cabinet to reveal the most miraculous sight he had ever seen. It was Anita. She was alive, and weeping. She immediately stood up and shouted, "Thank you, God! Get me out of here! I want to go home!"

Ron Eastwood scooped Anita up into his arms, and she clung tightly to his neck as he quickly carried her out to safety. She was crying and kept pleading, "Don't let go of me!" The crowd began cheering loudly, and several people were shouting, "They found her. She's alive! These guys are real heroes!"

Anita did not notice the noise of the cheering or the media taking pictures as they stepped outside. She was still terrified that somehow her captor could be lurking in the crowd with the gun to shoot her. Ron fought back the people as he rushed over to put Anita in a squad car to wait until the ambulance arrived. A Tri-State Ambulance pulled up within seconds. Ron carried Anita over to the waiting ambulance, which would take her to the Lutheran Hospital ER. Ron had to pry Anita's shaking hands off his neck. "It's going to be okay now, Anita," he reassured her. "You're safe now. Don't worry, hon. These people are going to take you to the hospital, and then we'll make sure you get back home to Kokomo as soon as possible." Tears ran down Ron's cheeks. It was just such a miracle that they had found her alive!

As the ambulance pulled away, he dropped to his knees and thanked God. The Kokomo officers and FBI agents were all in shock at the success of this case. Phil Lyons had already called Jack Roberts to give him the okay to return to the residence on Clinton Street. The scene that emerged as Jack and Curtis Hoover pulled up was an emotional one. The whole Kokomo dream team came together in a group hug. The veteran officers and FBI agents wept together and talked in excited tones. "We did it, boys!" Jack shouted. "Praise God, she's actually alive! Pinch me so I know I'm not dreaming!" Curtis gave Jack a pinch that made him yelp, and they all laughed. Nothing could dampen their spirits.

"So, did she seem all right to you?" Jack asked Ron when they were alone in the street.

"Yeah," Ron answered. "She was surprisingly coherent for being held captive in that metal box and all. She just didn't want to be left alone, and she kept saying that she wanted to go home."

"Okay. We have to search the suspect's truck and get him a transport to the jail for booking. Then I'll go over to the hospital to see how Anita's doing. I don't want her to think that we've abandoned her."

Jack walked over to the sidewalk and took a seat on the curb to call Deputy Don Howell in Kokomo. He had waited all week to make this call.

Don answered eagerly, "Hello."

"Don! We did it, buddy!" Jack shouted into the phone. "We just apprehended our suspect and found Anita alive in the house. She's at the hospital right now. She's okay, and as long as everything goes as planned, Phil and I are going to bring her home to her family by tomorrow!"

Don gasped. "Oh, Oh, my God," he stammered. "This is a miracle!" He yelled over to the rest of the officers at the station, "They did it! Anita is alive and coming home soon!" Jack could hear shouts of joy in the background.

"Don," Jack interrupted, "I need you to call Anita's parents and tell them the news. This is going to reach national news, and I don't want them to find out from the TV reports."

"Sure thing. I'll call them right now. I'm just in shock, Jack. You guys are heroes. Her family's going to be truly grateful."

"Just tell them she won't be home until tomorrow, but I'll make sure that she calls them this evening."

"Okay, Jack. I'll tell them. We're all proud of you guys. Go celebrate!"

"We couldn't have done this without you guys at home. That address was crucial to finding her. We'll all celebrate once we get back home with Anita."

———————————

Don Howell decided to go over to the Wooldridge home to let them know the good news in person. He pulled into the long driveway, and before he could get out of his squad car,

Anita's parents and older brother were at the front door, their faces stricken with fear until they saw Don smile from ear to ear. "They got her!" Don shouted out. "Anita's alive!"

"My baby's alive!" Anita's mom shrieked with happiness. "Thank the Lord! She's alive! She's really alive!" She was jumping up and down and nearly stepped on Gerald's hand: he had fallen to his knees in shock and joy. He slowly stood back up with tears streaming down his weary face. He walked over to Don and embraced him, sobbing. "Thank you!" he said sincerely. "Thank you for finding my baby girl!" Daniel hugged his mom and quickly got on the phone to call the rest of the family.

When they had calmed down, the family began to ask questions. "Where is she?" Carrie Ann asked. "I want to see her right now."

"Our officers found her and her captor in Wisconsin. We don't have all the details yet, but she's in the hospital there to check her over. Once she's medically cleared and questioned, she'll spend the night at a hotel with the police. Then they'll fly back with her tomorrow afternoon. You can meet her at the airport. Jack said that he'd make sure she calls you guys this evening from the hotel."

"So she's okay, right?" Gerald asked. "That son of a bitch better not have hurt her!"

Carrie Ann put her hand lightly on his arm to calm him down. "She'll be okay, honey. She's alive, and that's all that matters. We'll get through this as a family. You have to be strong for her right now."

Don left the joyous family and returned to the station in great spirits.

CHAPTER 50

Jack had just gotten off the phone with his wife to tell her the amazing news. Dorothy was thrilled for him and the team and was already planning a celebration for the guys at their home when they returned tomorrow. "Wow! I feel so honored to be married to a real-life hero!" she had said. "I'm so proud of you, Jack. You never gave up on her. I knew if anyone could bring her home, it'd be your team."

Jack had had to wipe away the tears on his cheeks. "Thanks for all your love and support, honey. It means so much to me. I can't wait to get back home to you! Love you."

"Love you too. Get some sleep tonight!"

Now Jack could focus on the task at hand. He needed to get the handcuffed suspect out of the squad car and over to the red truck to conduct a thorough search of his vehicle. This sounded easy enough, but there was still a large crowd of onlookers and media teams lining the street, causing a chaotic scene. Jack asked the officers to keep the crowd back while he started blocking off the crime scene and providing himself with some space to work.

With the help of Ron Eastwood, Jack led the suspect out of the squad car and around the crowd toward the truck.

All of a sudden, amongst the sea of noises, a voice clearly boomed above the others, "That man is innocent until proven guilty in a court of law! Don't forget that!" His voice rang out like the voice of God from above, and the sound lingered in the air as the swarm of faces all turned to catch a glimpse of the man who had tried to rain on their parade. As quickly as he had appeared, the small, stocky man vanished into the crowd.

The officers shook their heads in disbelief and went on like it hadn't happened. Tom Steele seemed amused by the whole incident, almost as if he had planned it. Sergeant Lipinski took charge and announced to the crowd, "All right. Quiet down. This is a crime scene investigation here. Everyone needs to back up and give us room or leave the premises. There is nothing more to see here. Go home now and watch it all on the news tonight."

When Jack arrived at the truck with the suspect in tow, he was informed by several La Crosse officers that the FBI evidence response team had already completed a thorough search of the truck at a different location and had brought it back only temporarily. They had found wood protruding from the back window of the topper on the truck and a gray backpack in the back. Within the backpack, they had found a woman's wig, a dress, a stun gun, and numerous nylon wire ties. These were all taken into custody by the FBI to be used later as evidence in the federal-court hearing.

Back home in Kokomo, Deputy Don Howell had obtained an Indiana search warrant for the suspect's mother's residence. They firmly believed that Anita had been taken to this residence initially before being transported to Wisconsin. Don walked up to the front door and knocked several times before he heard a woman's voice yelling, "Hang on. I'm a comin'!" Daphne Steele eyed the officer up and down before asking, "Who are you, and what do you want? My son ain't home if that's what you came for."

Don, wearing his uniform, asked her politely, "Ma'am, could I please come in and talk with you for a minute? I do have a search warrant for your home if you refuse."

Daphne Steele stood up straight and looked alarmed. "What the hell for?" She allowed Don inside, and they climbed the stairs to the front room where she had the TV blaring. She quickly shut it off and sat down in her old recliner to hear an explanation.

"I'm sorry to have to tell you this," Don explained, "but your son Tom has been arrested in Wisconsin for kidnapping Anita Wooldridge and taking her across state lines. He's also being charged with carjacking Anita's vehicle, among other things."

Tom's mother shrugged the officer off with a wave of her hand. "You guys got the wrong guy again. The first time my son got sent to prison it was all just a big mistake. He was gonna marry that girl, and he changed his mind at the last minute because she cheated on him and all, and then she wanted to get back at him for breaking up with her. My son doesn't have it in him to kidnap anyone. He stays to himself and doesn't bother anyone."

"I know this is hard for you to believe," Don calmly replied, "but we have proof that your son was the one that took her."

"No, I don't believe it," Mrs. Steele objected. "There were two guys at my house earlier that bought my son's old car, and they were actin' pretty fishy to me. Maybe you should find them and question them."

Don laughed, "Those were our undercover officers. They were trying to get information on where your son was living in Wisconsin. When you gave them the Clinton Street address, they were able to locate your son and arrest him. They found Anita locked inside a metal box in his home."

The reality was sinking in for Mrs. Steele. She could not speak. She began choking and said that she had to have a cigarette to calm down her nerves.

Don informed the grief-stricken mother that she would have to find another place to stay for a few weeks since her home was now considered a crime scene and needed to be searched. Daphne Steele did not argue with the officer anymore. She seemed resigned to the idea that her son was guilty of this unfathomable crime. She nodded her head yes and headed outside for a cigarette. Don felt sorry for the old woman. The news seemed to have taken the last bit of integrity she had away from her, and she walked a little more hunched over now, as though she could fall over at any time.

CHAPTER 51

While in the ambulance, Anita talked briefly with a La Crosse police officer named Keith, expressing to him how relieved she was to have been rescued. "Why didn't you make any noise when our officers entered and were asking if anyone was in the house?" he asked politely.

"He'd trick me and pretend that he was the police every so often. If I made any noise, he said he'd kill me, and I believed him. I was scared it was just him pretending to be the police again." Anita told the officer and the EMTs that she didn't think that she had any physical injuries that warranted immediate attention: she just felt beat up. Still, they rushed her over to the ER for a thorough exam. Anita stripped off her socks and told the paramedics, "I feel so dirty! My hair is greasy, and I want these socks off. I had to wear the same dirty pair of his socks all week. I just want a shower!" They all assured Anita that she could get cleaned up at the hospital. She was relieved to hear this and vowed to herself that she would never take hot showers and privacy for granted ever again.

Mr. Steele had been apprehended and taken to the La Crosse County Jail for booking. He was cooperative with authorities, yet evasive. "What do people call you?" Officer Stein asked him at one point.

"I suppose they'll be calling me whatever they want from now on."

"Do you have any idea why you are here?" the stocky jailer asked during the booking procedure.

"I have absolutely no clue why I'm here."

Tom was booked around 9:30 p.m. and then escorted to St. Francis Hospital, where samples of his blood and hair were taken as well as ink impressions of his fingers, hands, and elbows. When Sergeant Lipinski was asked whether they should cuff only one of Tom's hands to the bed rail while they retrieved the samples, the sergeant quickly denied that request. "Take my advice," Mr. Steele stated. "It's better this way." He made it clear that, if given the opportunity, he would become violent. Tom was not remorseful in any way for what he had done to Anita. He just wanted this whole booking process completed so that he could eat and get some sleep.

CHAPTER 52

Anita's slender, pale fingers trembled as she picked up the hotel telephone to dial her home phone number. She had called this number a thousand times, yet the numbers felt foreign to her now. She was both apprehensive and eager to hear the sound of her parents' voices on the other end of the line. Anita had waited so long and had prayed so hard to be able to speak to them once again, but it all felt so surreal now. She did not have any idea what to say to them or how she would ever be able to describe to them the nightmare that she had experienced.

Anita had just endured three long hours of a thorough checkup at the Lutheran Hospital in La Crosse. Her treatment there had been conducted by a male ER doctor, a registered nurse, and an empathetic female social worker that had never once left her side. The doctor had done a physical examination and had taken blood work and finger and elbow prints. They had used a sexual assault kit on her and had taken numerous photographs of her bruises, the residue from the electrical tape, the marks from the electrical ties, and the stun gun contact points. They had been thorough, meticulously gathering as much evidence as possible to help convict her captor. It had been intrusive and humiliating at times, but the staff were all friendly and comforting.

Anita had apologized repeatedly to the entire staff, "I'm so sorry! I haven't been able to shave for eight days. I really smell! I didn't want to shower there with him watching me." The staff had all assured her that she was fine and not to worry, but she had remained highly self-conscious of her appearance and odor. Anita had always had good grooming skills, and it felt foreign to have let herself go completely all week.

FBI Agent John Helton, Captain Jack Roberts, and Deputy Major Phil Lyons had all talked with Anita at the hospital and had taken more photographs of her injuries to use as evidence. A La Crosse police officer had visited her in the hospital to ask her if she had been sexually assaulted by her captor. Anita had tearfully responded, "Yes. Repeatedly. The last time was just this morning."

Though she was being poked, interrogated, and bombarded by strangers telling her their names and titles, it had felt like a warm blanket covering her on a chilly winter night, just being around other people. It had been wonderful to be treated like a human being once again. The nurses and aides had all been diligent about making sure that Anita was as comfortable as possible. The majority of the staff had heard the news of Anita's miraculous rescue and empathized with her and her family.

After her examination, Anita had taken a long steaming hot shower at the hospital. They had given her a razor, so she could finally shave the long stubble that had grown over the course of her week in captivity. That had been the best feeling, to shower in private and to wash all the filth and smells off her body and hair.

An FBI agent's wife had been kind enough to go to the local Walmart and purchase an outfit in Anita's size, including undergarments, and essential toiletries that she might need for the night and flight home. She had rushed to do this as soon as she had learned that Anita had no clothing with her other than what she had been kidnapped in eight days prior. Anita had been overcome with gratitude.

"I hope that the clothes fit," Julie, the agent's wife, had said. "I wasn't sure on the sizes so I just guessed. Also, I brought over my makeup bag. You can have whatever you might need for the next day. Feel free."

Anita had hugged Julie. "Thank you so much," she had said sincerely. "You don't even know me, and yet you did all of this for me. My mom can't be here tonight, so it feels good to have you mother me a bit."

"It was my honor," Julie had said. "You still haven't seen the best part! I snagged my husband's FBI jacket from his desk. Thought that after everything you've been through, you deserve it! Also, it's pretty darn warm!"

Anita had smiled for the first time since being rescued. "I will always cherish this." She had put on the oversized blue jacket and immediately felt a sense of safety. She wore it the rest of the night.

Snug in her new clothes, Anita was sitting down with the FBI secretary, who had not left her side since leaving the hospital, to make the tearful call to her family. She had been assured at the hospital that the police officers in Kokomo had already notified her family that she had been rescued and was, in fact, alive. Anita was unsure just how much information they had given her family, but she was not ready to discuss the gruesome details with them yet. Filled with apprehension, she dialed her phone number and heard the phone ring.

Carrie Ann and Gerald Wooldridge reached the telephone at the same time and held it as they gushed frantically into the receiver, "Hello!" The eager parents refused to believe that their baby girl was still alive until they heard her voice. There was a short pause and then, like music to their ears, they heard, "Mom, Dad, it's me." All three began sobbing. Anita's parents hugged each other tightly, and Anita squeezed the FBI secretary's hand for assurance. She had not been left alone since she was rescued at her own request. Even though she had been told that her captor was already locked behind bars, she was still too terrified to be by herself. She even questioned a few times whether all of this was real or just her mind playing tricks on her. Would she wake up to find herself in the nightmare once again? It was too much to even ponder.

The Wooldridge family bawled together for several seconds, and then Gerald spoke in a hoarse, raspy voice, "We love you, Anita! We're going to pick you up at the airport tomorrow and bring you home. Okay?"

"Okay, Dad. I prayed that this day would come. I'm so sorry—"

"Don't you ever say you're sorry, honey!" Carrie Ann stopped her daughter's cries of guilt. "You did nothing wrong! We love you so much, sweetie! You have no idea how worried we've all been. Just hearing your voice is a miracle!"

They wept together until Gerald said, "Get some rest now, and we'll pick you up tomorrow. You need some rest after all you've been through."

"I will, Dad, but I need to call Daniel and Melanie first. Then I have to go to the police station to give my statement. I'll be happy to just sleep after all that. Oh, tell Sarah that I will be in her wedding this Saturday. The only thing that kept me going these last few days was the hope that I'd make it home in time for her."

Anita's parents were not surprised by their daughter's will to honor her commitment to her best friend, even after all she had just endured. "We'll tell her. Just focus on you for right now. We love you! Goodnight, sweetheart," her mother said tearfully.

When the phone call ended, Anita's parents started screaming and dancing in celebration. Gerald, falling to his knees, screamed, "It's a miracle! Our baby's alive!" They hugged and screamed joyfully and then called their extended family and close friends to tell them the wonderful news: they had just heard Anita on the phone and would be able to bring her home tomorrow. They slept soundly that night for the first time in a week with the peace of knowing that their daughter had survived. Both Gerald and Carrie Ann knew that the details would not be pretty, but they also knew that they could get through it all as a family.

Anita picked up the phone receiver to call her older brother, Daniel. She longed to hear his comforting voice. She knew that, as the sensible yet fiercely protective member of the family, she could count on him to help her through this. She trusted his opinion and advice more than anyone else's, and she needed him now more than ever. Daniel picked up on the second ring. "Hello! Anita?"

Anita could only sob into the receiver at first and then managed to croak, "Yeah. It's me."

Daniel let out a long sigh of relief; he had been holding his breath since he had heard that his little sister had been abducted. He paused and said, "How you doing, sis?"

Anita answered honestly, "I'm hanging in there. I just want to come home!"

"You're going to press charges against the creep, aren't you?" he asked hesitantly. Daniel knew how compassionate Anita was by nature. Anita answered without hesitation, "Of course! He'll pay for what he's taken from me!"

Daniel was filled with relief once again. "Thank God! I just wanted to be sure that we were on the same page. I'll help you through the trial and everything. You just focus on getting some rest tonight and coming home tomorrow. I love you, sis! My prayers have all been answered!"

"I love you too! See you soon." She hung up the receiver and felt whole again at once. Her family would help her through this, and someday it would all be okay again. It had to be.

It was now nine o' clock in the evening, and her stomach was growling fiercely. Jack called her on the hotel phone to ask if she was ready to go over to the City of La Crosse Police Department Detective Bureau to give her taped statement regarding the abduction and weeklong captivity. Anita sounded weary as she answered, "Yeah. I'm tired and really hungry, but I might as well get this over with, so I can get some sleep. I just talked to my family, and they're all celebrating at home. I wish I could be there with them."

Jack was sympathetic to her plight and offered, "I promise to make it as brief and painless as possible for you. I'm sorry you don't have your family here with you, but we can definitely stop on the way and get you some food. Now that I think about it, I haven't eaten all day. I'm hungry myself." Anita agreed to head over with Jack and Agent Helton to grab a bite to eat first.

The three of them got into Agent Helton's car. "We can go somewhere that isn't busy if you want," Jack offered. He wanted her to feel as comfortable as possible in his care.

"No. Just the opposite," Anita answered. "I want to be around lots of people! I never want to be alone again. We can go to Burger King or something quick like that. Not Kentucky Fried Chicken, though. That's Tom's favorite place to eat. Just the thought of it turns my stomach!"

"Okay then," Agent Helton said. "There's a Burger King on the way to the station. We'll be there in seconds."

"I don't have any money with me," Anita said, "but I'll pay you back as soon as we get home."

The men were shocked that she would even consider trying to pay for her own meal. She was such a mature young lady for her age. She also expressed her fears that she hadn't been able to pay her bills this week and worried about late fees. "This meal's on us, Anita," they assured her. "Don't worry about it."

As they ate their greasy dinner, Anita slowly started to relax and feel normal again. It was amazing to her how food actually tasted good again when she wasn't in fear for her life. She felt so safe sitting next to these men who protected people for a living. Anita appreciated how reassuring and accommodating they were to her. She knew they were going above and beyond their job description to take her out to eat, and they seemed to genuinely care about her well-being. They would always be her heroes.

As they ate, Jack made a comment, saying that he would like a few minutes alone with her captor after what he had done.

But surprisingly, Anita seemed to defend the man who had put her through hell. "He wasn't always mean to me. He did buy me my favorite gum, fed me whenever I agreed to eat, brought me a fan when it was hard for me to breathe in the box, and he even brought me a pillow once to make me more comfortable." Jack and Agent Helton were both familiar with the psychological phenomenon known as Stockholm syndrome, where hostages show signs of loyalty toward their captor, regardless of what the person has done to them. It is a strong defense mechanism that the victim uses in order to mentally survive the abuse. They justify in their heads that their perpetrator isn't all bad.

The men, startled by her response, exchanged worried glances. Jack firmly tried to shake her out of this state of mind. "You listen to me right now, Anita. This man did you no favors, okay? He hurt you, and he's going to pay for what he's put you through. We're going to make sure of it."

Anita shook her head yes and looked down at her half-eaten food.

"It's okay, Anita," Agent Helton added. "You'll get through this. It's just going to take some time for you to get back to a sense of normalcy." They finished up their dinner and headed over to the police station. It was nearly midnight before the interview was completed, and they were all exhausted. They drove back to the hotel, and Anita thanked the men before heading into her room for some needed sleep. It seemed like the longest day of her entire life, filled with a mixture of torture and celebration. Anita cried herself to sleep that night while the kind FBI secretary slept soundly in the twin bed beside hers. Anita thanked God for sparing her life and remaining with her throughout this ordeal.

As Anita slept, the rest of the Kokomo investigators, except for Jack and Phil, celebrated their victory at a local bar in La Crosse. Despite their exhaustion, they were all too hyped up to sleep. They stayed out until after four in the morning, rehashing all the events of the week. They were still in disbelief that they had actually pulled it off. Around eleven o'clock, the national news showed footage of the officers carrying Anita out of the home and arresting her captor. The newscasters praised the officers' work and discussed how it was a miracle that Anita had survived. The men toasted each other while the locals cheered for them and offered them congratulations. They left the bar in good spirits, bonded for life by this humbling experience.

FRIDAY JULY 3, 1998

CHAPTER 53

Anita and the Kokomo officers ate a buffet breakfast at the hotel in La Crosse that morning. Anita was anxious to return home to her family and friends but was dreading the flight back. She had never been on a plane before; her family vacations had always consisted of driving in their family vehicle. After discussing her fears with the men at the table, Jack decided not to cramp Anita into the tiny six-passenger Indiana State Police aircraft when she was already feeling anxious and claustrophobic from the ordeal she had just gone through. He and Phil Lyons made the decision to take a small plane to Minneapolis and then fly to Indianapolis on a larger commercial flight. The other members of the Kokomo team would fly back on the Indiana State Police aircraft together.

The officers were extremely protective of Anita, and she felt safe in their presence. "I want to thank all of you for working so hard to save my life," she announced at the table. "I could never thank you all enough." Anita was crying as she spoke, so the officers tried to lighten the mood. "Ahhh! We didn't have anything better to do," Curtis cracked.

They all laughed, and Jack spoke up, "We're just so blessed to have found you alive and to now be able to take you back home to your family and to the community that has prayed for your safety all week."

"Really? I didn't realize so many people would care."

"You wouldn't believe how many calls we got every day wanting updates on you," Ron said. "The whole town cares about you. You're going to be a real celebrity when you get home!"

"The whole week I prayed for my family and that God would help you guys find me."

"We could all feel those prayers, Anita," Jack replied. "God opened doors for us every time we hit a wall. It truly is a miracle that we were able to find you alive. We all feel honored to be a part of your rescue."

The two groups said their good-byes, and Anita, Phil, and Jack all headed for the small plane that awaited them. Anita was jumpy as she buckled herself in and kept asking, "What's that noise? Are we in the air yet?" She closed her eyes and breathed deeply. Jack tried to distract her by telling jokes and helping her to laugh. They reached the Minneapolis-St. Paul airport with no problem, and at a newsstand, Jack bought ten newspapers with Anita's rescue on the front page. The three of them headed for the ticket counter.

Anita had to laugh when she walked out of the airport restroom to see both Jack and Phil standing at the entrance, waiting to escort her back to the ticket counter. "Man, I feel like I'm under arrest or something," she joked.

Jack laughed. "Hey, we mean no harm. We just don't want to lose you again. We have our reputations to uphold and all." They walked up to the ticket counter, where a blond young man assisted them. Jack asked for three government-discounted tickets to Indianapolis on the next flight. The man behind the counter requested to see their government IDs, so Jack and Phil placed their badges and IDs on the counter. The man looked at Anita and asked, "Where is your ID, ma'am?"

"She's in our custody," Jack answered.

"Do you have an ID for her?"

"Yeah. Here's her ID right here." Jack threw down the newspapers he had just purchased and pointed to Anita's picture. "That's her right there," Jack clarified. "She was just rescued, and she has no ID on her."

The man at the counter looked flustered and said that he would have to get his manager. "That's fine," Jack responded. "We'll be here." The manager came out and listened in awe as Jack explained the story to the man. "Look, she has no ID on her. We wanted her to get a discounted flight to save taxpayers some money, but it doesn't really matter to me at this point whether it's discounted or full price. We just want to get this young lady back to her family today."

The manager gave Anita the discounted ticket and told them the flight to Indianapolis was leaving in one hour. They headed through security and then over to their gate, where they sat down to wait. They were all tired and ready to get home. Anita was thinking about her best friend's wedding that was still scheduled for the next day. She was adamant that she was going to be in it. It was the only thing that she could focus on and feel excited about.

As they waited, a complete stranger walked over to her and asked her timidly, "Aren't you that girl from Indiana that was rescued yesterday?" Anita nodded her head yes. The rather large woman began sobbing. She hugged Anita and cried, "Oh, honey, I prayed for you! I cried so hard when I learned they had found you alive! You're a walking miracle, child! God bless you!" Anita, shocked at being recognized by a stranger, was completely taken aback by the attention. She tried to express her gratitude but was relieved when the lady walked away. Still, she could feel the stares of the people around her that had overheard the conversation and felt compelled to look at her as if she were now on display. Anita had never enjoyed being in the spotlight, so it took some time for her to get used to it all.

The flight home took them through some stormy weather, and the plane hit several turbulence bumps, which petrified Anita. Her knuckles were white from clutching the arms of her seat. Jack and Phil both seemed relaxed and at ease in the air. Anita tried to convince herself that it was just mind over matter and that they would be safely on the ground soon enough. She wanted to read one of the newspapers Jack had bought to distract herself, but she was still without her contacts and had blurry vision. Jack handed her his bifocals to see if they helped her see more clearly, but she could not see a thing. Nonetheless, the men got a good chuckle out of seeing her with the large glasses on.

As she laid her head back and tried to nap, she overheard Jack and Phil talking quietly about a teenage boy sitting just a few rows ahead. "Look at that kid up there," Phil said to Jack. "He has a red, white, and blue mohawk! Can you believe that?"

"No! It's good to be so patriotic, but if he were my kid, I'd get him down and shave that mohawk right off! He'd be sporting a buzz cut instead."

Anita couldn't believe they were talking so freely around her. It helped her to realize that they were just normal people like her own family. Until then, she had put the officers so high up on a pedestal that she had felt slightly uncomfortable around them. Now she liked them even more because they were so real around her.

After nearly two hours in the air, the plane finally started its descent. Anita was so excited to land and be greeted by her friends and family. She said a few tearful good-byes to Jack and Phil as they were walking to the gate, thanking them for all their help in rescuing her.

She started to search the crowd for her family's faces when Anita heard a woman screaming, "It's her! Anita! Thank God!" She ran over with open arms and fell into her mother's embrace. Anita felt other arms wrapping her tightly in a squeeze and realized that it was her father and brother. Her sister and the rest of her family were there too, as well as several close friends, her boyfriend Scott, and the media. Anita was blinded by all the bulbs flashing in her face, but she did not care. She was finally home for good.

It was a tearful reunion, one that Anita would remember for a lifetime. She had never seen her family so choked up. Her typically reserved father actually picked her up and swung her around in the air like he used to when she was a little girl. He was sobbing and saying, "My baby is home! Thank you, Lord!" When they got a minute alone together, her father whispered in her ear, "I'm sorry I couldn't protect you from that man, honey. It nearly killed me to think that you were out there somewhere and I couldn't do a damn thing! I'll do whatever it takes to help you through this. I won't let you down again!"

"Dad, please don't blame yourself for this," Anita pleaded. "I'm so sorry you and Mom had to go through this too. We'll all get through it together."

Anita took her family and friends over to introduce them to her heroes, Jack and Phil. "These are two of the men who rescued me." They thanked the officers profusely.

"Thanks for the recognition," Jack announced, "but Anita is the true hero here. Our gift is bringing her back home to all of you."

Gerald shook both of their hands. "I can never thank you enough. We'll forever be grateful and indebted to you. You're all heroes in my book!"

As Anita's family celebrated on the ground, the other three members of the Kokomo team were flying through the same storms the commercial plane had gone through. Every storm cloud the tiny plane hit felt like they were being sacked in a football game. Chuck Wilson was white as a ghost, counting down the minutes to landing. It was a miracle that he was able to keep his breakfast down: he was feeling so nauseated. The men were running on adrenaline, but the exhaustion was starting to set in. They were ready to get home to their loved ones and celebrate their victory with the community.

Even Chuck Wilson would have willingly endured the flights to La Crosse and back again if it meant achieving this wonderful outcome. The men would savor this experience for a lifetime. Anita's rescue would forever be the highlight of their careers, and they regretted nothing. The men believed that God had guided them and kept them safe throughout all the bumps and trials they had faced. It soon became clear that the nation as a whole was touched by Anita's inspirational story. Her testimony made it clear that miracles do still happen and that the good guys could still pull out a win here and there.

JANUARY 1999

CHAPTER 54

On January 9, 1999, Victor Thomas Steele was finally brought to trial at the Birch Bayh Federal Building and U.S. Courthouse in Indianapolis, Indiana. By his request, Tom acted as his own attorney during the trial that lasted five full days in court. Several days were cancelled due to an ice storm that hit during the course of the week, which ended up being a pain for the multiple officers and FBI agents that made the drive to Indianapolis daily. Anita was grateful that the State of Indiana supplied her and her mother with a hotel room in Indianapolis for the entire week of the trial.

Tom had enforced his right to be brought into the courtroom without shackles on his legs. He was also allowed to wear street clothes and appeared to be in the height of his glory. Tom looked as though he felt in control, despite the fact that two armed U.S. Marshalls escorted him into the courtroom, standing on guard to keep him in line. He seemed to be confident that he could convince the jury of his innocence. In his mind, he had done Anita a favor by choosing her and taking care of her for eight days. His defense strategy was to introduce the idea that Anita had been working with the Indiana State Police and the FBI to frame him because he had successfully sued the Indiana Department of Corrections for unfair treatment during his last prison sentence.

Walking through the massive double doors to enter the federal courtroom, spectators were immediately struck by how large the room was. The structure was intimidating and made people feel small in comparison. It had high cathedral ceilings with architectural murals throughout. The judge's seat was positioned higher, giving her a look of full authority. The witness chair was to her right, positioned lower. In front of the judge's bench was a podium where the attorneys were to stand one at a time to question the witnesses. Behind this was where, on the right side, the two prosecuting attorneys and the case agent sat during the whole trial. On the left side was the defense table where Tom sat.

Tom was forced to have a seasoned attorney join him in case he needed any assistance or legal advice. The Honorable Judge Elizabeth Allen-Parker wisely demanded that an attorney be provided to the defendant so that any appeals for a mistrial due to lack of proper legal advice would be quickly dismissed. This well-known attorney, Rodney Davidson, was a law professor at Indiana University from Bloomington. He came fully prepared to give Tom any advice he could to assist him in his defense case. But Tom saw this man as an annoyance and did not want to take any advice from him. His suspicious nature led him to believe that Mr. Davidson was only there to sabotage his defense, and he believed he knew more about the law from reading legal books in prison than this prick they had sent to him.

Behind the prosecution and defense tables, there was an iron railing that kept the audience from proceeding any farther. The audience was filled with around thirty people, though it had the capacity to seat around seventy. In the audience was Christopher Owings, an intelligence research specialist through the U.S. Attorney's office that had worked closely on the case. Other police officers involved in the case and the members of Anita's family not ordered to testify filled the rest of the seats.

The one person missing from the audience was Anita's father. He could not handle sitting in the same room as her captor, hearing the disturbing details of what his youngest daughter had endured. Gerald was afraid he might jeopardize the case if he were present, so he stayed at home. Anita's older brother Daniel, her older sister Melanie, and her brother-in-law Ben all came daily and took extensive notes.

Anita stayed in a nearby hotel and sat outside the courtroom every day with Kimberly Vandorf, a paralegal specialist who also served as an FBI victims advocate. Kimberly was there the whole five days to support Anita. Since Anita's rescue, Kimberly had been a huge support, driving Anita to appointments with the police, getting her into counseling, giving her legal advice, and checking on her almost daily. Anita considered Kimberly to be not only her advocate but one of her true friends. As they sat outside the courtroom doors, Kimberly helped Anita prepare to testify.

Everyone allowed into the courtroom had been advised prior to entering that it was standard procedure that all witnesses would be separated and were not allowed to discuss the case until after their testimony was given. People were not allowed to come in and out of the courtroom as they pleased and could not express their emotions while inside. The judge was very firm about keeping order in her courtroom; she would not allow the trial to become a circus show. The family and officers had had nearly six months to prepare for this day, and they were ready to get it over with and put it behind Anita. Tom had used that time to concoct his defense scheme. He was ready to shine.

The courtroom was deathly quiet once everyone took their seats. Melanie could hear several people clearing their throats and the sound of the attorneys rustling through the papers spread out in front of them. They were all anxiously awaiting the entrance of Judge Allen-Parker. The back door opened, and the judge strode in, immediately taking charge of the room with her authoritative presence. The bailiff announced loudly, "All rise." Everyone stood up, and after the judge had walked up the steps and taken her seat, they were allowed to be seated.

Judge Allen-Parker was an attractive, stern-looking female in her fifties. She had seen many cases like this one but was still always amazed by a defendant brazen enough to refuse counsel when facing such serious charges with the possibility of life in prison. Judge Allen-Parker put her glasses on and began looking at the documents in front of her.

"This is the case of the United States of America and the victim, Anita Wooldridge, versus the defendant, Mr. Victor Thomas Steele," the judge announced. "The prosecution is asking that Mr. Steele be tried by a federal jury for the charges of kidnapping, carjacking, illegal possession of a firearm in a kidnapping, and the use of a firearm in the commission of a felony. The defendant will not be tried or charged with a sex crime in this courtroom today as there is no federal criminal law covering those offenses. Prosecutors in the states of Wisconsin and Indiana do have the right to file these additional charges in their respective state courts at a later date. Again, we will not be trying Mr. Steele for that offense today. Are we all clear?" She looked up briefly to address the prosecution table. They nodded their heads in agreement. "Good," she continued. "Now let's proceed. Prosecution, you may call your first witness."

The U.S. prosecuting attorney, Richard Hall, with the help of his assistant U.S. attorney, Elaine Bradford, found the file they needed to question their first witness, the neighbor that had observed a man with a backpack approaching Anita's home on foot the morning of her disappearance. Mr. Hall rose and stated, "Your Honor, we call to the stand Mr. Fred Taylor." Fred was escorted into the courtroom, taking his place on the witness stand, where he was sworn in by the judge. "Mr. Taylor, on the morning of June 25, 1998, can you recall what you were doing?" Mr. Hall asked.

"Well, I hung around the house most of the morning. I know I went outside to get the newspaper around ten o'clock like I always do."

"Okay. Do you recall seeing anything out of the ordinary?"

"Yes. I saw a rather stocky man carrying a dark backpack approach the Wooldridge home, which is directly across the street from me. He was on foot, and I just thought he was one of those pesky salesmen or a Jehovah's Witness or something. I do remember thinking it was odd, though, that he wasn't dressed up like they usually are. I just thought it was because it was so hot out or something."

"Mr. Taylor, did you see this man talk to Anita Wooldridge?"

"No, I didn't. It was really hot, and I wanted to get back inside, so I didn't pay attention after I saw him standing at her front door, ringing the doorbell. I never would have guessed that this kind of thing would happen right there on Center Road during the day. I just feel awful about it. Maybe I could have stopped it from happening if I'd had any idea."

The judge stopped the witness and reminded him to only answer yes or no to the questions. He said apologetically, "Sorry, your honor, I'm just a little upset. It won't happen again."

Mr. Hall continued, "Mr. Taylor, does the man that you witnessed approaching Ms. Wooldridge's home on that particular morning resemble the defendant, Mr. Steele?" Mr. Hall pointed directly at the defendant for emphasis.

"I never got a good look at the man's face, but Mr. Steele's frame seems the same as the man I saw."

"Did you see this man approach or leave the Wooldridge residence at any other time ?"

"No. That was the first and last I ever saw of him. I never saw Anita's car leave that morning as I had to go get some gas for my lawn mower, and then I stopped by the hardware store after I got my mail."

"I have no further questions for this witness, Your Honor. Thank you, Mr. Taylor."

The judge asked Mr. Steele if he would like to cross-examine the witness. Tom rustled through his papers on the desk for several minutes, and the judge started to lose her patience with him. Tom cleared his voice and took the stage. He asked the witness in a very cocky manner, "Mr. Taylor, do you wear glasses?"

"Yes. I do."

"On the particular morning that you claim you saw a man of the defendant's build approach the Wooldridge home, were you wearing your glasses?" Tom asked, speaking in the third person.

"Yes. I could see just fine." After his first failed attempt to discredit the witness's testimony, Tom tried again. "Mr. Taylor, you testified that you thought that it was odd for a stranger to be approaching the house in such attire, right?"

"Yes."

"Okay. Then why did you not stay to watch or report this to the authorities?'

Fred stammered, "W-W-Well, I said that I feel real bad that I didn't. I should have."

Tom was getting excited now. "So, Mr. Taylor, you weren't alarmed enough to call the authorities. You never saw the man enter Anita's home. You don't know if Anita came to the door. So, it could have easily been someone selling something, and Anita might not have been home. The fact is that you don't really know whether Anita was even home at that time, do you, Mr. Taylor?"

"I guess I can't say for sure since I never saw her that morning."

Tom smiled smugly from behind the podium. It was obvious he took great pleasure from what he viewed as his first victory in the proceedings. "I have no further questions for you then," he said as if questioning the witness was a waste of time. "You are dismissed."

The judge asked the prosecution if they had further questions for the witness. "No, Your Honor," Mr. Hall said. "The witness can be dismissed now."

"Thank you, Mr. Taylor," Judge Allen-Parker said. "You may step down now and leave the courtroom. You will not be needed any further and are excused for the remainder of the trial."

The judge asked the prosecution to call their next witness, Anita's mother, Carrie Ann Wooldridge. Anita's brother and sister were asked to leave the courtroom so that if they were called as a witness at a later time, they would not know their mother's testimony. After she was sworn in by the judge, Mr. Hall asked her, "Mrs. Wooldridge, on June 25, when was the last time you saw your daughter Anita?"

"I was the last one to see her that morning before I left for work. Anita was still sleeping, and I woke her up briefly to see if she was still going over to the high school with the cleanup crew. She told me it'd been cancelled and that she and her boyfriend, Scott, planned to go over to her grandparents' later for lunch."

"So Anita did not appear upset when you talked to her? She just confirmed her plans for the day?"

"No, she wasn't upset. She was really tired and wanted to sleep for a few more hours before Scott picked her up for lunch."

"Mrs. Wooldridge, has your daughter ever worked with the police or disappeared without telling anyone?"

"No," she replied emphatically. "Anita has never been involved with the law. And she's always been a good kid. She's very reliable. If she says she's going to do something, she does it. I've never known her to just leave and not call us. She wouldn't have blown off her grandparents and boyfriend or missed work. That's not Anita at all."

"So, when you went home for lunch that day, and her boyfriend told you he couldn't find her, were you alarmed?"

"Yes. I couldn't figure out why she would leave without her glasses or contacts in and why the window screen was torn out in the kitchen."

"What did you do next?"

"I couldn't get a hold of my husband, so I called Anita's older sister. Melanie said she hadn't heard from Anita since the day before when Anita had watched her two kids. She told me to call 911 because it sounded like a forced entry, and she was worried something might have happened to Anita. I wanted to wait for my husband to return home. I kept thinking that maybe he had removed the screen for some reason and that this really wasn't happening. But I decided to call 911, and I did report her missing."

"Did the dispatcher send an officer out at that time?"

"Yes. An officer was at our house within the next twenty minutes."

"Did you, any other family members, or her boyfriend remove or touch any evidence in the house when you entered it that afternoon?"

"No. After I called 911, they advised me to wait outside, and we weren't allowed to reenter our home until the crime scene was investigated fully."

"Thank you. I have no further questions for this witness, Your Honor."

Tom wanted to rip this bitch apart on the stand. *If she even thinks she can outsmart me, she's mistaken. Anita's mine, and she'll never go back to her meddling family.* He attempted to approach the stand, but the two guards started to come forward, stopping him in his tracks. Tom backed up but was proud of his ploy to intimidate the witness some. He stared her down as he asked, "Did your daughter ever mention the defendant's name to you before she was allegedly abducted?" He was surprised when she did not look away from his penetrating eyes. Instead, she shot him back a piercing glare.

"No. She never mentioned your name to me. There was never any reason for her to."

"Was your daughter familiar with any law enforcement officers before the alleged abduction occurred?" Tom continued.

"No. Not that I am aware of. She has never been in trouble with the law before."

"Yet, don't you find it odd that the Kokomo officer that allegedly pulled her out to safety grew up in a house near your own home?"

"No. It's a coincidence. Anita had never met Deputy Eastwood prior to him rescuing her. He's years older than her and no longer lived in that home when Anita was growing up." Carrie Ann was not backing down; she was fueled by her intense anger toward the man that had destroyed her family's sense of peace and safety. She wanted to choke him but decided to beat him on the stand instead.

Tom seemed to ponder her answer for a few minutes. It was a tactic to distract her on the stand. She waited patiently for the next question.

"My point here is that Anita could have had ties to the officers that allegedly rescued her and been coerced into framing the defendant as a favor to them."

"Objection," Mr. Hall interjected. "The defense is trying to lead the witness with his own theories. He isn't even asking our witness a question, Your Honor." The patient judge began guiding Mr. Steele through the correct process of formulating his words into questions. The Wooldridge family members in the room were growing rather irritated: it seemed that she was trying to help him win the case. The prosecution attorneys explained to the Wooldridge family later that the judge was only helping the defendant through the trial process to prevent him from being awarded a mistrial down the road.

Tom asked Carrie Ann a few more useless questions and then announced suddenly, "I'm done with this witness now." He seemed to thrive on the power he had inside this courtroom to dismiss people whenever he felt like it. The judge thanked the witness for her time and excused her for the remainder of the trial. She then ordered an hour-long lunch break. When the trial resumed, Anita would take the stand.

CHAPTER 55

Anita was sitting outside the courtroom with Kimberly Van-dorf, waiting to be called in. They both knew her testimony would be key in achieving a conviction. Anita had not been able to sleep a wink the night before in the hotel room. She had borrowed her friend Jamie's mother's navy blue suit to wear today. It was too large for her and covered every square inch of her body, yet it still looked professional. She did not want to give her captor the satisfaction of gazing at her body any further. The thought of being in the same room with him again and having to answer his questions made her want to vomit. To keep her distracted, she and Kimberly tried to talk about Anita's new job at Chrysler's transmission plant in Kokomo and why she and Scott had broken up a few months ago.

Anita held no hard feelings toward Scott for the breakup. He had been the number one suspect for some time during the investigation. Dealing with the loss of his girlfriend while being falsely accused of hurting her was too much for him to handle. The whole experience put so much strain on their relationship that it just could not work, and they ended it on amicable terms. The conversation successfully distracted her because, before she knew it, Anita was being called into the massive courtroom.

All eyes were glued on Anita as she walked in and took a seat in the witness chair after being sworn in. The twelve jurors had remained poker-faced until now, but several of the older, grandmotherly women on the jury looked sympathetic toward this poor young girl who had to face the man that had allegedly hurt her. Tom waited patiently for his turn with Anita. For roughly an hour, the prosecution asked her questions regarding her experience with the man who had kidnapped, beaten, sexually assaulted, and threatened her life for eight days and the evidence that had already been introduced. When the prosecution was done, Tom leapt eagerly to his feet. He kept Anita on the stand for an hour and a half despite asking her only about twenty questions.

The judge had to prod Tom along several times, even asking him if he was done with this witness or just thinking of his next question. He would rustle papers around, attempt to get closer to the stand to intimidate her, and clear his throat incessantly. Tom was stalling: he loved having his trophy near him and wanted to remain in control of her for as long as possible again. "Isn't it true that the week you were allegedly abducted by the defendant you were really staying in a hotel?"

"No. I wish that were true, but it's not."

Tom continued, "Did you receive money and fame by appearing on television and talking to several magazines about your alleged abduction?"

"I was paid for my time and travel by one of the magazines for my story," Anita admitted. "That's not why I agreed to talk about it, though. I wanted to help other victims."

"Just answer the questions, Ms. Wooldridge," he countered.

Tom focused in on the gag and the stun gun for his next set of questions. "The prosecution has presented into evidence pieces of the gag they found strewn all over the house and garage of the defendant's mother. Yet, you testified that the defendant took the gag off you in the garage. So, why would it be found all over the house too?"

"I don't have any idea," Anita answered. "All of that seems like a blur to me." Tom remained on that question until Anita could take no more of his game and snapped at him, "I have no idea why. You were there. You go ahead and tell them why."

The judge seemed to stifle a smile but reminded Anita, "You do need to answer the questions, Ms. Wooldridge, but let's move on to your next point, Mr. Steele. We don't have all day."

Tom picked up the stun gun, held it up in the air for all to see, and asked Anita, "So the defendant used this tool to abduct you…allegedly?"

"Yes. You zapped me with it three times and were angry that it was supposed to have taken me down on the first zap."

Tom stared Anita down and then continued on while holding the apparatus in his hand. He started pushing the button down, playing dumb, "I don't even know how this thing works."

"All you did was push the button, and it worked on me."

"Are you aware that the defendant only has one testicle, Ms. Wooldridge?" Tom asked bluntly.

Anita answered the question honestly, "I'm not sure. I'm not sexually experienced, and I was being raped, so I wasn't paying attention to your anatomy." She believed he was just asking the question so that, if she agreed with him, he could argue that, since he has two testicles, she could not have been raped by him. When he finally ran out of questions for her, Anita was overcome with exhaustion. As she walked out the double doors of the courtroom, she fell dramatically to the floor. There was a gasp in the crowd as the guards at the door picked Anita up off the marble floor and carried her out. It had taken everything out of her, and it would take her another week to mentally and physically recover from seeing her captor again.

Howard County Sheriff's Deputy Ron Eastwood was called in as the prosecution's next witness. He testified to finding Anita locked in the defendant's home inside a metal box. The jury was on the edge of their seats as the actual metal cabinet was dragged loudly into the courtroom for added effect. It was used to convince the jury that a human being could fit inside of it. The jury members all seemed disappointed when the box was opened up and Anita was not inside.

Tom's mother, Daphne Steele, was called in by the prosecution to testify after Ron Eastwood had been released as a witness. Tom was sure his mother had been forced by the prosecution team to testify against him until he cross-examined her. "Why would the defendant bring Anita back to your home when he knew that you would be home soon that day?"

"Son," his weary mother said, ignoring the question, "I believed that you were innocent the first time you got yourself in some trouble, but you need to fess up now. Tell the truth…that you hurt this poor girl real bad. You're dead to me if you don't."

Tom seemed flabbergasted that his own mother had turned on him when he desperately needed her. His confidence level seemed to fall a few notches after hearing those words. He said nothing else to his mother; he just turned and walked over to his seat. The judge dismissed Mrs. Steele, and she did not return for the remainder of the trial or the sentencing, making it clear that she was done with her son for good. He had humiliated her for the last time.

Captain Jack Roberts was the last witness for the prosecution to take the stand. Jack was able to provide the jury members with the ample evidence he had obtained. He brought in shell casings from the two rounds of bullets he had fired from the suspect's pistol to prove that the gun was in good working order. Jack also testified about the evidence found at the defendant's mother's home, the La Crosse residence, and the Wooldridge home, as well as the evidence found in Anita's car and Tom's truck. He submitted as evidence a stack of papers, on which the suspect had taken notes in his own handwriting, regarding a list of potential female victims to abduct, allowing him to argue that this act was premeditated and well planned. Jack also testified that he had walked the distance from the suspect's mother's home to where they had found Anita's abandoned car to prove that the suspect would have had enough time to walk back to his mother's home after getting rid of her vehicle.

Lastly, Jack testified that the defendant, Mr. Steele, had told him at the time of his arrest that he had made several mistakes and was surprised that the police had not apprehended him sooner. The elbow print lifted from Anita's car had been matched to the defendant's elbow impression but was not used as evidence in court as they did not want to overwhelm the jury with a brand new form of evidence.

The defendant only had one question for Captain Jack Roberts on the stand. "Did the Indiana State Police ask you to help them set me up to settle a vendetta against me?"

"Absolutely not," Jack answered. "If they had, I would have refused. I take my job seriously and don't have the time to make up an investigation just to settle some score. I had never even met Anita Wooldridge before this case."

Tom Steele looked defeated and knew that he had nothing further to ask this man. Jack had obviously done his research and knew his facts. Tom simply turned and walked back over to his chair to sit down. Judge Allen-Parker cleared her throat. "Are we to assume that you have no further questions for this witness, Mr. Steele?" Tom just nodded his head yes.

The only witness Tom called in to testify for his defense was his lifelong friend, Jimmy. To the audience and jury, it appeared to be a pathetic attempt on his part to see if Jimmy would still be his friend after this. It didn't seem like he had a strategy with this witness, even though so much was at stake.

"You've known the defendant since you guys were kids, right?"

"Yes," Jimmy admitted.

"Wouldn't the defendant have confided to you that he had taken the girl if he really had? I mean he told you everything."

Tom was shocked when his friend failed to cover for him. "You wouldn't have told me if you were going to do this! You know I would've turned you in…are you crazy? You're on your own. I wish I'd never known you. You disgust me!"

When he realized he was alone, Tom's confidence seemed to deflate even further.

The judge asked the prosecution attorney, "Mr. Hall, do you have any further questions for this witness?"

"No. The prosecution rests, Your Honor," Mr. Hall responded. "We have no further questions for this witness and are ready to proceed to final arguments for the jury."

"Let's take an hour break," Judge Allen-Parker ordered, "and then the court will reconvene to hear closing arguments from both sides." She stood up and exited the courtroom.

An hour later, the prosecution team was poised and ready to go. The defendant did not appear worried as he sat, doodling on a sheet of paper in front of him. In fact, Tom Steele seemed oddly confident, almost delusional, that he had a good chance of winning just by giving a good closing argument. It would be one of his last opportunities to take the spotlight and shine.

The prosecution argued that the main pieces of evidence presented during the trial, on top of the live victim's testimony, were enough to grant a conviction on all counts. The defendant paid little attention to the prosecution's closing argument. At one point, he absentmindedly picked up the wooden dowel from the nearby evidence table and began sliding it through his fingers. It made the same *swoosh* sound Anita had earlier testified about: she had told the courtroom that her captor did it out of habit whenever he was bored or thinking. Mr. Hall directed the jury's attention over to Tom, catching him in the act. It seemed to be the end for Tom.

The prosecution's argument was clear, convincing, concise, and filled with pleas to put Anita's captor behind bars for life so that she could feel safe and move forward. Tom Steele was on his own as he stood up to give his final argument. He had no friends, family, or supporters in the courtroom now. Even the lawyer they had forced upon him looked convinced that he was guilty. Tom knew it was up to him to convince the jury of his innocence with what he felt was a plausible explanation.

Tom began by walking up as close to the jury as he was allowed and letting out a pitiful sigh. "Ladies and gentleman of the jury, I am the true victim here in this case. If I had known that suing the State of Indiana for mistreatment in prison and winning a measly five thousand dollars would lead to all of this, then I would never have done it. I'm here to tell you that I took a fishing trip in La Crosse the week of the alleged abduction. I was going to go home and retrieve the rest of my belongings and move there the next week. The Indiana State Police concocted this whole case and planted all this absurd evidence against me while I was gone."

Tom continued after a slight pause, "Somehow, they even got my own mother to go along with their plan. The whole investigation was a scam. They had Anita set up in a hotel room the whole week. She agreed to all of this for the fame and money she received for interviews following her alleged rescue. If there is even one of you that can feel my plight, that thinks that I could be telling the truth, then you have to find me not guilty of these ridiculous charges today. By law, if you have even an ounce of reasonable doubt, you must acquit me. Please, do what is right and show our law enforcement officers that they do not have the power to bully a private citizen and waste taxpayers' money. I did not kidnap Anita Wooldridge. I hope you will all find that to be true. Thank you."

Tom walked slowly back to his seat, casting a smug look over toward Jack Roberts. He felt triumphant and was confident that he had planted at least some seeds of doubt in several of the jury members, who had also possibly felt bullied a time or two in their own lives by law enforcement or the government.

"Now I'll allow the jury to go into the deliberation room until they can reach a verdict," Judge Allen-Parker announced. "We'll reconvene when the jury has made their decision." With that, the judge left the courtroom, and the members of the jury stood up and filed out of the courtroom as well.

Tom took this opportunity to rudely get rid of his lawyer, who had, in his mind, been useless. "You can get the hell out of here now," he ordered. "Don't even bother returning for the verdict. I don't need help from you or anyone else." Rodney Davidson was dumbfounded by how arrogantly this man was behaving in his dire situation. But he could not say anything before the courtroom officer led the defendant away in handcuffs. Tom was taken back to his holding cell to await his verdict.

Several FBI agents who had attended the trial decided they would take an early dinner. They asked Rodney Davidson to join them since he had been so rudely dismissed. Bob Thorton, the FBI profiler, asked Jack to give them a call as soon as he heard any news, and they left to dine at St. Elmo's Steakhouse in downtown Indianapolis. Jack, Anita's brother, and the prosecution team all remained nearby, waiting for the call to return to the courthouse for the verdict.

Three hours later, they were called back into the courtroom to hear the verdict. It was dead quiet in the large courtroom as the spokesman for the jury read aloud, "We, the jury, find the defendant, Victor Thomas Steele, guilty on all counts of kidnapping, carjacking, and illegal possession of a firearm in a kidnapping felony charge." For a moment, nobody moved or made a sound. Tom's shoulders sank down as low as the table in front of him. He appeared to be in a state of complete shock as the officers came over to cuff him and remove him from the courtroom before an incident could occur. The judge and the jury members all silently filed out one by one, and the prosecution team, Jack, and Anita's brother walked out together. They were in good spirits but were not able to fully celebrate until they learned what his sentencing would be. Jack left the group to call Bob Thorton and let him know the good news. Daniel called Anita to let her know the verdict as well.

Bob and the other FBI agents from Quantico were throwing stories back and forth, having a good time getting to know Rodney Davidson at the restaurant table. They had enjoyed appetizers, savored their steaks, and had thrown back a few beers during the pleasant conversation. They had avoided the topic of the trial as they did not want Rodney to feel uncomfortable sitting with the opposing team. Even though he had no real ties or investment in this case, he still needed to act ethically and not discuss it with the men from the other side. As the men were deciding on dessert, Bob's cell phone rang loudly. Everyone stopped talking and looked at Bob; the waitress did not know what to think of their silence. It seemed like only an hour had gone by. It was a good sign that a verdict may have been reached in that short a time. They all knew that should mean good news for the prosecution team, bad for the defense.

Bob quickly answered his phone, "What's the verdict, Jack?"

The other men could hear the answer as Jack yelled into the phone, "Guilty! They found him guilty on all charges! Yeah! The sentencing won't be for another few weeks, though."

"Get over here and celebrate with us, Jack! You've earned this one. Great job! Does Anita know yet?"

"Yeah. Her brother just called her and her parents to let them know. They were relieved, but they don't want to celebrate until we find out how long he has to serve in prison."

"That's understandable." Bob had gotten to know Anita and her brother Daniel well since she had been rescued. He had invited them to the Quantico FBI Academy Headquarters and had been impressed with Anita's spirit and willingness to talk openly about her ordeal. Bob had become as protective of her at these conferences as he would have been with one of his own children. He had made the trip over for the trial because he truly cared about Anita and had wanted to show her support as well as to make sure that her captor was sent to prison for good.

Jack showed up shortly to celebrate with the FBI agents. Rodney Davidson politely said his good-byes and congratulated Jack on winning such a successful case. Jack stayed with the men for an hour but was eager to get back to the Kokomo station and let his team know the good news. He also wanted to get home to Dorothy to tell her all the details. She had been his number one supporter throughout the case, and Jack wanted to share this triumph with her.

Two weeks later, the prosecution team, Jack, Ron Eastwood, Anita's brother and sister, and Tom Steele all reconvened in the federal courtroom for the sentencing hearing. Anita had wanted to be at the hearing but, at the last minute, had decided to stay home. She did not want to grant her captor another opportunity to see her or violate her in any way. She had control now: she never had to be in the same room as the man who had violated her again.

"I will now give the defendant the opportunity to express any remorse that he might want to share with his victim's family,"

Judge Allen-Parker began. "Mr. Steele, do you have anything you'd like to say?"

Tom was stone-faced and stated casually, "No. I don't think I do."

Judge Allen-Parker continued, "All right then, does Anita's family wish to say any words before the sentence is read?"

Daniel stood up. "My family has been through enough, Your Honor. We have my sister safely back home with us, and we're ready to have all of this behind us so Anita can move on with her life. We beg you to give the defendant the maximum sentence possible so that we can all feel safe again. Thank you, Your Honor." Daniel sat down, wiping the sweat from his brow, to wait for the sentence to be read.

Melanie and Daniel held hands as the judge read the sentence, "I hereby sentence the defendant, Mr. Victor Thomas Steele, to serve life plus twenty-five consecutive years in a state prison for the crimes he has been charged with." With that, the judge briskly removed herself from the courtroom.

Tom showed no expression regarding his sentence. He had already planned out an appeal and could not care less what the judge had decided. Anita's family could finally celebrate once they walked outside the courtroom. They hugged and jumped up and down in victory. They called Anita immediately. She was eating lunch with Kimberly nearby, waiting for their call. Anita answered the phone eagerly, "What'd they give him?"

Daniel was whooping and hollering on the courtroom steps. "She threw the book at him! He'll be dead before he gets the opportunity to walk out those prison doors. We did it, sis! I'm so proud of you! Now we can put this nightmare behind us!"

Anita was so relieved to hear the news and vowed that her captor would never take another day from her again. She was finally able to exhale. She felt safe again. Free. Anita said a prayer of thankfulness as she hung up the phone and attempted to get back to the normalcy of everyday life that she had once taken for granted. She never would make that mistake again.

EPILOGUE
BY ANITA WOOLDRIDGE

Have you ever had that feeling where you're somehow walking, but you can't feel your legs moving, and you're talking to people, but later you have no idea what was said the whole conversation? That's how I felt when I was first rescued and in the weeks that would follow. Everything was so surreal for me. I know now that I was in a state of shock from the torture that I had endured, and was still trying to grasp the idea that I was actually alive and had really been saved.

Everything was whirling so fast in front of me; everyone wanted to introduce themselves to me, talk to me, and hug me. I felt numb and could not feel their touches. It was so overwhelming to me. I just wanted my normal life, like back before this nightmare began, but I was a celebrity for the moment as no one could believe that I was still alive and that I could look so "okay" after all that I had been through. People would just stare at me with bewildered looks on their faces like they could not understand how I could go on. I might have looked and talked the same on the outside, but I was a changed person inside.

The world just seemed different and was such a blur. It was like being on a roller coaster ride that I could not get off of. I no longer could smell the deep fragrances of a summer breeze and the birds seemed to be without song. It was strange coming home to the same house that I had been abducted from. It felt comforting, but at the same time, it was my safe haven that had been tainted by the abduction. I had so much to tell people and felt so lucky to be that needle in the haystack that was found. I was one of the rare 1 percent of victims that actually come home alive after being abducted that long. The problem was that the world at large was not ready for me and the gruesome details that I had to tell.

The day after I returned to Kokomo, I was maid of honor at my best friend Sarah's wedding. She kept telling me that she would understand if I did not want to come and be around so many people that soon. She assured me that she would not be mad if I was not ready, but I assured her that I needed to do this. The persistent thought that had kept me alive during my captivity was the hope that I would be able to see her wedding and be with my friends and family again.

I had kept track of the days on the mole's computer calendar. I counted down the days until the wedding and prayed desperately that I would be home by then to see it. The wedding was held at the church that I had attended since the tenth grade, and my pastor, who just so happened to be Sarah's father, married them. He said tearfully during the ceremony, "Miracles do still happen today, my friends. We have our own miracle in the fact that Anita is back home safely with us today. We are so blessed." I don't think that there was a dry eye in the house at that point.

People wanted to talk to me at the reception about what I had been through, but I told them all that I would tell them whatever they wanted to know a different day. Today was Sarah and her new husband's day and I did not want to take the spotlight away from them in any way. This day was one of the most memorable of my entire life, because I felt so alive, loved, and free again. The feeling was like a rush of pure adrenaline. I felt like I wanted to dance through the streets, run in a field, anything to keep feeling this alive. Unfortunately, this high did not last even the entire evening. I went through these intense emotions that fluctuated between rushes of energy and happiness to feelings of rage and despair. I, at one point, would just hit my head on the wall over and over to take my mind off the intense pain I felt inside. I was so moody during the first few weeks of being home that the people closest to me no longer knew what to say or how to help me.

I saw a therapist shortly after returning home, and she told me that I was suffering from post-traumatic stress disorder, which is common in victims of traumatic events. During the first few weeks of returning home, I would occasionally, upon waking up in the mornings, find myself in a dissociative flashback state. I would feel as if I were right back in the box or being raped again and there was nothing I could do to stop it. I was helpless until I woke up screaming or whimpering from the episode. I would wake up drenched in sweat and felt the rest of the day like I had been victimized again. It was torturous getting through those first few weeks of adjusting to being back home.

I went back to work at UPS a few weeks after returning home. My coworkers were all very supportive, and it helped to get back on a normal routine. It took my mind off things, but it was hard for my family at first. One evening, I had to work late, and I forgot to call to tell my parents. They became alarmed when it was three hours past the time I normally would have returned home from work. I received a frantic phone call from my mom and had to apologize and assure her that I was fine. I appreciated everyone's concern, but at the same time, I felt almost smothered by everyone watching me so closely. It was like living in a fishbowl at times.

Six months after I returned home, I was told by my U.S. attorney that the animal who had degraded me in every form possible, was now being allowed to be his own defense attorney and would be able to cross-examine me in the courtroom. The mere thought of being in the same room with him again and having to answer his questions set me into a complete explosive rage. My poor mother had never seen her daughter behave or talk the way I did that day. I dropped to the kitchen floor, bawling like a baby and screaming at the top of my lungs. I ran through the house throwing anything that I could get my hands on. For the first time, I was shouting obscenities into the air.

"Screw his civil right to defend himself. I can't even believe he has any rights after what he did to me! What about my damn rights as a victim? Don't I have any? He is such a jerk! I wish he would just die and leave me alone!" I was mentally and physically exhausted and very hoarse after my meltdown. This was the day that I started smoking cigarettes because I felt so stressed out, and I thought that the nicotine would calm me down. It is a nasty habit that I wish I had never started and would never recommend to anyone. I justified it in my head, though, that at least I had not gone to drugs or a bottle to cope. I soon found that it is just as hard an addiction to quit.

It was almost as if I hit kind of a rebellious streak because of all the anger welled up deep inside me and the growing dislike of all the characteristics of myself that the mole had been attracted to: my submissiveness, shyness, and compassion for all. I wanted people to know that from now on I was not someone to mess with ever again. It took me many years to get all of that poisonous anger out of my body, but that day with my mom was a good start to the process. I only stayed with my first therapist for a short while, and then when the acute symptoms seemed to be gone, I said, "I'm fine. I can do this on my own from now on." I made it a few years on my own, really struggling, before I decided to find a new therapist.

I went to Angela Roegner in 2002 for several reasons. She had also grown up in Center. Her dad had been my basketball and softball coach growing up. I was friends with her younger sister in school. She was closer to my age, and I thought that she already would be familiar with my story. I trusted her when I went into the office, which helped quicken my difficult process of healing and closure. I opened up to her right away, and she said, "Wow, Anita. How have you made it these last few years on your own? It was such a miracle that you were rescued. You are so strong. You are such an inspiration to people." The problem was that I did not feel strong at all. I felt like a coward that was hiding from my problems.

I would love to be able to say that I had no emotional scars from my kidnapping; I hate to give the mole the satisfaction that he continued to have an impact on me even as he sat in prison. But I won't lie just to get to him because I want other victims reading this book to know that I was seriously damaged. I want all of you that have suffered through similar pain to hear that I eventually overcame this pain and suffering but will never fully forget. I want you to know how I pulled myself, step by step, out of the dark, sinister world of depression. I came to Angela in a serious state of depression and panic. I was living with my friend Monica at the time. We both were depressed, feeding off each other's misery. It felt like I had fallen into a dark hole and could not pull myself out of it. I could not see any light or opening to head toward. I was enveloped by this darkness daily and had a hard time getting out of bed at all. I no longer even cared how I looked, I had a sarcastic comment on my tongue at all times, and people were noticing how bitter I had become. I had walls up that pushed all of the people closest to me away. My only daily contact was with my dogs, coworkers from the Chrysler plant, and my roommate. I had stopped cleaning the house and would not allow people to come over. My family and close friends were worried for me. They had all encouraged me to get back into counseling.

Would I ever have developed depression if I had not been traumatized? Probably not, but I will never know for sure. Angela said, "You may have had the predisposition genetically for depression, but it might not have ever come out since your life before the trauma was rather peaceful. The trauma that you experienced brought on a major depressive episode. You have to start fighting the depression if you ever want to get your life back again."

I took this to heart. It felt good to hear that I could possibly someday have my bubbly, positive personality back and that

I could get control back gradually. In my past therapy, I had not yet been ready to fully forgive my abductor or even myself. I hadn't been ready to deal with the demons in my head that haunted my dreams and caused me to panic and cry during the day. I was still extremely angry and scared to be alone but, at the same time, afraid to be around people.

Angela explained to me, "I know that this is going to be a tough road for you, Anita, but you'll have to forgive yourself as well as the man that did this to you in order to fully let go of all the pain, anger, and fear that you have buried deep inside. I want you to look at forgiveness as a means of freeing yourself for good from your perpetrator. It doesn't mean that you ever have to have contact with him or that you'll ever like him in any way. It also doesn't ever mean that what he did to you was okay. All it means is that you're going to get all of the raw emotions out, either by talking or writing on paper through journaling. After you choose to forgive and let go of these emotions regarding the abuse for good, you have to look at it as an ordeal that made you stronger and move forward with your life. In essence, it will be a new start. I'm not saying that you'll never have flashbacks or nightmares of the abuse anymore, but if you do, you'll remind yourself that you have put closure on that and that it no longer controls you. This reassurance, using your support system, praying to God for strength and peace, and taking an antidepressant daily will allow you to manage those symptoms and will help you to not relapse back into a state of depression and helplessness."

I have to admit, it really scared me to think that I would have to forgive this man, even though I knew that, through Christ Jesus, we are all ultimately forgiven if we repent. Still,

I had yet to even hear this man admit to hurting me, let alone get an apology from him. Part of me felt like he did not deserve forgiveness, but the moving on and being at peace part Angela spoke of was like a child being offered candy. I craved being cleansed and free from these demons. My mouth salivated at those mere words of hope. I told her, "I'm ready. Sign me up. But I don't do morning appointments!" She laughed, and we then started this lengthy process of "letting go" on a weekly basis.

The first step was her referral to her father-in-law, my psychiatrist for life (I will never allow him to retire!), Dr. Roegner. He was also someone that I knew growing up, as his children went to Taylor High School as well. It was also very important to me that my treatment team were God-fearing Christians. They both understood and encouraged my deep faith in the Lord and his power to heal. They both assured me that it was not a weakness to take an antidepressant daily and an antianxiety medication as needed for the panic attacks. The medicine would stabilize my mood and allow me to then put closure on my past issues in order to return to my previous functioning level.

I was amazed that within a month's time I no longer cried uncontrollably, and the black cloud started to evaporate. I started to enjoy my life again and no longer wanted to sleep it away. My sense of humor returned, and I started to take pride in how my house looked and my appearance again. I regretted not taking the medicine years earlier. It was like a miracle. I believe that God healed me and that he wants me to take the medicine in order for me to keep the demons at bay. Occasionally, I will still have a mild depressive episode, even with the medicine, but it is less severe and does not last as long.

The second step was learning a list of techniques to utilize daily to fight off the depression. We worked on cognitive-behavioral strategies first, such as telling myself positive statements every day to combat all of the negative thoughts that were flowing in. For years, I had felt like the devil kept telling me, "You'll never get through this. You might as well end it all now. Give up! God was never with you. He *let* this happen to you. He doesn't love you. Wake up!"

I just never could seem to shake these negative thoughts off, until I found Angela. She reminded me, "Your perpetrator violated and harmed your physical body, but he was unable to touch your soul because God would never allow him to go that far. Don't let the demons control your thoughts anymore. The devil wants you to believe these negative thoughts and make you self-destruct, so that he can one day take your soul with him."

It helped me to tell myself positive statements every day like, "I will make it a good day today" or "God loves me. He is with me at all times." My testimony is so powerful in helping others to see that they too can make it through any negative experiences if they keep faith in God and know that his love for his children is unfaltering. I have read in the Bible that his children who suffer here on earth will be rewarded greatly in heaven. I often joke that I want the king-sized suite in heaven for enduring all of this!

Another tool I learned to use daily to feel better is helping others. I volunteer as a youth group teacher at my church and feel rewarded every time that I am allowed to influence a child's life. I have cried many tears of joy when these kids choose to turn their lives fully over to the Lord and are saved eternally. It helps me to feel valuable and worthy of another day of life. I was also encouraged to find hobbies and spend time with my loved ones regularly. I enjoy scrapbooking family albums for myself, friends, and family. There is no greater gift than to look back on all the memories that pictures provide you with. I have numerous snapshots of myself and the people that I love the most, smiling from ear to ear on trips or holidays.

It helps me to remember all the good times that I've had in life and how blessed I truly am. I started making jewelry for people as another fun hobby. I love to travel to see my friends in other states, and last year I got to take a trip with my teenage niece to Niagara Falls. I will never forget the views, especially at night when the water is lit up and turns different colors. The experience that we shared on the road together is priceless.

Angela urged me to use daily exercise as an anger outlet, to let out any stress or frustrations and to give myself more energy and strength. It acts almost like an antidepressant by sending out endorphins into your bloodstream and making you feel better. I had always been active prior to my abduction and knew that I needed to get back into a sport. I joined a women's softball league and started to feel better physically. I now try to exercise at home and feel better when I muster up the energy to do it. It also helps me to spend time with my animals. My dogs have given me the most comfort of all. They are always there for me and make me feel loved and protected. You would have to kill them to get to me.

The next step that I had to work on was feeling more in control, which helped to deescalate my panic attacks early on. I identified that my triggers to panic were people who come up behind me and startle me, enclosed spaces such as getting an

MRI or hearing tests at work that were given in a small booth, being in crowds of strangers, or passing by a Kentucky Fried Chicken restaurant. Certain smells or sights brought on panic for me.

I learned to talk myself through these situations. I would tell myself, "I'm in control. I need to calm down. Everything is okay. God will give me peace." At the same time, I would envision myself in my calm place, in a fishing boat with my dad on the lake, and take deep breaths from my diaphragm. Slowly, in and out I would breathe until my heart slowed down and I felt at peace again. This, on top of taking a Xanax if it was a bad attack, helped me to no longer fear losing control. Just knowing that I had a plan in place to manage the panic attacks was enough to make them occur less frequently. I can now calm myself down in record time when it does happen on rare occasions.

Another issue I had to face was my other addiction that came on since my abduction: food. I looked good at age twenty-one, but when I got back home, I hated my body. I hated all the things that the mole had found sexy or appealing about me. I could never scrub myself clean enough in the shower and still felt so disgusting. I started eating more to hide my body so that men would no longer even look at me. It was also a way of punishing and further isolating myself from others. As the weight packed on, it started to match how I saw myself. I also drew comfort from food. It became my best friend and only joy at the time. It was the one thing I did feel in control of. I was adamant that I was going to eat whatever in the heck I wanted after all that I had been through. No one could tell me what I was going to eat or when I would eat it ever again.

My eating was a double-edged sword in the end, though, because I eventually no longer felt control over my large eating habits, and it made me feel worse about myself every day. This is an issue that I continue to struggle with, but I am more at peace with it as I have cut back on portions and try to choose healthier foods when I can. I am convinced that, since my self-esteem has increased through this whole healing process, soon I will be able to kick my bad habits and treat myself better. As a result, I will be able to lose the weight and feel better about my appearance. That, like therapy, is going to be a process, and I have to remind myself to be patient and to not beat myself up about it.

The last part of my therapy process is the forgiveness/closure issue that I so wanted to avoid in the beginning. Oh, I am so glad now that I was pushed to work on it. Angela and I decided that God had brought us together in this therapeutic relationship for a reason or purpose. He had laid upon both our hearts, separately, his desire for this book to be written by us and read by the world at large. I joked several times that my story would make a best seller, and Angela chimed in that she would write it for me as she had always wanted to write a novel. We were both initially just kidding around, but I think that it started to make more and more sense to write it as a means of gaining closure.

Angela urged me, "It will be the final nail hammered down for you to reach full closure and freedom. Your testimony is so inspiring and needs to be told to people to give others hope. You have always felt like God allowed you to go through all this for a reason. This is his reason."

I knew that letting my demons out for the whole world to see would be hard, but I also felt that if it helped even one person, then that is what God would want me to do. This book would help me to heal fully because I would then know that God had a reason for sending me to the trenches and back. This is why he kept me alive and helped the police to miraculously find me. It all would make sense and be worth it to me if I could help other survivors to keep their faith in God and heal.

It has been a laborious process of retelling and writing in my journal the events that occurred, but it is finally all released from me. I feel fifty pounds lighter, and I have a sense of relief that all our hours of talking, research, and interviews with the FBI and police officers have paid off. Angela and I began this journey together and will now end it by having a bonfire, a closure party to celebrate. We will burn all my journals and her research notes to signify letting it all go for good. We are both ready.

Despite all of my success with moving on and letting go, this experience has taken its toll on myself, my family, and my relationship with men and friends. About four months after I was rescued, my father suffered a massive heart attack. All the stress had been too much for him to handle. He is the type that keeps everything in and avoids doctors like the plague. He hadn't felt good that day, and we had to rush him to the hospital when he began having sharp pains in his chest and shortness of breath. I had just gotten my dad back, and the thought of losing him again scared me to death. He had to stay in the hospital for over a week and then was sent home on a strict diet and warned to lower his stress,

He decided then that life is too short and actually retired from Delco Electronics that year. This is something we never thought he would do. On top of almost losing my dad a second time, my family suffered another blow. We received multiple reports from the FBI and the authorities that the mole was threatening to escape from prison and kill me, my parents, siblings, and even my niece and nephew. My sister became fearful for her children's safety and had to warn the school about these threats.

My relationships with men have also been greatly affected. I had been in a relationship with Scott for eight months when I was kidnapped. We had a good relationship, one I thought was going to be long term at the time. We broke up a few months after I returned home a changed person. We had not had sex yet, and when I got home, that was the last thing I wanted to consider doing for a long time. I know that it had to have been hard for him to have been questioned as the prime suspect initially. Then he was thrown into the limelight with me and had to hear all the disturbing details of what had happened to his girlfriend. Also, he was forced to deal with all of my emotions and probably felt like he took the brunt for what had been done to me. It just could not have worked out for us at the time. I hold no hard feelings toward him for moving on.

I then began dating my "celebrity" boyfriend, Ben, who stuck around only while I was still in the limelight. He was a wonderful means of support for me during the whole trial, and I thought that maybe we had a future together. Again, I think that it was all just too much for him to handle, and he started distancing himself from me after the trial was over. I've had a few relationships since then, but none have seemed to go anywhere. I still pray that God will bring into my life a godly man that can handle all my baggage and help me learn to love again. My trust for men is not that great, so this will have to be a very patient, loving person that can help me in breaking down the towering walls I have built up to protect myself. Right now, I just continue to enjoy my life, and I figure that I will know when the right man comes along.

I would like to share with you a few factors other than God, many prayers, my family and friends, therapy, and medication that have aided in my recovery. I started celebrating the day that I was rescued on an annual basis. I took in food to my department at work and told my coworkers that I wanted to celebrate another year of life. I often told people, "He took eight days of my life. He won't take any more from me!" I meant every word of that.

It was funny, though: I was laid off on July 2, 2007, the anniversary of my rescue. It had been such a busy week with friends and family that I actually forgot what day it was. Angela called me on my cell phone that day and said, "Congratulations! You made it through another year. I just wanted to let you know that I was thinking of you today." I asked, "What is today?" She said, "That's a really good sign that you've healed, Anita. This is great!" That whole week had always been hard for me in the past, and I felt so liberated that I had made it all week without even thinking about it.

Another factor that greatly helped me was that I stayed connected with the FBI and police officers that worked together to rescue me. About three months after I was rescued, I was asked to go to the FBI headquarters in Quantico to speak to agents with Bob Thorton, the FBI profiler who had worked on my case. They all said how rare it was to be able to speak to a live victim and find out how they can best help future victims when they are rescued. Bob trains FBI agents on how to crack a case successfully by using an outline of my case.

Bob gives credit to the Kokomo officers, who all went above and beyond their duties and thought outside the box during the investigation. They cared about me and still do to this day. They are all fiercely protective of me and my comfort level at these seminars. Bob always threatens to kick anyone out of the room if they ask me any disrespectful questions. When I speak at FBI training seminars, Angela and I both feel amazed that I am typically the only live victim in all the case studies presented. I feel fortunate, but at the same time, my heart goes out to all the victims that did not return home to their families.

I have also been on the Howard County Community Corrections Advisory Board since 1999. My purpose of serving on this board has always been to fight to prevent violent offenders from being allowed to join the work-release program and serve shorter sentences for good behavior. The statistics show that violent offenders are rarely rehabilitated. They almost always commit another violent crime when they get out early, and this needs to stop. These are often murderers or sexual predators who are highly dangerous and know how to play the system. The number one excuse is often that we don't have enough room in our prisons to keep them locked up. I will continue to serve on this board until I feel like I am no longer needed. It makes me feel good and safer to have a say on these issues in my community.

One of the most exhilarating forms of catharsis for me came about a year after my rescue when a good friend of mine, Lori, came up to me at work, telling me that she and her husband had just bought a home together. She was telling me about all the work that the old farmhouse needed, but that they thought it had good potential. She said they had gotten it at a good price because an elderly woman wanted out of it immediately. It was just too much upkeep for her to do alone. I was happy for them and told her that I would love to come by and see it soon. She then told me the address, and I was speechless for a moment.

I asked Lori slowly, "Is it an old farmhouse with an attic bedroom and a detached garage?" She answered, "Yeah. Why? Anita, are you okay? You look white as a ghost. What's wrong?" I told her, "That's the same house I was taken to at first when I was kidnapped. That was his mother's house. He raped me in that garage and in the attic bedroom."

We were both distraught. All Lori could do was say over and over, "I am so sorry, Anita. I am so sorry. We had no idea." To my delight and surprise, they decided to have the house and garage demolished and to rebuild on the land. Lori called me to tell me, "We wanted you to know that they are sending out the wrecking ball and crane tomorrow if you want to come over later tomorrow after they leave. You can help us knock this piece-of-shit house to the ground." I could never express to them how wonderful this sounded. I loved them for this.

The next evening, I went to the property with a professor I had bonded with. He came with me for support that rainy night. It was so liberating to go in there with my sledgehammer and go wild. Any structure that was still standing I knocked down with the full force and fury of a woman scorned. I screamed at the top of my lungs, and the rain made my dripping wet hair stick wildly to my face.

I must have looked crazy that night, but I never once cared. I threw rocks at the windows and crunched the glass on the ground with my boots. It felt dangerously good to get my anger and fury out in such a physical way. I believe that God sent that opportunity to me as he knew that I needed to see that hellish house go down. This experience still gives me chills and a sense of empowerment when I recall it.

I wish that every survivor of abuse could be granted this same opportunity. We all deserve it to heal our wounds and feel somehow in control again. I thank my friend for being so loving and understanding in that situation. I could never repay her for this. I also thank God, my family, friends, and countless others that have been there for me over these times of hardship. May God bless all of you and the countless other survivors of abuse that know exactly how I have felt. I pray that this book will reach you and guide you to peace as well.

Lastly, I have to tell you the most ironic, twisted part of my whole story. I have recently had to hire my U.S. attorney back as I am being sued by the mole for a million dollars and an apology for all the pain and suffering that he has gone through during his past ten years of incarceration. He is also suing the attorney that represented me for the same things.

Now mind you, he has already exhausted his appeals during the past nine years. His appeals have always been denied, and I was never even bothered by the U.S. Attorney's Office up until now. They have tried to spare me any further distress. But they were forced to contact me about these recent charges as it might actually make it to court this time. This is unbelievable to me as he has not even paid the filing fee yet to do this. I just assumed that since he has already exhausted his appeals that he would no longer be able to harass me in any way. I was wrong.

Apparently, I just happen to be lucky enough to have a per-petrator that reads up on his rights daily, and he found a loop-hole that makes all this legal. He has wasted numerous Colorado taxpayer dollars on filing all these charges and appealing his case hundreds of times over the years. It is amazing to me that someone convicted of a crime of this nature could then sue his victim for his own pain and suffering while serving his punishment. Enough is enough. I have tried to put it out of my head until I hear of a court date, but the anger does start to well up again if I let it.

My first response to the poor U.S. Attorney caseworker who had to break the news to me was, "I don't think that Mr. Steele is going to like my apology because all I have to say is that I am sorry that he has spent all these years in prison and still has not accepted God into his life and asked for forgiveness for his crime, or even admitted to doing this to me. I'm also sorry that he had to go out and abduct girls to get sex because he was too disgusting to get a girl willingly. That is about as sincere an apology as he'll ever get from me. As far as the million dollars, good luck getting something that I don't have."

The new caseworker assured me that my perpetrator would not have a case and that all of this would be okay. She apologized for even having to tell me. I realize as well that the mole never expects to win the case or receive money or an apology. To him, it is still about control and finding a way, even from prison, to let me know that he can still get to me. It does irritate me, but I will not let it set my progress back. It just makes me stronger and more passionate about "letting go."

I would like to end my story with a passage that I found by an unknown author. I thank whoever did write this as it gave me the extra strength and perseverance that I needed every day to fight off the demons. One of my friends gave it to me, and having this nearby to read aloud has helped me through some of my darkest hours of despair. I hope that it touches you and gives you peace as it did for me:

"To come out of the darkness and into the sunshine, it helps to remember that you are in a tunnel, not a cave. You will get through this if you just hang in there, and keep on walking through the tunnel."

―――――――――――――

Please contact us at 8daysindarkness@gmail.com if you or your group would like the authors of this book to speak at your conference or group meeting regarding the topics in this book.

ACKNOWLEDGMENTS
BY ANGELA ROEGNER

Anita and I were reluctant to thank specific people, as we are unable to name all the wonderful people that have helped in rescuing her and in assisting us in compiling the information contained in this book. Nonetheless, we are going to attempt to thank as many as we possibly can to express our appreciation and endless gratitude to them. We need to begin by first and foremost thanking God for Anita's safe return and for pairing the two of us up to fulfill his ultimate purpose of getting her remarkable story out to the world.

I am thankful to Anita and her family for having the courage to once again be thrown into the limelight and share their painful experiences with us. They are fiercely private and protective of each other as a family. The only reason they are willing to do this is to positively impact the lives of others. I pray that the public will appreciate their willingness to share this inspirational story and that their privacy will be respected in the future. I further pray that this book will act as the final piece that Anita needs in order to fully move on with her life and be at peace.

Anita and I both want to express our gratitude to the dedicated staff of Synergy Books for investing their time and expert knowledge in our project and believing in a first-time novelist. They have been essential in guiding us throughout the intimidating process of getting our book refined and published. We also need to thank the entire Phenix & Phenix literary publicity team for their enthusiasm regarding our project and their hard work in gaining various media opportunities for the distribution and release of the book.

Anita wants recognition given to her parents, her older sister Melody, and her older brother Daryl for all of their unconditional love and support throughout her ordeal. She also thanks her entire extended family for providing her with constant love and encouragement throughout the past ten rough years. She also wants the entire community of Kokomo, Indiana, recognized for going above and beyond in offering support to her family. They hung posters and words of encouragement in local businesses and on street signs and poles around the entire city until she was rescued, and developed prayer chains for her safe return home.

Anita would like to thank her best friends, namely, Jamie, Michelle, Denise, and Kelly, and countless other friends and coworkers for all of their prayers and support. Without Anita's faith and the combined support from the people who have stood by her, she is convinced that she never would have made it through this ordeal or gotten to where she is today. These genuine people have lifted her up with words of encouragement or humor when she needed it the most. She is forever grateful to all of them. Recognition is also due to her pastor and her entire Baptist church family.

We also want to fully recognize the brave, dedicated Howard County Sheriff's Department deputies, the Kokomo Police Department officers, the City of La Crosse Police Department officers, the local FBI agents, and the FBI profilers, all of whom put their egos at the door to work together diligently and bring Anita back home safely.

We both want to thank Major Steve Rogers, Sheriff's Deputy Don England, retired FBI profiler Steve McVey, retired La Crosse FBI agent Jeff Hill, FBI victims' advocate Cathy Vatauw, and FBI profiler from Quantico Robert Morton for their extra help in sharing the crucial details of this investigation process with us for the purpose of this book. Major Steve Rogers was always available to us by phone, and allowed us to do countless hours of research and interviews in one of the interrogation rooms at the sheriff's department station. Steve's professionalism and dedication to his work are to be commended.

I would like to thank my loving, supportive husband, Chris Roegner, for allowing me to embark on this time-consuming project. I know that, at times, he had to have felt neglected and frustrated, believing that I might never finish. He has always provided me with honest feedback, even when I did not want to hear it. He often urged me to take a breather when I needed to and frequently reminded me to enjoy the journey of the writing process.

I also want to thank my three precious children for all their love and any sacrifices they have made to allow me the time to write late into the nights. Austin, my fourteen-year-old son, had only one request—that I not embarrass him. I hope that I can come through for him. I am so proud of the responsible young man that he has become. It is hard for me to fathom that he is now nearly an adult himself. The years have flown by so quickly.

Austin often helped me out during the writing process by watching his little sisters and praying for me. He has overcome a rare blood disease and has always impressed me by never complaining about his own plight, but always just plugging forward. I am proud of him for his honor roll grades and talents in golf and playing the guitar and saxophone. His encouraging words and successes in life mean the world to me.

My seven-year-old daughter, Lexi, has also been a godsend to me. She is my prayer warrior, praying every night that Mommy would finish her book soon. She is relentless in her prayers and never gives up until God grants her requests on his time. She offers me sweet kisses, and her smile can light up any room on a daily basis. My other daughter, Kaitlin, is four years old and is cute as a button. She has had to sacrifice hours of precious time playing Go Fish and reading books together lately. Her endless chatter and questions in my ear while I am writing have taught me both the virtue of patience and the ability to multitask. She too has prayed nightly for our book to get done. I feel so blessed to have such wonderful, prayerful children. I am honored to be their mother.

I also need to give full recognition to my parents, Dan and Brenda Roe, for always supporting and believing in my writing skills even when I doubted myself. They are awesome grandparents to my children and have watched them numerous times so that I could write. Their love and support over the years have been priceless to me. I also must thank my two best friends—who just happen to be my sisters—Lori Murrell and Jennifer Budenz, for always having my back and believing in me.

I want to thank my mother- and father-in-law, Marlys and Don Roegner, for watching the kids for me numerous times to allow me to write. What's more, Don, who is the psychiatrist in our office, happens to be stuck in a room with me every week for supervision meetings, and has been kind enough to listen to me vent about any frustrations I had with this overwhelming project. He has offered me his wisdom and insights on a regular basis and, like his son, often reminded me to slow down and enjoy the process. I further need to thank my neighbors and close friends, Kyle and Jessica Caylor, for allowing my girls to come over and play with their daughter, Erika, on countless weekends. They have given me such support and friendship, and I will forever be grateful to them.

My brother-in-law, Tony Budenz, hates to be in the limelight in any way, but his helpful assistance in the editing process of this book must be noted. He was a great help to me in developing the "dark side" of the mole's character. Tony and my sister, Jennifer, were always there to assist me in computer "issues" and allowed me to write at their house on several occasions, away from kids and other distractions. Recognition also goes to Kelly Uncapher, the best secretary and friend that anyone could ever ask for. She typed out several initial drafts of the story for me in a timely manner.

Also, thanks to my friends, Kim Thatcher and Lisa Blacklidge, for kidnapping me for girls' weekend getaways on multiple occasions when they could tell that I was feeling stressed out. Also, thanks goes to Cathy Amaya, my church bible study leader and good friend. I am so blessed to have her in my life and to know that she prays for me and the success of this book daily.

Lastly, I would like to thank Anita for having the faith in me to write her remarkable story of survival and unfaltering love for the Lord. You are an amazing woman whom I feel honored to know. You inspire me daily to go on despite any challenges that ever come my way. This gift that you are giving to the world by telling your story is priceless.

RECOMMENDED RESOURCES
WEB SITES:

"Are You Ready to Recover from Sexual Abuse?" Soul-Expres-sions-Abuse-Recovery. http://www.soul-expressions-abuse-recovery.com.

Boulware, Carol. "Carol Boulware, MFT, PhD." Carol Boulware. http://www.psychotherapist.net.

"Center for Sexual Abuse/Assault Recovery Education." The University of Florida. http:// www.shcc.ufl.edu/care.

"Healthy Place: America's Mental Health Channel." HealthyPlace.com, Inc. http://www.HealthyPlace .com.

"Sexual Abuse Survivors in Recovery Anonymous." Sexual Abuse Survivors Anonymous. http://www .sexualabusesurvivors.com.

"Sexual Recovery Page." Recovery Web. http://www
.recovery-man.com/sexual.htm.

"Survivors & Friends." Survivors & Friends: Support for
Survivors of Sexual Abuse, Parents & Partners. http://
www.sandf.org.

"The Lamplighter Movement." The Lamplighters. http://
www.thelamplighters.org.

BOOKS:

Bolich, G. G. *Brick By Brick On the Road Through Oz: Recovery from Sexual Abuse Trauma*. Nashville, TN: Thomas Nelson, Inc., 2007. This book provides the reader with a powerful step-by-step model of how to heal from sexual abuse trauma as the character, Dorothy, demonstrates.

Demuth, Mary. *Watching the Tree Limbs*. Colorado Springs, CO: NavPress, 2006. This novel reveals an inspirational story of a young girl who suffers from sexual abuse and manages to eventually break free from the bondage of guilt and shame to heal through a spiritual journey of faith and forgiveness.

Ells, Al. *A New Beginning/Daily Devotions for Women Survivors of Sexual Abuse*. Nashville, TN: Thomas Nelson, Inc., 1992. This book of 365 daily devotions is written by sexually abused women and their therapists to provide the readers with hope to assist them through the healing process.

Fehlbaum, Beth. *Courage in Patience: A Story of Hope for Those Who Have Endured Abuse.* Clearwater, FL: Kunati Inc., 2008. This novel portrays a young woman who suffered sexual abuse from her stepfather and found the courage to come forward and to heal from her experience.

Fredrickson, Renee. *Repressed Memories: A Journey to Recovery from Sexual Abuse.* New York, NY: Fireside, 1992. This book stresses the importance of recovering repressed sexual abuse memories in order to fully heal.

James, Cynthia. *What Will Set You Free.* Parker, CO: Thornton Publishing Inc., 2007. This book endeavors to help in setting you free from the bondage of pain, shame, and suffering that many sexual abuse victims struggle with during the recovery process.